THE FUTURE OF THE WORKPLACE

INSIGHTS AND ADVICE FROM 31 PIONEERING BUSINESS AND THOUGHT LEADERS

Bill Fox

The Future of the Workplace: Insights and Advice from 31 Pioneering Business and Thought Leaders

Bill Fox
Henderson, NV, USA

ISBN-13 (pbk): 978-1-4842-5097-6   ISBN-13 (electronic): 978-1-4842-5098-3
https://doi.org/10.1007/978-1-4842-5098-3

Managing Director, Apress Media LLC: Welmoed Spahr
Acquisitions Editor: Shiva Ramachandran
Development Editor: Rita Fernando
Coordinating Editor: Rita Fernando

Cover designed by eStudioCalamar

Distributed to the book trade worldwide by Springer Science+Business Media New York, 233 Spring Street, 6th Floor, New York, NY 10013. Phone 1-800-SPRINGER, fax (201) 348-4505, e-mail orders-ny@springer-sbm.com, or visit www.springeronline.com. Apress Media, LLC is a California LLC and the sole member (owner) is Springer Science + Business Media Finance Inc (SSBM Finance Inc). SSBM Finance Inc is a **Delaware** corporation.

For information on translations, please e-mail rights@apress.com, or visit http://www.apress.com/rights-permissions.

Apress titles may be purchased in bulk for academic, corporate, or promotional use. eBook versions and licenses are also available for most titles. For more information, reference our Print and eBook Bulk Sales web page at http://www.apress.com/bulk-sales.

Any source code or other supplementary material referenced by the author in this book is available to readers on GitHub via the book's product page, located at www.apress.com/9781484250976. For more detailed information, please visit http://www.apress.com/source-code.

Printed on acid-free paper

This book is dedicated to the forward-thinking leaders who contributed their time, intellect, and wisdom to the Exploring Forward-Thinking Workplaces conversation. Thank you for being part of this journey.

Contents

About the Author

Bill Fox helps CEOs and leadership teams have a new type of strategic conversation that engages and leverages the collective voice, energy, and wisdom of the entire team to attract, retain, and grow exceptional people and results. Bill brings a forward-thinking approach that helps people discover how to advance beyond managing change, best practices, and working harder or even smarter in today's rapidly changing times.

In his interview series, Exploring Forward-Thinking Workplaces, he leads an ongoing twenty-first century conversation with global business and thought leaders that is uncovering exciting new solutions to our most vexing workplace challenges.

Bill is the cofounder of Forward-Thinking Workplaces 2.0 (www.forward-thinkingworkplaces.com). He has over three decades of experience in project management and in leading successful transformation and software development projects in the technology, financial, and manufacturing industries.

Bill is also the author of *Be a Workplace of the Future NOW*,[1] a series of six books that reveal the most intriguing insights from his conversations with global leaders, and the interview collection *5 Minutes to Process Improvement Success*.[2]

www.linkedin.com/in/billfoxstrategy

https://billfox.co

twitter: @billfoxstrategy

---

[1] Bill Fox, self-published, 2019.
[2] Bill Fox, self-published, 2012.

Foreword

The world of work is always changing. Before the 1800s, most people worked on farms and were craftsmen, with plenty of room to be creative. After the advent of the Industrial Revolution, we became more productive with the introduction of assembly lines and machinery. The unfortunate side effect of this was that the work became tedious and boring. People on the assembly line did the same tasks over and over again. Ford Motor Company had to double their workers' wages to convince them to do this kind of dreary work. Regardless, this assembly practice made Ford the richest company in the world. Other companies followed suit and this boring work process became commonplace. Unfortunately, this system has lasted for over 100 years.

But the world of work is still changing. Instead of designing work for machines and slotting people in to work with them, a new horizon is shining, and we are finally realizing that people can be very productive as we expand their capabilities. Canon Corporation has workers that can build an entire copier with over 1000 parts in 3 hours with a 30% increase in productivity and also sustaining high quality. Honda has new assembly lines in Thailand and in Columbus, Ohio, with the worker up on the line building an entire subset of the cars, rather focus on one piece per person. In both instances work is being designed for people, not only machines. These innovative business and thought leaders have so much to teach us, if only we could keep an open mind and listen.

The Future of the Workplace is a stimulating and interesting book to read and share with others. Like Socrates, the world's greatest teacher, Bill Fox asks some interesting questions in this book, resulting in exciting responses. As you read this valuable book, ask yourself these questions and write down and share your answers with others. Asking questions stimulates creativity!

Please read this wonderful book and share it with all of your friends and associates.

Norman Bodek
President, PCS Inc.

Acknowledgments

I would like to thank my family, friends, colleagues, interviewees, and readers who supported, encouraged, and inspired me in this work. I would also like to thank my editors at Apress, Rita Fernando and Shivangi Ramachandran, for their patient and professional editorial help. And special thanks to Sue Elliott, who contributed her superb editing skills to helping me with the Introduction, and to Norman Bodek for writing a wonderful and thought-provoking foreword.

Introduction

The future is already here, and it's unexpectedly and suddenly different than we'd planned or imagined—even just yesterday.

Today, we're living in a state of constant whitewater, besieged by an avalanche of ever-increasing information, with interruptions coming at us from every corner.

New times and new challenges call for innovative forward thinking. Yet most organizations are still mired in the Industrial Age. In that bygone era, methods like best practices, working harder, and even working smarter may have served us well, but now they keep us stuck living in the past.

To step into a better future, we need to shift into more modern ways of being and working. These new ways allow us to sense changes early and to adapt swiftly and intuitively.

To do this, we must interact with each other differently: with an open mind, listening to every voice, ready to discover whatever is there for us to see. And we must give ourselves the freedom to act upon what we discover.

This book will help you bridge the gap between the Industrial Age and the Forward-Thinking Age, with new insights and strategies you won't find elsewhere.

INDUSTRIAL AGE	FORWARD THINKING AGE
Newtonian Physics	Quantum Physics
Age of Science and Mass Production	Age of Intention and Wisdom
Command and Control	Everyone is a Leader
Separation into Parts	Connected and Part of Whole
Best Practices, Working Harder and Smarter	New Questions, Mastery and Exploration

Advice, Experience, and Tools from 31 Experts

This book contains Forward-Thinking Age conversations with 31 pioneering leaders of tomorrow—today. These top business and thought leaders come from many different countries and industries. They span the business, psychological, and spiritual domains.

Yet they all have one thing in common: Their work demonstrates a deep understanding of how to navigate the shifts that are occurring today.

Together, these interviews illuminate how—together—we can uncover new and better solutions to our most vexing challenges.

The advice, experience, and tools shared by these experts can help us create a future in which every voice matters, everyone thrives and finds meaning, and change and innovation happen naturally.

As one reader who chose to remain anonymous said

> This conversation invites and allows whole beings to show up. Like whole food, whole beings are more nutritious to the system they exist within.

In addition to questions specific to each leader, there are six core questions that I ask in each interview:

Question 1: **How can we create workplaces where every voice matters, everyone thrives and finds meaning, and change and innovation happen naturally?**

This question helps get at the essence of what's missing in most workplaces, and it opens up a space for people to freely describe how to create an ideal workplace. As Joseph Jaworski said

> We do not describe the world we see, but we see the world we describe.[3]

Change and innovation may be top of mind for most organizations today, but they still struggle to implement it. The 31 answers to this question reveal how organizational change and innovation can occur naturally, if we start with the inner change of the human participants.

Question 2: **How do we get an employee's full attention and best performance?**

This question deals directly with one of the top priorities for today's bottom-line focused executives, and you'll find that the responses are practical and actionable.

---

[3] *Synchronicity* (Berrett-Koehler, 1996).

Question 3: **What do people really lack and long for at work?**

Even in the best of companies I worked for, there was always something that would dampen my enthusiasm and my engagement. Often, it was office politics. Sometimes it was a bully. Many times, it wasn't safe to share my true thoughts or what was really going on. Then there was the meaningless work, even in organizations with a grand purpose. And this was just the tip of the iceberg.

So I asked, "What do people really lack and long for at work?" Few people talk about this, and even fewer try to address it. But we can't move forward if we don't.

You'll find that the answers to this question provide more than just increased awareness: They provide the means to do something about it.

Questions 4 and 5: **What is the most important question leaders should ask employees?** and **What is the most important question employees should ask leaders?**

Every organization I've ever worked with has had an "us" vs. "them" dynamic to one degree or another, at one or more levels. My intention with these two questions is to bridge the gap between levels and help people see one another's perspective.

The answers to this question will help you see that, too often, we are still asking the same old questions—or not asking questions at all.

You'll also discover just how important it is to create a space for questions to be asked, as well as for us to listen to each other.

Question 6: **What is the most important question we should ask ourselves?**

This question has been one of the most popular among readers of the interviews, and with good reason. I can't think of anything that's had a greater impact on my life than asking myself new questions. These 31 experts will introduce you to powerful questions that you've likely never heard or asked yourself before.

As Kurt Wright says in *Breaking the Rules*[4]

> The energy around an unanswered question may very well be the most powerful motivating force in the universe.

---

[4] Philadelphia, PA: Kinect Publishing, 1998.

Final Note

The interviews in this book were thoughtfully selected from a collection of more than 70 interviews that make up an ongoing conversation called *Exploring Forward-Thinking Workplaces 2.0*. In truth, all 70 of the interviews belong in this book, but we had to limit our choices due to the economic constraints of publishing and the attention spans of most readers.

I hope you will feel moved to share what you found most intriguing about this book. You can reach me by email at bill@billfox.co.

If you'd like to know the story of how this work came into existence, I invite you to read "Find Your Own Way to Go Deeper to Move Forward"[5] on my personal web site.

To your great work life and success!

---

[5] https://billfox.co/find-your-own-way-to-go-deeper-to-move-forward/

Howard Behar

Former President, Starbucks

The Person Who Sweeps the Floor Chooses the Broom

Howard Behar is a well-known business leader, author, and speaker who has influenced the lives of many men and women. During his time as president of Starbucks International, the company grew from 28 to 15,000 locations. His latest book is *The Magic Cup: A Business Parable About a Leader, a Team, and the Power of Putting People and Values First.*[1]

I was moved to reach out to Howard after reading one of his articles on leadership. I have been a longtime admirer of the Starbucks Coffee experience and often wondered how something as mundane as coffee became such a big part of so many people's lives and our culture. After reading Howard's book, *The Magic Cup,* and interviewing him, the veils began to lift.

Bill Fox: How can we create workplaces where every voice matters, everyone thrives and finds meaning, and change and innovation happen naturally?

Howard Behar: I have this little saying, "The person who sweeps the floor chooses the broom." What I mean by that is the person who has a responsibility in certain areas is given the authority, responsibility, and accountability. That means you've got to give them room to make mistakes and to grow primarily as people first, and then as employees.

---

[1] NY: Center Street, 2016.

© Bill Fox 2020
B. Fox, *The Future of the Workplace*,
https://doi.org/10.1007/978-1-4842-5098-3_1

The keyword here is trust. What makes a family healthy? What makes it so the kids can strike out on their own? What makes it so our partners can stretch out on their own? It's the trust we build with each other—that's what has to happen in organizations too. When you have trust, it's amazing what can happen.

When there's trust it's amazing how people can begin to use their own creativity because they lose that fear of being judged. They lose the fear of making mistakes.

They go out there and do things that serve each other and serve their customers. It's not complicated. It's half building trust and caring about each other while encouraging each other. As a leader, it's giving them responsibility and accountability to let them "choose their broom."

You know it's not really employees and customers. That's a word we all use to describe with who we work and do business. It's one human being serving another human being. That's what it is. At the end of the day, that's what we were put on the earth to do. It doesn't make any difference what your job description is or what your title is; we're all servers of human beings.

Bill: What does it take to get an employee's full attention and best performance?

Howard: I think, first of all, it's about always being open and honest. Lots of communication. Setting expectations so that they're clear and getting agreement on those expectations. It's primarily what I talked about in the previous question, if people feel like they're trusted and that they have responsibility and accountability, they'll give you their attention. It's just automatic.

Employees want to hear you because they know you want to hear them. It's the same thing that happens in a family. What allows your kids to give you their attention? It's when they feel trusted and not judged. When that happens, they open up to communication that gets closed down when they're not. When you're constantly after them, when you're always setting rules and regulations, then what happens? They close down.

It's that whole dynamic of letting them be, setting expectations, gaining agreement on those expectations, and let them go for it.

That's the same thing that goes on in a company or organization. It's that whole dynamic of letting them be, setting expectations, gaining agreement on those expectations, and let them go for it. It's amazing how they listen and give you their attention when that's done.

Bill: What do people really lack and long for at work?

Howard: Being treated with respect and dignity. Being dealt with as a human being and not an employee. They're not seen as an asset, but they're seen as a person with all their good points and all their flaws—they're accepted for that.

What do people long for at work? Being treated as a human being and not an employee.

I say you want to be able to wear your *hat*, whatever *hat* you choose to wear. I'm not talking about the roles we play; I'm talking about our values no matter where you are.

When people are allowed to be themselves at work, whatever that is—within the context of achieving the goals of the organization—then that just happens. That's what they long for. It's the same thing our significant others long for— they can be themselves when they're with us.

Bill: What is the most important question leaders should ask employees?

Howard: What can I do to support you in the attainment of your own goals in the context of obtaining our family or our organization's goals?

Bill: What's the most important question employees should ask leaders?

Howard: The one I particularly like for new hires is, What's the gap between what we say we do and who we are and what actually happens? What's the intrinsic reward, recognition, and penalty structure inside the organization not what's stated? How do I live within that gap? And another question every employee should ask, What happens to me if I make a mistake?

What's the gap between what we say we do and who we are and what actually happens?

Bill: What is the most important question we should ask ourselves?

Howard: Who are we? What are our values and how are we going to bring those values to life in our daily lives, our work, our family, and our spiritual life?

Bill: In your book *It's Not About the Coffee,*[2] you state that one of the most important things is for us to discover our truth. Can you share your story?

Howard: I began that journey in earnest when I was 26 years old. Up until that point, I never thought about who I was, what I stood for, what my values were, or what I wanted to accomplish in my life. I was just happy having and living my life.

At 26, somebody asked me a question, which seems like a throwaway question. I was in the furniture business at the time. My boss asked me, "Howard, what do you love more, people or furniture?"

I had grown up in the home furnishings industry, so I always thought I wanted to be the best in the home furnishings industry. I was confusing that with who I was. Once I asked myself that question, it began a process of self-discovery. Trying to figure out, "Howard, who are you?" "Do you love furniture?"

I came to the conclusion it wasn't furniture that I loved, but it was people that I loved. Now I loved the creativity of furniture, and I enjoyed working in that context. But what I loved was working with people, being with people, and learning from people.

And most importantly, learning to manage me. Learning to figure out who I was, what my mission was, what my values were, and how I was going to live my life—that journey has never ended. It's constantly in my head. I'm always trying to deal with "Who am I?"

Key Takeaways

- Give people room to make mistakes and grow as people first.

- Remove the fear of being judged.

- It's not really employees and customers.

- Always be open and honest.

- Attention follows when people feel trusted and not judged.

- Treat people as human beings and not as employees.

- Allow people to be themselves at work.

- What can I do to support you?

---

[2] NY: Portfolio, 2007.

- What happens to me if I make a mistake?
- Who are we?
- What do you love more, people or furniture?
- What do you really love?
- Always ask, "who am I?"

Gwen Kinsey

Transformation Leader

How Do We Create That Environment That Uses Natural System Wisdom?

Gwen Kinsey is a transformation leader who learned strategic change management through self-directed experience. She is a former president and general manager from the television industry who shares what she learned about leading organizational change to help transformational leaders create what's next.

Gwen was the first person I met when I attended a leadership breakfast event in the Washington, DC area in 2013. We immediately connected, and we've collaborated on several important projects since that first meeting, including speaking at the Chesapeake Bay Organizational Development Conference in 2014. She has been a mentor to me and her support and encouragement have been a source of ongoing help.

Bill Fox: How do we create workplaces where every voice matters, everyone thrives and finds meaning, and change and innovation happen naturally?

Gwen Kinsey: Workplaces are a microcosm of what's going on in the world. The schisms and splits that are impacting us aren't just happening at work, they're happening everywhere.

© Bill Fox 2020
B. Fox, *The Future of the Workplace*,
https://doi.org/10.1007/978-1-4842-5098-3_2

Joseph Campbell perceived over 70 years ago that healing this artificial split between I and We would be the challenge of our time.

I'm reminded of Joseph Campbell and the work that he did. In his book *The Hero with a Thousand Faces*,[1] Campbell talks about the natural tension between finding value in individual purpose and community purpose. What's amazing is more than 70 years ago, Campbell saw that this perceived gap between individual purpose and community purpose would widen. Campbell knew that this schism would be the challenge of our time. He said that healing this artificial split between I and We is our foundational work. Our Job with a capital J is to figure out how to balance that natural polarity.

In our workplaces, we spent these same seven decades getting smart about what processes we could create to help individuals reach discreet, replicable goals. We used mechanization and efficiency frames. We designed systems to refine individual control—control for efficient replication becomes our primary focus. We used that same frame in our education system. We stopped teaching children how to learn and started turning out employees. Heck we even apply efficiency goals to our private lives. Only we're figuring out that time management systems can't help us control much at all.

Our systems are breaking down. The problem is we've missed an essential question: How do we balance the natural tension between what's best for the individual and the community at large?

This dynamic is a natural part of every living system in nature. Ask yourself in nature, which has more value: the individual or the community? Nature treats this a false choice. Both are important to a healthy ecosystem.

Nature provides terrific insights for what dynamics must be present to balance this polarity of purpose between the individual and community.

One dynamic is that the purpose of community is to improve the life, health, and sustainability of everything within the entire ecosystem. The community can't endure unless it serves and benefits all.

Another dynamic is that the purpose of each living entity is to serve through its role within the community. An individual can't stay healthy and relevant unless it adapts within the community as the community changes.

---

[1] CA: New World Library, 2008.

So, to create a world where every voice matters, everyone thrives, and innovation happens naturally, we need to heal the artificial schism between individual purpose and community value. Unfortunately, our ego gets in the way. Ego is the unconscious thinking part of our brain that has us behave as though human purpose can be independent of a healthy community. Nature knows better.

We are struggling because we've designed our ways of interacting and systems for control and replication.

They aren't designed to bridge the artificial split between I and the community of We.

To balance both we have to shift from ego-centered thinking to adaptive, natural system wisdom.

Bill: What does it take to get an employee's full attention and best performance?

Gwen: Can I let the contrarian in me come out? I think this is the wrong question. That question points us to how do we influence somebody so that we can control their behavior to suit our goal. Control doesn't allow for "what else is possible here?" If an employee can't see how they make a difference with my unique contribution, it's tough to get excited.

This question brings to mind what I find in workshops. When I do a workshop on feedback, for example, the word accountability comes up regularly. Managers ask, what do we have to do to have people be more accountable? How do we control people so that we get them to accomplish our goal? I always tell folks accountability is an outcome. It's an outcome that comes from a natural process of people being authentically involved and connected in purpose.

That's not the same as buy-in. It's sweat equity. That's the term I like to use. Sweat equity means you feel connected to something. Your heart is in it. You feel a passion about it. You sense the connection between what it is that you're doing and why that matters to you as well as why that matters to the community. As a result, when that connection is alive, you are accountable because what matters to you is on the line. That's the outcome. Another question for forward-thinking organizations is, "How do we facilitate our natural system wisdom?" That's different.

I think a lot of what you read in the business press reflects leaders wrestling with the symptoms of that artificial split between individual and community. Instead of wrestling with symptoms, I help people address the root cause, designing a natural systems way of integrating I and We instead of reflexively going for that control mechanism.

Bill: What do people really lack and long for at work?

Gwen: Here are a couple of ideas about that.

In my leadership work, I started off studying engagement strategies. As I peeled that onion, I kept coming back to the balance between I and We. If people feel like they're valued and contributing members of a community working toward something bigger than themselves, that's an important precondition to well-being. Of course, none of this matters if people aren't earning a living wage.

People also want to be free from living in a constant state of fear. Today's rate of change triggers an underlying fear that things are unstable. People who are worried that their relevance is uncertain live in fear. That reflects a wider perspective of where are we as a society and as a workplace—we're in between. Accelerating technological advances and intertwining of global communities feeds this.

We're in a state of transformation. Our entire economic system is being challenged. Our political institutions are being challenged. We have this incredible friction driving a desire to go back to the way things were. Back feels more familiar and safer. Unfortunately, our known solutions were formed by the world in the way that it used to be. Life is different today, so fear is going to be present while we navigate in-between.

In my executive coaching, I see the best antidote for fear is a compelling vision of something more powerful than fear. It's always something that is very important to my client. Worth transcending fear. When they imagine possibilities that enable them to take even one concrete step forward, their fear is more manageable.

People want and need to participate in creating what's next. As organizations, we need natural systems that help people to sense, adapt, and prototype toward things that really matter.

Can we help them learn their way into the future? How can we create an environment where people feel they are a valued and contributing member of a community? It's not about buy-in, it's about participation. They have to be able to see their contribution matters and, at the same time, have space to grow so they won't be left behind.

Bill: What's the most important question leaders should ask employees?

Gwen: What are you noticing? What else are you sensing? What should we be paying more attention to? I realize that's more than one question, but I want to illustrate the importance of asking people to look outward and share what they're observing. What questions help them open their lens? Ask yourself, what do they see that I'm missing? Because when those kinds of conversations happen, they surface more good stuff we get to work with. It not only helps engage an individual who feels valued, acknowledged, and appreciated, but more importantly, those additional perspectives generate more possibilities.

Ask that lens-opening question. Whatever that looks like to you. It's not only good for problem solving, but it's also good for helping people to learn and grow.

That doesn't mean we use all possibilities, but we have more to work with before we begin a collaborative sorting process of which ones offer the best opportunities with the least downside. Now we're getting somewhere. We're germinating seeds for innovation and creating new solutions. Ask that lens-opening question. Whatever that looks like to you. It's not only good for problem solving, but it's also good for helping people to learn and grow. Allow them to figure something out. Or to learn on the fly. Or to just think about something from a looking outward perspective.

Bill: What's the most important question employees should ask leaders?

Gwen: Let's invoke that collective awareness. "How are we doing?" That might not be the best question, but I'm looking for what's that opening question that moves the conversation to something broader and something bigger than just me if I'm that employee. Having employees think that way is a good thing. Those are the conversations that serve us in that in-between space.

Bill: What's the most important question we should ask ourselves?

Gwen: I have a favorite question, and I learned to ask it years ago. I started asking it of other people, but then I realized I had to ask myself the same question. In my first job as a sales manager, I had people coming in my office all the time asking me questions. It was exhausting because it seemed like the more questions I answered, the more questions I got. Then it dawned me that people weren't asking me their real questions. What they were really looking for was either validation or they were looking for ideas because they hadn't taken the time to think through what they were trying to do.

For whatever reason, I realized the more I gave them, the more they asked. I just decided my new question was going to be, "What's your real question?" I started asking people that because what I realized was a lot of times, they either hadn't thought something through especially if they were encountering something for the first time.

By me giving them an answer, I precluded their learning. But by my saying, "What's your real question?" I could start asking questions that helped them think through their problem. For people who were looking for validation, well that was just a way of calling out the fact that they were looking for exactly that. When I started saying, "What's your real question?", it completely changed the dynamic I had with my employees.

When I want to explore something, or I have an answer and it's not working, or I'm getting pushback, I'll take a step back and ask, "Well, what's my real question?"

Then I thought, what about me! Every time that I start thinking I want to explore something, or that I have an answer and it's not working, or I'm getting pushback, I'll take a step back and ask, "Well, what's my real question?"

What I'm trying to do is set up for myself the same thing I did for others. Questions set the trajectory for where we go for answers. Whatever that question is sends us in a particular direction. Start off with thinking about what should that question look like. For me, it's "What's your real question?"

Bill: Do you have any final thoughts on what we've talked about here today?

Gwen: I think I'd go back to where we started, and that is attending to the larger social dynamic of balancing I and We.

Back in March I read a *New York Times* article[2] that Google had done some research looking for the highest performing sales and marketing teams in their organization. They did this huge metadata analysis. They looked at people's talents, when they were hired, their education. They looked at many things to try to decide what do the best teams look like, and how do we replicate that?

---

[2] www.nytimes.com/2016/02/28/magazine/what-google-learned-from-its-quest-to-build-the-perfect-team.html

> It's not about pieces and parts as much as it is how do we create that environment that utilizes natural system wisdom?

At the end of the survey and analysis, what they recognized was that it was about the people dynamics. That points to that perspective between I and community as opportunity. What does that social architecture look like? How do we create that environment that utilizes natural system wisdom?

Key Takeaways

- Management systems don't help us control much at all.
- We've missed an essential question.
- Heal the schism between individual purpose and community value.
- Control doesn't allow for what else is possible here.
- Accountability is an outcome that comes from people being authentically involved.
- People need to feel valued and part of something bigger.
- People want to participate in creating what's next.
- Ask that lens-opening question.
- Surface more to work with.
- Ask questions that close the in-between space gap.
- What's the real question?
- Questions set the trajectory for answers.
- How do we tap into natural system wisdom?

John Bell

Former CEO, Jacobs Suchard

Voices Will Matter, People Will Thrive and Innovation Will Become Ingrained in the Culture if…

John Bell is the author of *Do Less Better*,[1] a transformational leader, corporate director, and former CEO at Jacobs Suchard. You can learn more about John on his blog *In the CEO Afterlife*[2] where he reflects on leadership, branding, and life. John's latest book is a fictional novel called *The Circumstantial Enemy*.[3]

I met John Bell in 2013 after he commented on an article[4] I published at the Lead Change Group. Since that time, I've learned a lot from John and his book *Do Less Better*. John's expertise in branding has been very helpful in our messaging of this work. John frequently shares and comments on our posts on social media.

Bill Fox: How can we create workplaces where every voice matters, everyone thrives and finds meaning, and change and innovation happen naturally?

John Bell: I read this question three times before realizing that the answer can be found within the question. Voices will matter, people will thrive, and innovation will become ingrained in the culture *if* people find meaning. So if

---

[1] New York: Palgrave Macmillan, 2014.
[2] www.ceoafterlife.com/
[3] London: Endeavour Media, 2018.
[4] https://leadchangegroup.com/leadership-means-no-more-silver-bullets/

© Bill Fox 2020
B. Fox, *The Future of the Workplace*,
https://doi.org/10.1007/978-1-4842-5098-3_3

people can find meaning, you can satisfy the question. But that begs another question, "How do people find this elusive meaning in their work?"

Voices will matter, people will thrive, and innovation will become ingrained in the culture if people find meaning.

In my experience, the starting place is a corporate purpose that not only resonates with employees, but it binds them together. Sure, we'd all prefer a moral purpose, such as working for a company that is saving lives or saving the planet. But, that's not to say that people can't be inspired by a company vision that thrills customers, pleases people, and brings fulfillment.

For example, I'll share my experience with Apple. When you are a tech neophyte like me, you can spend a lot of time talking on the phone to technical support people. When I got my iPhone, I spent a lot of time talking to the techies at Apple. I was blown away by their work ethic and their desire to help. They can't do enough for you, so I asked one of the reps about their process, "Are you not on a quota because you're not rushing me here or anything." The rep said, "No, there are no quotas at all. We are judged by the satisfaction of the customer." He went on to say that if you do an excellent job, you get a better choice of work hours and scheduling. Now, there's a voice that matters.

At L.L. Bean, the idea of selling really good apparel and outdoor equipment at a reasonable profit and treating customers like human beings is worth the effort. For Wegmans Food Markets, it's all about caring, respect, empowerment, and making a difference. Organizations that walk the talk create Work that Matters. And when you have work that matters, you have more voices that matter and people that thrive personally and professionally.

Bill: What does it take to get an employee's full attention and best performance?

John: Generally, every employee needs to know that the work they are doing, no matter how menial, is meaningful. As an example, what would happen to a restaurant if the floors weren't swept and the kitchen wasn't scrubbed? Management's job is to continually reiterate the importance of cleanliness, reward for it, and ensure that this success factor is shared with everyone. Even though somebody may have a very boring or tough job, there's a reason for it. We as leaders have to share that, honor it, respect it, and make sure everyone in the organization knows it.

Every employee needs to know that the work they are doing, no matter how menial, is meaningful.

I'll share a personal example on rewarding performance. When I was a CEO, we had a very lucrative bonus plan in place. But because the company was unionized, half of the employees were excluded and that created a "them and us" wedge. The union didn't like "variable" compensation because they want to know exactly what they're getting. There can't be any variables, it's a fixed deal. So when it was time to renegotiate the contract, I had to find a way to include a bonus plan. Once we had the regular wage rates and benefits settled, we simply added the bonus element. Even if it was zero, they had a contract they could live with. And the results were phenomenal! The following year, everyone got a bonus because the company was profitable and growing. I'd walk into the plant and employees would walk up to me and say, "John, we've got a lot of inventory in the warehouses, are things slowing down?" They were worried because bonuses were based on sales and profits. Because it was the same for every employee, you didn't have to go through every employee's performance to pay them a bonus. Of course the payment wasn't zero, and the "us and them" mindset soon dissipated.

Now, to be totally frank, in our desire to get an employee's full attention and best performance, one must be very careful in recruiting the right people. I met with every employee before we hired them because I like to start with mindset first, to ensure that there is a cultural fit. If the fit isn't right, there's no need to discuss skills. So back to that union example—if you don't get the right headset from the start, a unionized employee's tenure could be a headache for a very long time.

Bill: What do people really lack and long for at work?

John: Some people work to live and others live to work. I think that's critically important before you even address someone to know which ones you have and to value each of them. Times are changing. I watch my kids balance their personal lives and their business lives way better than I ever did. My parents came out of the war and their parents were out of the depression so you're affected by that. Success meant making money and working hard, so we did and eventually we realized that's not all there is. There has to be satisfaction in the work and there's an immediate need to pay the bills, so we have to realize that.

Some people work to live and others live to work. You've got to know where people are coming from.

I got into marathon running in my late 30s and early 40s. So I started running at lunch and some of the employees wanted to run with me. I once asked one of the employees, "Why don't you run with us?" He said, "John, I'm on my feet all day long!" I said, "Oh gosh, you're so right. Thanks for clearing my head on that." You've really got to know where people are coming from.

What do they want? I think they want to be appreciated. I think they want to do things that have a purpose. This idea of purpose has been around a long time, but it is so important and was even more so for me running small- to medium-sized companies that were competing against giants. Purpose is such an opportunity to bind a team together and us against them. It's a very competitive situation and the people I had working with me were the same. Winning is important and business was the game.

Bill: What is the most important question leaders should ask employees?

John: I believe there are two equally important questions. Question one is, "What do you think we should do?" The operative words are "you" and "we" in this question. But this question will soon become meaningless if management doesn't act on the suggestion or at least take the time to explain why the suggestion might not be appropriate. That said, more times than not, there will be something that comes out of the discussion that can be implemented or looked into. So the key to success is engagement, building trust, and inspiring the employee to be a voice within the company.

Question one is, "What do you think we should do?" The operative words are "you" and "we" in this question.

The second question is, "How can I help you achieve your objectives?" Again, this is an opportunity to engage, to better understand an employee, and to determine what motivates them. In some cases, are they motivated by career or by craft? Everybody thinks "career" is the name of the game. I had a lot of frustrated employees who just never got past a certain level. A university professor I had a long time ago said, "It doesn't always have to be career. Why not craft?" What do I mean by that? One of our employees was a purchasing agent and he was really good at his job, but he wasn't the greatest when it came to leadership and mentoring. He was thinking about leaving and we said, "We'll do everything we can to make you a specialist, the best purchasing agent in the country. What would that entail?" Bottom line, he took more courses, joined trade associations, and he's still with the company some 20 years later... and still in purchasing!

Bill: What's the most important question employees should ask leaders?

John: I think the answer to this question depends on the situation. If a company is losing money and is at risk, the question will be very different from one that deals with a project or the future of a new initiative. Ultimately, the question is either about the company or about the employee. The common thread is that both questions ought to be about the future of the company or the employee. I believe talking about the future is a great conduit for the engagement that we must have.

Bill: What is the most important question we can ask ourselves?

John: Is this worth the effort? I'm asking this question all the time. It better be worth the effort. If it isn't and you are satisfied with mediocrity, you'll never be happy in your work. Likewise, if you strive for excellence in an organization that blocks your ability to realize excellence, you'll never be happy in your work. A matter of excellence is a shared responsibility between the company and the employee. The company must create an environment in which achievers can achieve. Then it's up to the employee to make it happen.

Is this worth the effort? I'm asking this question all the time.

Bill: What prompted you to write your book *Do Less Better*?

John: Early in my career, I was faced with the challenge of turning around a near-bankrupt company that was mired in complexity. Too many products, too many brands, too many categories, and no competitive advantage for any of them. By closing or selling the majority of the brands, we trimmed the company down to a shadow of its former self. We decided to become an expert in one category—it happened to be coffee—and by focusing on coffee, and nothing else, we were able to swim out of a raging river of red ink. We called the means to that end the "do less better" strategy.

When I became a consultant, I saw a similar pattern of unnecessary complexity in both troubled and successful businesses. Today, business complexity has reached pandemic proportions—big keeps getting bigger. Almost everyone is stuck in a paradigm of doing more and more. Never has the need for simplicity and focus been greater than right now. So where there's a problem, there must be an opportunity. A book on how to cut through the complexity clutter is that opportunity.

Almost everyone is stuck in a paradigm of doing more and more. Never has the need for simplicity and focus been greater than right now.

Bill: In the book you discuss the advantages of doing less rather than more. What do you mean by that?

John: That's just another way of saying think less rather than more, and get really good at whatever that less is. I'll use the analogy of a mountain range. There's so many opportunities at the top of each mountain in the broad range. But can you really get to the top by spreading yourself too thin, by diluting your resources to do so? By putting all of your resources (and expertise) against climbing just one mountain, you have a better chance to reach the pot of gold at the summit.

Bill: What makes this book different from other books on focus?

John: This isn't the first book on focus, nor will it be the last. But the element that separates this book from the rest is *how people can successfully cut through complexity and achieve focus.* The "how" is the ability to make tough strategic choices.

And sometimes, especially when transformation is required such as it is at J.C. Penny and Hewlett-Packard, some very tough sacrifices are required. Now, there's a difference between tough strategic choices and tough strategic sacrifices, and I point this out in the book. Tough strategic choices are about the business. Tough sacrifices are about *you.* Tough sacrifices claw at your emotions because they require that you do something that you don't want to do. And these are the sacrifices that rob you of sleep, sober your disposition, heighten your stress, and choke your patience on the little things in life.

So why should today's leaders make these sacrifices? Because the essence of sacrifice is giving up something of value for the sake of other considerations.

Bill: What is the reader's takeaway? If just one idea what would that be?

John: How about I give you the one big idea and three corollaries?

1. The most important takeaway is the fact that leaders and managers don't have to keep doing more and more to be effective and successful. Doing less, and doing it better, is a viable strategy at all levels of an organization.

2. The best strategies require sacrifice. Because these strategies are concise, they also tell you what not to do. That keeps complexity at bay.

3. The specialist always beats the generalist. Doing less better because of product, market, and customer sacrifice ensures viability and strengthens competitiveness.

4. The small guy doesn't need deep pockets to outmaneuver giants. Creativity, nimbleness, and ingenuity are the best bargains in business. They cost nothing.

Key Takeaways

- Help people find meaning in their work.

- Corporate purpose that resonates and binds together.

- All work is meaningful no matter how menial.

- Eliminate the "us and them" mindset.

- Understand what each person values.

- Purpose is an opportunity to bind people together.

- What do you think we should do?

- How can I help you achieve your objectives?

- It's about the future of the company or employee.

- Is this worth the effort?

- Become an expert in one category.

- Never has the need for simplicity and focus been greater.

- Think less rather than more.

Norman Bodek

Owner, PCS Press

Discover the Spirit of Self-Reliance

Norman Bodek's mission is to teach managers how to teach their employees how to be successful in life and also to teach teachers how to teach their students how to be successful in life. Norman played a prime role in introducing Lean to the West. He is a cocreator of the Shingo Prize and is a Shingo Prize winner. He has written hundreds of articles; and when he owned Productivity Press, he published 100 Japanese management books in English, over 250 published books on productivity and quality, and has written seven books including his *How to Do Kaizen,*[1] *The Harada Method,*[2] and *A Miraculous Life.*[3]

I first met Norman Bodek in 1992 when he was the owner of Productivity Inc. and Productivity Press where our shared interests in workplace productivity brought us together. We reconnected more recently through his work with the Harada Method. Norman has a gift for finding extraordinary people and ideas and making them more visible and available to help people and businesses.

---

[1] Vancouver, WA: PCS Inc., 2010.
[2] Vancouver, WA: PCS Inc., 2014.
[3] Bodek, Norman, 2018.

© Bill Fox 2020
B. Fox, *The Future of the Workplace,*
https://doi.org/10.1007/978-1-4842-5098-3_4

Bill Fox: How can we create workplaces where every voice matters, everyone thrives and finds meaning, and change and innovation happen naturally?

Norman: The key to this question is what I received from two people, Takashi Harada, inventor of the Harada Method, and Venu Srinivasan, chairman of TVS Motor—a $7 billion company in India.

The Harada Method is a systematic system that allows the individual to take responsibility for defining their own path in achieving self-reliance and professional excellence.

The Harada Method, which I teach and cowrote a book with Takashi Harada, asks people to pick a very strong goal that excites them and motivates them to be successful in life. It asks people to state their purposes, what they value for themselves and others, to pick a goal to attain those purposes, to carefully analyze their strengths and weaknesses, to select the tasks and routines to help them attain that goal, and to monitor their daily progression working with a coach.

It is systematic system that allows the individual to take responsibility for defining their own path in achieving self-reliance and professional excellence. The subtitle of my Harada book is "The Spirit of Self-Reliance." That's what the Harada Method does. It gets you to pick a goal so that you can become self-reliant in your life. You pick a goal to be a master at something that serves other people's needs.

People come to work and often do boring and repetitive things. Give them a chance to be self-reliant and to align their goals with their work, and you will see a workplace where everyone thrives and finds meaning and where change and innovation will naturally happen.

Most employees are completely dependent upon their employers making virtually all the decisions, as if the employer knows better. Often, they don't, for the person that does the job really knows it the best.

Venu Srinivasan's TVS Motor manufactures motorcycles and automotive parts. In 1996, Venu started Srinivasan Services Trust (SST) to share his success with others. Now after 20 years, SST has uplifted over 1.2 million people, in India, out of poverty.

The key to SST's success is helping people to become self-reliant.

SST's consultants go into an impoverished village and normally gather 15 to 16 women together, to form self-help groups—most of the women are unable to read or write.

I went to India to one of these villages and saw women in four groups of 15 each make chapatti flatbread. The women own collectively the factory, take a weekly salary, and give out a bonus at the end of the year. They make thousands of chapattis daily and sell them to the surrounding companies and villages. Instead of living in shacks without running water, they now own their own brick/cement houses with all of the modern conveniences.

In the past, I owned Productivity Inc. with 127 people publishing newsletters, books, and running conferences, seminars, study missions to Japan, and consulting in JIT (just-in-time) methods. Often the staff would come to me with questions; I foolishly always gave them an answer as if I was the only person intelligent enough to do it. Of course, now a little older and a little wiser, I should always have turned around and asked them to come up with a solution to their question.

Taiichi Ohno, VP Toyota, and Dr. Shigeo Shingo, two of my authors, created the Toyota Production System (Lean), and both were masters of this. Each had a different management style: Ohno would command you. He'd go to you and say, "Look, you have six people working in your area. Do it with four." Then he'd walk away. He'd never tell them how to do it. He would just demand the impossible. Ohno just demanded people to do the impossible because he never knew if they could do it or not, but he knew if he didn't ask, they'd never do it. He was probably the best manufacturing manager of the last 100 years. Often, managers tell people the what and the how to do things not allowing them to be creative.

Dr. Shingo would turn to the people, managers, and engineers and say to them very simply, "How can you improve the value adding ratio on this process?" When people are asked, they do come up with amazing answers. Dr. Shingo was a great master and teacher. He could solve probably any manufacturing problem presented to him. But, he would turn to the people, managers, and engineers and say to them very simply, "How can you improve the value adding ratio on this process?" That was his main question, "How can you improve the value adding of what you do?" Then he would let people come up with the answers. When people are asked, they do come up with amazing things.

I had a student who was in charge of Lean in a big hospital in Arkansas. I asked him to pay me something to train him over zoom.us. He told me he had no money in his budget and that he would have to ask the president of the hospital. I finally suggested he pay me $125 for an hourly session. My student said, "I'll have to ask my president of the hospital!" He told the president that another sister hospital system in Indiana saved $1.5 million from my training.

The president, believe or not, said, "Sorry, there is no money in the budget for you to be educated."

It's amazing that people are not empowered in any way to spend money on their own improvement or even for the benefit of the company. They have to always go ask for permission as if the senior knows more or is more capable. The whole idea of asking for permission is a system that seems to exist throughout America and the world.

But the great, great teachers have set up a system that doesn't require permission. They trust people to make the right decisions for their organizations and themselves.

I published a book *The Happiest Company to Work for*. This book is about an amazing company called Mirai in Japan that runs on this principle: Everybody is a boss. Everybody makes their own decisions. If they made a mistake, they got $6.00 but told never make it again. That's the simple way to approach it. It really gets people to be self-reliant and very careful at the same time. Mirai has never lost money and has more patents than any other company, its size, in Japan.

Bill: How do we get an employee's full attention and best performance?

Norman: One, go back to Ohno and what he said: Command people to do great things. Two, use Shingo's method of asking questions. And third, praise, sincerely—specifically, the heck out of people.

Praising people is part of the Harada Method. Just praise them. Recognize their strengths, what they do well, reinforce them, and be a coach and support them.

Try to minimize all criticism. And don't blame people for mistakes because everybody learns from their mistakes.

We go to industry, and we rip people apart. Everybody's afraid to make mistakes because they're going to get fired. Well, that's crazy, that's the way they learn! Stop this nonsense and then you'll build up a dynamic workforce.

Mr. Kazuo Inamori was the founder of Kyocera—probably was the best top manager in Japan. He created a great corporate vision, purpose, and mission that I highly recommend you study. He also started KDDI, which is a very large wireless mobile company in Japan.

Bill, that is a great missing key in American corporations, the lack of a clear vision of how their organization will grow and how they serve the benefit of the world.

A few years ago, Inamori was asked by the Japanese government to take over and run Japan Airlines because they went bankrupt. Two years after he took over, they made over $800 million. He focused first on what was good for the employees, then got them to work their "tails off" to give great customer service, and then the result will be fantastic profits. He got everyone in the airline to believe in his philosophy and to focus on improving their "attitude," increase their "efforts," and to improve their "skills and capabilities."

According to Kazuo Inamori, to have a wonderful life, one should embody and live by these ideals:

- Everyone should notice the importance of having ideas and enthusiasm.
- Think back to the origin of what went good or bad.
- Become a gentle person with a big ambition.
- Live nobly and continue to chase your dreams for the future.
- Believing strongly inspires courage.
- Always to be positive.
- Be sure to pursue the infinite possibilities in which luck lives.
- Work harder than ever to do one thing well harder than anyone else.
- Ignite your heart.
- Do not spare any effort.
- Never give up with a fighting spirit.
- Improve step by step giving the essential effort.
- The effort not to lose to anyone.
- Be sincere and correct.
- Overcome failure and be honest with yourself.
- To live with the high goals.
- Do always creative work.
- Overcome calamity and difficulties believing in miracles.

- Keep your heart pure.

- Keep your heart filled with love.

- Have an "Altruistic heart."

- Self-sacrifice—willing to act for the people of the world.

- Will the universe to be harmonious.

- It is a good idea to have the "wind" on your side.

Bill: What do people really lack and long for at work?

Norman: Everybody is different of course. It's hard to generalize because many people just lack. They lack enough money, they lack comfort, and they lack understanding.

We end up trying to change others and change events. We can't. We're given a life and you have to learn to accept it, be detached from it, and grow without end. That's pretty much the key.

Our educational system is so bad; we don't teach people how to pick a goal. We don't teach people how to master something. How do you graduate high school without a skill to make a living?

At a minimum, you should teach people how to be a plumber, a carpenter, how to cook, and so on. Certain fundamental things that they can make a living at instead of going through school for 13 years and going to work at a fast food restaurant.

Bill: What is the most important question leaders should ask employees?

Norman: Very simple. Number one, how can the organization serve you better? Number two, how do we give you the right tools? And number three, how do we give you the right opportunities so that you grow? And number four, "How can we serve the customer better?"

The other important thing is that we want to give people challenging work. We don't do that. We try to simplify it. Canon is a beautiful example. Canon had an assembly line to make their copiers, but then they went to conveyor belts. In a conveyor belt, you have a takt time of 2 minutes before the copier goes to the next person, each person doing the exact same thing over and over again. It is a crime.

Then Toyota taught them how to set up cells. Canon now has people capable of making an entire copier by themselves, installing and testing over 1,000 parts. It takes 3 hours to do it, and the copiers are superior in quality. One woman says that every time she completes a copier, she feels like she made a new baby.

Honda is now doing this in their new assembly line in Columbus, Ohio. Everyone should have the aspiration to be a master at something that other people need. I go to Japan often; I've been there 92 times. When I go, I love to go visit masters and Japanese living legends. I went one time to a place that had a living legend making pottery. I'm looking at this plate, and it was selling for about $2,000. And that's for a new plate! It wasn't an antique. Yes, real skill has real value. If you can pick something that you can become a master at, then you can have a great life—a wonderful life.

Bill: What is the most important question employees should ask leaders?

Norman: I want to do the best possible job for this company, so what should I do better for you? What can I do better for this company?

And of course, the CEO and managers should have an open ear to listen to the people. They're filled with marvelous ideas, but we don't have systems that work that way.

We have a screwy system where we reward the power with more money instead of dispersing the power throughout. Getting people to really be responsible, learning, and self-reliant is the challenge.

Bill: What is the most important question we should ask ourselves?

Norman: Are we growing? Are we maximizing our skills and capabilities? Are we serving others to have a great life?

Bill: Do you have any closing comments or observations you'd like to share?

Norman: I have spent the last year with creative geniuses developing a Harada Method APP—to help people improve themselves and the world. I hope people will test it. I thank you Bill for this opportunity and I wish you great success in selling the book—you deserve it.

Key Takeaways

- The Harada Method is a systematic system that allows the individual to take responsibility for defining their own path in achieving self-reliance and professional excellence.

- Give people a chance to be self-reliant and to align their goals with their work.

- Asking people to do the impossible because if you don't ask, they'll never do it.

- Ask people to make improvements, then let them come up with their own answers.

- Set up systems that don't require asking permission.

- Trust people to make the right decisions for their organizations and themselves.

- Try to minimize all criticism and don't blame people for mistakes because everybody learns from their mistakes.

- Companies should have a clear vision how their organization will grow and how they serve the benefit of the world.

- Give people challenging work.

- The CEO and managers should have an open ear to listen to the people. They're filled with marvelous ideas.

Lance Secretan

CEO, The Secretan Center

How to Stop Following the Herd and Break Out of the Mundane

Lance Secretan is a former Fortune 100 company CEO and is a pioneering philosopher whose bestselling books, inspirational talks, and life-changing retreats have touched the hearts and minds of hundreds of thousands of people worldwide. He is the author of 22 books about leadership, inspiration, corporate culture, and entrepreneurship. In his latest book, *The Bellwether Effect: Stop Following. Start Inspiring!*,[1] he proposes a theory that explains how and why leaders are attracted to, and seduced by, trendy ideas, and the process by which these ideas then become mainstream—and how we can change it.

I first heard of Lance Secretan when a colleague posted an update on LinkedIn about *The Bellwether Effect*. I was so intrigued by what I had just learned that I purchased the book. *The Bellwether Effect* is a book about the problems we create when we copy what others are doing and don't do our own thinking. I share this same belief, and it's one of the key reasons why this interview series exists.

Bill Fox: How can we create workplaces where every voice matters, everyone thrives and finds meaning, and change and innovation happen naturally?

Lance: The first thing we need to understand is to stop focusing on the processes and mechanics of the business quite as firmly as we have and put less emphasis on quantifying everything.

---

[1] Ontario, Canada: The Secretan Center Inc., 2018.

B. Fox, *The Future of the Workplace*,
https://doi.org/10.1007/978-1-4842-5098-3_5

We need to move things up a notch, so we are (1) inspiring all the time and (2) understanding the larger picture of what we're doing.

We just don't make widgets. We actually try to do something important in the world, and how does that transpire and how does it affect the world? I think Starbucks has done a terrific job of doing that. They aren't just making coffee. They're creating a "third place." That's their dream.

Bill: What does it take to get an employee's full attention and best performance?

Lance: It's funny that you ask that question. I'm not sure we need to do that. I think we need to get leaders' full attention. If we've got the full attention of leaders, then I think the employees would be fully engaged and there wouldn't be an issue. I think if a leader can't get the attention of the employees, that's a leadership problem—not an employee problem. The leader needs to really understand how to inspire and serve people, which is a subject we'll talk about later.

As I said in the book, everybody's afraid at every level. Leaders are afraid they're going to get ripped off by employees, get called out by shareholders or by the press or, who knows. Maybe they groped somebody 30 years ago and don't even remember it because they were in high school at the time and so on. So many people wake up today wondering, what's going to happen and will I survive the day? Well, we need to take that away. That's one of the things that holds us up. You can't perform at a high level if you're always frightened.

Bill: What do people lack and really long for at work?

Lance: I think a sense of being valued and a feeling that their contribution is of importance mostly. I make a lot of speeches publicly and around the world.

In every speech I ask this question: What proportion of the population do you think would give up what they do if they had a free choice?

I run this like an auction. I say let's start at 50%. Do you think 50% is a reasonable number? Immediately people say no, it's 60%. Then somebody will say no, it's 70%. Then somebody says no, it's 80%. Eighty percent is where we always end up.

Just think about this. Our history of, let's say, 100 years and, in particular, 40 years of the leadership development industry has been short. We're at a place where 80% of the population doesn't want to go to work. Why is that? Why have we created so many processes and so many environments that are so disrespectful and disenchanting to employees as well as for the leaders? The result of this is we've created miserable workplaces. And business is one of the three legs of our society, by the way—the other two being religion and government. Our liberal democracy depends on business. If we lose business, we lose everything. Unless you're a communist nation.

Bill: What is the most important question leaders should ask employees?

Lance: How may I serve you? It's the great question from the Knights of the Round Table. Lancelot would have discovered the Holy Grail if he had asked that question. That was the key. He never discovered where the Holy Grail was, but the person who would find it had to ask that question. If they had done so, they would have found the Holy Grail. So it is for us in our day to day life. Every leader needs to ask every follower, "How may I serve you?" That's the purpose of a leader.

Bill: What is the most important question employees should ask leaders?

Lance: On occasion, my wife would say to me something like "Treat me like a customer." And I think that's actually quite a good question to ask leaders. Leaders are asking us all the time to provide top notch customer service. All I really need from a leader is for the leader to treat me the same way that they're asking me to treat the customer. It's as simple as that. In the end, we should be treating each other and all of us, not just customers and employees but vendors, government regulators, unions—whoever is involved in making whatever it is we do happen. We should be treating each other the same way, which is to make sure that we're inspiring each other.

Focus is an important aspiration too I think, and I believe employees get excited by that as well. They like to know what's going on and where are we heading. What are we trying to do here? A lack of focus, vision, direction is very discomforting for employees. Employees like to know there's a clarity around the direction of the organization.

Bill: What is the most important question we should ask ourselves?

Lance: I think the most important question is something around, "Am I doing the work that sings to my soul—my calling?" I've just written a blog this week that talks about not giving up on our dreams. I was talking to a young man last week who has given up his college education in order to play music. He has a gig opening for a very big Grammy Award winning band. People are criticizing him for giving up his education. But I'm trying to support him by saying, "You know, you're following your dream and hardly anybody does that. That's the most important thing you can be doing."

Cornell did a big study on this. The biggest regret is between the three personalities: the actual self, the ought self (ought to be doing this), and the aspiring self (my dream). When people get in the later stages of their life, the one thing you'd think they would say is, "Well, the gap between my ought and my actual is too big." In other words, my responsibilities or how I should have behaved as a father, as a provider, as a spouse, and so on. But that's not what they say. The biggest gap is between the actual and how I never followed my dreams. That's something we want to be sure to ask ourselves, "Am I following my dream?" If you're doing work that you can't stand with people that you hate, you're clearly not following your dream. It's a miserable life. Stop doing that. Yes, it's going to be difficult. Yes, you're going to have to sacrifice. Yes, it's going to be tough. You'll probably starve. You probably won't even have a house to live in, but it will be worth it.

When we follow the herd, we stay with the mundane and sometimes even the immoral or criminal.

We're whores when we do that. We're prostituting ourselves and we're falling short of our potential. In other words, we're not anywhere near achieving our potential, and we're robbing ourselves when we do that. Yes, it's a journey and there's a price to pay to get to where you want to be. We won't always make it either. But you won't always make it the other way either, so you may as well go for it!

Bill: You've just written a book called *The Bellwether Effect*. What is a Bellwether and why did you choose that title?

Lance: Bellwether is a 13th-century word that describes a ram that has a bell tied around its neck. When the flock gets lost, the shepherd can find the flock because the ram leads the flock, and the shepherd can hear the bell. Typically, in the highlands where the sheep roam, it gets very misty and foggy at night. You can't find your way anywhere, so you're listening for the bell.

There are companies that essentially are the same. In the earlier era, the 1970s and so on, we had companies like IBM, Proctor & Gamble, Honeywell, and General Electric. These were Bellwethers because what they did was set the tone. You'd keep reading about them in *Harvard Business Review*, *Stanford Journal*, and elsewhere. People would talk about them. You'd see articles in *Fortune*, so they were always pioneering and coming up with new business processes. The trouble was it quite often worked for them, or at least they tinkered with it, even if it didn't work. But then a lot of other people would simply copy them. That's the Bellwether Effect.

They often copied them without understanding what they were doing. A good example of that is GE, which started something called stack ranking, which basically meant you ranked all your employees, then fired the bottom 10% based on performance. Very ruthless, very crude, and extremely violent emotionally for people. But what happened is other companies copied it. At one point, 80% of big companies had a stack ranking system. It added greatly to the pain of the employee's experience. It's just one of the many processes that we do in business where companies, in an unthinking way, copy Bellwether companies. As a consequence, they get themselves into trouble.

Bill: What question is at the heart of your book?

Lance: I think the question at the heart of the book is, why are we doing damaging things without thinking about it? Why do we thoughtlessly implement stuff like employee surveys of various kinds like engagement surveys and performance reviews?

Performance reviews are one of the most maligned, reviled, and hated processes in business, yet 80% of businesses do it. Nobody loves doing a performance review. Nobody loves having them done to them either. Yet we continue to do them. That's the Bellwether Effect, and it leads to what I call dissonance, which is the gap between what leaders think is happening and what employees say is happening. The gap between the thought and the experience.

I like to say to clients I work with, "Would you do this with your spouse?" Let's take a performance appraisal. Would you say to your honey, "Hi honey, we're going to sit down and have a little conversation. We're going to discuss your key performance indicators and your budget. We'll do some 360 surveys to see how your colleagues think about you."

You wouldn't get three words out of your mouth before you'd be backing out the door. Well, if you wouldn't do it with your spouse, why would you do it at work? It's just as uncomfortable, diminishing, demeaning, and demoralizing at work as it is at home. That's a good example of the Bellwether Effect, which we copy mindlessly and it's doing terrible damage.

I did a piece of research into the characteristics people most admire in great leaders. There were things like "visionary, builds great teams, motivates, strategic thinker", and so on. I did a survey of what do people think of when they think of a great romantic relationship. Here you have words like "intimacy, vulnerability, passion, truth, trust, love, caring, and humility."

So, we have these two different lists of words where we expect to get up in the morning and say, "Goodbye honey, I'm going to go to work now. I'm going to be visionary, motivational, a great team builder, and a strategic thinker." Then at the end of the day, you say, "Hi honey, I'm back. I'm going to be intimate, compassionate, passionate, caring, loving." Why would we do this? This is ridiculous. We are one whole human being, and we need to be those things we admire in relationships—everywhere. Because those are the things that build great relationships whether it's at home or anywhere else.

We love people who are truthful, compassionate, caring, and loving. Those are the people we are drawn to. Those are the people who inspire us. The whole idea of the warrior at work, the great leader who is a General Patton type of cardboard cutout, is simply obsolete. It doesn't fit with what people want and need today.

Bill: What are the key takeaways you'd like readers to get from your book?

Lance: The first one is to make sure that we understand the difference between motivation and inspiration. There's a clear difference between these two. We have become very good at motivating, which is a fear-based system. We essentially use bribery all the time in every place you can think of whether it's in marketing (buy this product or you'll be ugly), in religion (join my religion or you'll go to hell), in healthcare (follow this protocol or you'll die), in education (pass this exam or I'll fail you), in business (do what I say or I'll fire you), or in parenting (do what I say or I'll punish you). I mean, there's no end to this you see.

This is the system we've learned. This is the system we now practice. That's fear-based motivation. The idea is to exploit the behavior of others by manipulating and controlling others, and forcing outcomes from those people, which benefit *me*.

Inspiration is exactly the opposite of that. It is not about me, it's about you. It's not about exploiting your behavior, it's about helping you to become fulfilled, rich, and successful—rich in the sense not of money but of richness in your life. The whole idea is that we need to become as good at inspiring people as we have become at motivating them.

We need to motivate. There are times and places where that needs to happen. But it's the only thing we know. We have no idea how to inspire people. The way I summarize this is, motivation is lighting a fire under someone, and inspiration is lighting a fire within someone. There's a big difference. We need to know when to be inspiring and when to be motivational.

■ The big takeaway from this book would be, can you be inspiring?

Do you know how to inspire? Do you know how to inspire all the time even when you're having a bad day—even when you don't feel inspiring? That's the great test. When we get cut off in traffic, we have a choice. We can flip the bird, or we can smile. Everywhere in our lives, we have these choices and the choice should always be to be inspiring.

Bill: What is the purpose of leadership?

Lance: That's a great question. I think we've come to think about leadership as heroic and in a context of the military or corporate life. Sometimes we see it in politics but not always.

Here we are where we only think about leaders that way, whereas a mother is a leader. A student at school is a leader. The kids on the playground are leaders. We're leaders in all kinds of aspects of our lives. Indeed, sports celebrities and entertainers, they're leaders too.

We need to reframe how we see this because I think leadership is about influencing outcomes in many ways. It's about serving people. It's about building relationships.

All leadership is a relationship. It either works or it doesn't. If it doesn't work, you're an ineffective leader. If people will follow you anywhere because they have a great relationship with you, then you're an effective leader.

Bill: What's wrong with the current state of leadership and how do we fix it?

Lance: Yes, we've got a lot of things wrong with it. One of the things that's increasingly become obvious to all of us is that the compensation system for leaders is out of whack. We should be sharing a little more evenly across all people that achieve results—not just the leader. When leaders get paid $50 and $100 million a year, it's just not sensible it seems to me. I think that needs to change. And I think we need to be more democratic. I don't mean socialist. I mean democratic in the sense of fairness and sharing the spoils of what gets accomplished. It isn't just the leader who does all these things. Very often it's the employees who make the leader successful and great—or appear great. So, that would be one of the things we need to change about leadership.

I think we also probably need to slow down a little. Leaders spend a lot of time these days working on the inconsequential—about a third of their time, or more for a lot of them, is drained by email. If you think about a leader in front of a computer doing emails all day, that's a foolish waste of time. The things a leader should be doing are external. A leader effectively should be out representing the organization in the world, in the marketplace and elsewhere, and also internally—in listening and talking and hearing.

I've done a lot of objecting to employee engagement surveys because I think they're pretty useless. I don't think a performance appraisal is listening. I think if you want to hear, you sit down with an employee and say, tell me, what's going on? In a supermarket, instead of doing broad market research surveys about baked beans, for example, the CEO of the baked bean company could go into the supermarket and ask the person who just picked the competitive brand, why did you do that? That's research. That's how leaders could become more effective.

Bill: In your book, you say, "If I were CEO of a major enterprise again, one of the changes I would make would be to replace the word "leader" with "coach," or even "partner." Why is that?

Lance: We've got this misunderstanding about what leadership entails. Many people think it means creating a strategic plan and then telling other people how to get there. Leadership is actually about coaching the best out of everybody that's on your team. What's remarkable, and I certainly found this when I built a Fortune 100 company when I was running Manpower Ltd., is the idea of having great people. When I say great, I mean people with potential. People who are smart, intelligent, hungry, ambitious, creative, innovative, compassionate, and caring—all those things. Then we need to facilitate the development of those people. Help them with their growth. Help them to achieve and to dream because they can do that.

Years ago, when I was at Manpower, I bumped into a guy who was a helicopter pilot in the North Sea in Scotland. I loved him. He was just fantastic. He had a great attitude. Very smart. Lovely man to be with. I offered him a job. I said, "We'll hire you." I went back to London where my offices were, and I met with my team and said, "I just hired this guy." They said, "What's he going to do?" I said, "Oh, that's a good question! I didn't ask him that! I need to talk to him."

I went back to him and said, "You know there's a little detail. We didn't talk about what you're going to do. Let's talk about that a little bit. What would you like to do?" Note that I was asking him what he thought, not "I think you should be doing this." He said, "You know. I fly missions out to the North Sea oil rigs. It's a cowboy business. It's unregulated. There's no insurance. There's no union—nothing. It's a mess. It's just unorganized people and they're crashing, burning, and literally dying regularly. People have accidents. It's just awful. What I think we should do is organize all these guys. Pull them into one organization and provide a master organization that supplies services to all the oil rigs in the North Sea." Now, that was a long way from anything we did. We didn't do anything like that at all. I said, "Okay, let's do it." We became the largest North Sea oil rig company in Scotland.

What's a leader supposed to do? The leader's supposed to find out what the potential is of employees and help them reach their dreams. They know what to do. I don't need to come up with a strategy.

Key Takeaways

- Stop focusing on processes and mechanics as firmly as we have.

- What we really need to do is get leaders' full attention.

- You can't perform at a high level if you're always frightened.

- What proportion of the population do you think would give up what they do if they had a free choice?

- Business is one of the three legs of our society—we can't lose it.

- How may I serve you?

- Would you treat me like a customer?

- Am I doing the right thing for the rest of my life?

- Am I following my dream?

- When we follow the herd, we stay with the mundane.

- There are companies that are essentially bellwethers.

- Why are we doing things without thinking about it?

- We are drawn to people who are truthful, compassionate, caring, and loving—those are the people who inspire us.

Sarah Rozenthuler

Founder, Bridgework Consulting Ltd.

How to Create the Right Conditions for Stunning Conversations

Sarah Rozenthuler is an expert on having big conversations and wrote a book about it. She is the author of *Life-Changing Conversations*[1] and a psychologist, leadership coach, and the founder of Bridgework Consulting Ltd. In her book, she talks about the seven strategies that are needed to help people talk about what matters most and shares some of those ideas here.

Bill Fox: How can we create workplaces where every voice matters, everyone thrives and finds meaning, and change and innovation happen naturally?

Sarah Rozenthuler: It's a big question with many dimensions to it. But if I just address the essence of it, one of the key things is to make the workplace psychologically safe and stimulating.

---

[1] London: Watkins Publishing, 2012.

© Bill Fox 2020
B. Fox, *The Future of the Workplace*,
https://doi.org/10.1007/978-1-4842-5098-3_6

People will only find their voice and share their thinking if they feel safe.

Early on our ideas might be half-baked rather than anything really polished because often we refine our thinking in conversation with other people. In order for people to share those early thoughts, they need to feel safe. The combination of psychological safety and making it stimulating is a really interesting combination, so everybody can thrive.

I think people are increasingly recognizing that we can all wear a corporate mask and that there are parts of ourselves that we think are more socially acceptable or presentable.

What is called for here in terms of making a workplace more innovative and more fulfilling for human beings is to help people drop some of that mask and show up more authentically.

While it's easy to say, I think that shift is actually quite challenging. Because in showing up more authentically, that also might be sharing parts of ourselves that feel more vulnerable and risky to share.

I like what the people at the Harvard Negotiation Project say about their work on conversations. One of the things they say is that difficult conversations are about difficult emotions. And actually, I think to break through to that more innovative and creative thinking and talking space, there's often a difficult conversation to be had because there's a diversity of perspective. Or there might be a degree of conflict. So actually, part of the journey is learning to manage difficult emotions in oneself and in other people. Inside of that, how much do I express? What's appropriate? Dropping the corporate mask sounds simple, but it's not easy.

To break through to that more innovative and creative thinking and talking space, there's often a difficult conversation to be had because there's a diversity of perspective.

Bill: What does it take to get an employee's full attention and best performance?

Sarah: It's really important that people feel listened to. That to me is just fundamental. If people are feeling sidelined, or if they're just feeling that they're an expendable resource or easily replaceable, they are not feeling valued as a human being. I know if that's going on inside me, I wouldn't be engaged. I wouldn't be giving my best thinking to a project. Feeling listened to is absolutely critical.

Feeling stretched and stimulated and involved is important too so that there's genuine curiosity from coworkers and other team members. For example, do people want to know what are your ideas or what has been your experience? Are you being asked to share your wisdom? What is the unique human being you are, what are you seeing? Are people properly engaged in a conversation? It's back to this combination of both feeling supported and safe, but also feeling stretched and challenged as well.

Bill: What do people lack and really long for at work?

Sarah: I think people really long for self-expression—to be in alignment with their heart's desire or passion. What is uniquely theirs to do. What I notice in people that I work with is even if that person can't express and articulate clearly what their purpose or their passion is, what they absolutely do know is when there's a lack of that. When people are not following their north star, they will notice that their energy is low. They feel directionless or burned out or chronically understimulated in some way.

I can relate from own experience. I've had times in my own career where I felt absolutely off my path, and it was such a painful experience for me. That's partly why I do the work that I do because the difference in terms of felt sense between feeling on our path and off our path is huge. So, I think change often begins with people when they notice what's not working even if they're not able to articulate actually what it is they want.

It's great if you can just say to yourself, "You know, I'm stuck." Then think through it in conversation and reflection to work out where that "stuckness" is coming from. What I think is often missing is that sense of true alignment with one's path in life and in work. At a deep level, I think that is what we're all seeking whether we're conscious of that or not. Even if we can't articulate it.

Bill: What is the most important question leaders should ask employees?

Sarah: I think it would be something along the lines of how could we come together in service of something greater than ourselves? To put it in its most simple terms, I think that's what teams and organizations are ultimately all about. It's about creating something that's greater than the sum of parts—a reflection of individuals working alone could never achieve.

I also think the service part of the above question, bringing something new and more valuable to the world, is an important part of that question of that mission. My observation on a personal level is that what truly motivates people at a deep level is that sense of being part of something larger that goes beyond my little life and needs. I think to the extent that any of this can move us out of self-absorption and into an orientation that is about serving the greater whole, that's the degree to which we feel fulfilled. We're willing to go the extra mile.

From a leadership perspective, that's the question I would be asking. It's a question on one level that might sound quite simple, but actually how you get a diverse range of human beings to pull together in the same direction is a challenge in and of itself. That's the question that I think is critical.

Bill: What is the most important question employees should ask leaders?

Sarah: It could be something around direction such as where are we going? But not in a conventional sense around a planned future or what are the strategic goals for the next 5 years?

I would be encouraging employees to ask me, "What's the future you're sensing into? What are you feeling what wants to emerge here? What's the marketplace really calling for in terms of this organization and how it needs to evolve and what that might mean for us as employees?"

What I would be hoping for from a leadership team is that sense of them scanning the horizon. At Oxford Saïd Business School, they use the term "ripple intelligence." What are the ripples coming through that can inform us about the future and how we need to be evolving? I think a leadership team really has a responsibility to be doing that sensing and feeling into the ecosystem and sharing that with employees. Then also hearing what the employee's sense of that is. That would be the dialogue I will be encouraging employees to stimulate with leaders.

Bill: What is the most important question we should ask ourselves?

Sarah: It would be along the lines of to what extent do I feel truly alive with life, with what life is calling me to do? It's getting back to this sense of right path. To what extent am I following my north star or not? I think actually we all intuitively and instinctively have a sense of that.

What I see in the leadership work I do is that when people start asking questions of themselves on that level—while in some cases that might be quite uncomfortable to ask that question as it might reveal some difficult feelings—it is truly catalytic. It's catalytic in terms of people's career and development because the difference between somebody being in a place of alignment and being in a place of misalignment is absolutely huge.

It's huge in terms of the energy they have to bring. It's huge in terms of their creativity, how their self-expression flows, and in how open they are to be connecting with other people. For me right now, the really critical question to be asking ourselves is around alignment. How much am I resonating with where I am in this organization and where I am in life? Not an easy question but that's where my own thoughts are. In the coaching work I'm doing, that seems to be a really strong emerging thread of conversation.

Bill: What has been your experience being in this interview?

Sarah: It's interesting. What I'm noticing is that I feel I'm thinking here with you. I had no idea what I was going to say.

What I'm noticing is a kind of *we* between us.

There's something about connectivity between human beings—how that works and how that can be more effective. There's a thread around purpose and passion. There's a thread around alignment between people in service of something greater between the individual and their own sense of calling in life. That whole territory feels really rich to me here. Just conversation, alignment, and purpose.

Bill: One of the concepts from your book *Life-Changing Conversations* that fascinated me was the idea of a conversation being an *aperture* through which life unfolds. Can you talk more about this idea?

Sarah: It's interesting that you picked up on the metaphor of the aperture, for which I'd have to acknowledge the work of David Bohm, the quantum physicist, and his ideas around dialogue. The fundamental question he was asking was, "Why is it when there are big things to talk about that really matter—and whether that's nation to nation or team to team or individual to individual—why is it that as human beings it so often ends in violence or silence?" As I said in my book,

> *"The word aperture fired my imagination and ignited all sorts of questions in my mind. What if, I said to myself, I was to see each conversation as an opening through which my life unfolded? What difference would it make to my life if I engaged with another person in a way that kept the space between us as expansive as possible?"*

He was bringing in insights from quantum physics to try and understand human interaction. That idea of an aperture. We think of an oak tree as coming from an acorn, but actually it's more accurate to see the acorn as this aperture through which the oak tree unfolds. And it's not just about the acorn. There have to be the right nutrients in the soil, the right amount of sunshine and moisture in the air.

But I just found that notion of aperture really evocative. This idea of a portal through which a whole entire massive oak tree could come into being. Then when working with different leadership teams and going into different organizations, I was seeing very clearly that when people could create the right conditions for a conversation—where they could talk about things that mattered without relationships rupturing—then it was amazing to watch what could unfold. Not instantly but over time. Whether that was a new strategy coming into being or operationalizing what was quite a challenging strategy. That's where I started making the connection in my own mind that a conversation can be like a doorway.

One of the ideas I tried to convey in the book was that on one level you could say, "Isn't having a conversation quite a simple thing?" And actually, no it's not sometimes. I've coached people who have waited decades before they had a conversation with a family member. In one case, literally 23 years with one client.

What I'm interested in is how do we help ourselves and how do we help each other get over the line? How do we cross that threshold to have that conversation? Because in that particular individual's case who waited 23 years, it's not an exaggeration to say that her whole life shifted by having that conversation that had been on hold for all those years. Things changed in her personal life and in her professional life. I'm still in touch with her, and she's absolutely lit up in terms of where she is now.

As a psychologist and as a practitioner and even in terms of my own struggles, having big conversations is what I'm really interested in. In an organizational setting, how wecan open up the conversation to help create openings where truly new thinking and ideas come in? In a more personal setting, it's about the wider context that might be a whole new relationship with a family member that has a tremendous impact.

Bill: I found your book *Life-Changing Conversations* brilliant and deeply profound. Will you be writing another book?

Sarah: My next book is about leadership. It's about how leadership teams can come together in the service of something greater than themselves. It's picking up on the movement of this whole purpose-driven business, which seems to be capturing more and more imaginations in the corporate world. And yet, it's not an easy journey to make.

What I'm writing about is what that calls for from leaders and leadership teams because I think it calls for a much greater quality of dialogue and thinking. It's taking some of the ideas of life-changing conversations and applying them very clearly in the leadership context by looking at that question of purpose.

BIGGER CONVERSATIONS

There were three big ideas that stood out for me in this interview that can lead us to having bigger conversations:

- People will only find their voice and share their thinking if they feel safe.

- Making a workplace more innovative and more fulfilling for human beings is to help people drop their mask and show up more authentically.

- Part of the journey is learning to manage difficult emotions in oneself and in other people.

So why is it important to have these bigger conversations? I asked Sarah in a follow-up interview and she said, "By enhancing our ability to talk together we can create the lives that we desire, for ourselves and for those whose lives we touch. If one of us finds the courage to talk, then another does, then another, this domino effect could even change the world."

Key Takeaways

- Make the workplace psychologically safe and stimulating.
- Help people drop the corporate mask.
- People need to feel supported, safe, stretched, and challenged.
- People long to be in alignment with their heart's desire or passion.
- Change often begins when people notice what's not working.
- How could we come together in service of something greater than ourselves?
- What truly motivates people at a deep level is being part of something much larger.

- What's the future you're sensing into?
- What are the ripples coming through that can inform us?
- To what extent do I feel truly alive with life?
- How much am I resonating with where I am in this organization?
- I feel I'm here thinking with you.
- Conversations about things that matter can be a doorway for the amazing to unfold.

Jeff Dalton

CEO, Broadsword Solutions Corporation

Making Every Voice Matter

Jeff Dalton is a process innovator, chief evangelist at AgileCxO, author, and CEO at Broadsword Solutions Corporation. Jeff's latest book is *Great Big Agile: An OS for Agile Leaders.*[1]

I first met Jeff Dalton when I interviewed him for my interview series book, *5 Minutes to Process Improvement Success.*[2] Since that time, I've met with Jeff several times at various conferences and training events. Jeff's sessions are always filled, and he always delivers valuable insights in a fun and entertaining way.

Bill Fox: How can we create workplaces where every voice matters, everyone thrives and finds meaning, and change and innovation happen naturally?

Jeff Dalton: We've been struggling with this question for 10 years at Broadsword, the company I founded 11 years ago. We started out as a traditional consulting firm with a leveraged model and different levels of performers—senior consultants, directors, and managers. We were a little bit like a traditional Big 4 consulting model, which is where some of us came from.

---

[1] New York: Apress, 2018.
[2] Bill Fox, self-published, 2012.

© Bill Fox 2020
B. Fox, *The Future of the Workplace*,
https://doi.org/10.1007/978-1-4842-5098-3_7

Last year we had a joint epiphany. We were out there in the world talking with our clients about agile, self-organization, and collaboration when we realized we weren't doing a good job at it ourselves! We really wanted to ensure that all of the smart people who worked at our company had a voice, but more importantly, felt like they were contributing and thriving in their own lives. We wanted them to feel like they were empowered to do the things they needed to do to be delighted. So I started what I call the "no victims" policy. There are no victims in our company—everyone is empowered to do what they need to do to be successful. They're empowered to resolve issues and be equals. No managers.

We wanted to ensure that all of the smart people who worked at our company had a voice by empowering everyone to do what they need to do to be successful.

Of course, you can't be successful without some level of organization, so in order to facilitate this policy, we've started to adopt a model called "Holacracy." I was literally Googling "self-organizing companies" when I ran across the Holacracy web site. I'm not sure how much you've been following Brian Robertson and his journey, but Brian created this model a number of years ago and has helped many companies find great success with self-organization. It's a constitution-based model where your organization is self-governing. In some ways, it's a supercharged version of what we've been doing with our clients—crisply defined processes where people have very clear defined roles in the constitution. They have a lot of input into each role, and their role is designed to give them the meaning they are searching for.

Obviously, we have some roles that have to be performed, but there are also elective roles so that people are focusing on the things that make them most empowered and most successful in their careers. One of the key concepts in Holacracy is "learning to separate role from soul." An individual at our company might have 20 roles. For example, I have a role such as "writer of proposals," and another like "reviewer of financials." I also have "teacher of classes" (a role others also have) and "planner of retreats." We're codifying all of the roles in our constitution and are starting to become proficient in this self-organization model where every employee is responsible for their own meaning and their own innovation. It's really starting to change the face of our company.

People needed coaching more than management, and I became concerned that too much oversight was stifling innovation.

For a while, we had a couple of dedicated managers—people whose job it was to direct the other people. We realized early on we were uncomfortable with this because everyone in our company is a high performer. People needed coaching more than management, and I became concerned that too much oversight was stifling innovation (another thing we always tell our clients!). We haven't fully implemented Holacracy yet, but we are on the path. The results have been overwhelmingly positive.

Bill: What does it take to get an employee's full attention and best performance?

Jeff: This is a complicated question, with many inputs and qualifiers. I've struggled with this idea my whole career. But if I'm proud of anything in my career, it's that I've done a decent job bringing great performance out of people. I think the way to do that is to encourage and motivate them to want to do it and to be excited about what they're doing.

I'm always reminded of the mantras of the Armed Services. The Navy says "People, People, People" is their focus. The Army says, "Process, Process, Process." And the Air Force says, "Mission, Mission, Mission." These are the things that you hear military professionals talk about as being what really drives them in their particular branch. What I've learned in my company is that people want to be excited about all three of those things, the mission is the most important one. It isn't enough just to give them a mission and a goal. You also need to focus on the people, making it easier for them to focus on the mission.

Finally, process is important too. Process is nothing more than a definition of expected behavior, and I find that the right amount of process guidance can be very liberating and a powerful force in growing your culture. So, it's a three-legged stool—and architecture of sorts. Laying out a very clear mission that's exciting to them, laying out a clear vision for a culture that helps people be successful, and laying out the process in a way that makes their job easier and more successful. All three things together have to be intertwined and work together.

Bill: What do people really lack and long for at work?

Jeff: It's interesting because it's really evolved over the last decade. When I was a young programmer and then consultant, what was most important was a solid career track, making more money, and moving up to be a partner, senior manager, or vice president. People were really focused on that. I've been excited this past couple of years because it seems like the workforce is evolving. People are more interested in the work environment with time and challenge being the most important things.

People want to have time to do the things that are important in their life. A career, making money, and moving up are the things that people do, but it's not the reason we work. We don't work to move up and get a new title. We don't work to make an additional $50,000 per year. Those things are nice and good things (and wholly necessary), but what we really work for is to spend time with our family, relax, read, and do other pursuits outside of our careers. And be challenged every day.

As part of our own Holacracy journey, we have implemented a couple of new policies. One of them is we have an unlimited Personal Time Off (PTO) policy. We have no designated vacation days by role. We used to say if you were a senior consultant, you got 3 weeks. If you were a manager, you got 4 weeks. Now we say, "OK, you take the PTO that you need to take to make yourself successful." That way people get ample vacation time, but more importantly, they get ample time to take off to do things that are important to them. All they need to do is collaborate with their peers to ensure nothing falls on the floor.

What we were finding with the traditional model of time management was that someone would use up their vacation, and then they would have to miss important family events or have to come to us asking special permission to get that time off. Who likes doing that? With the model we have now, it's much more about supporting the team and being collaborative. The person brings it to the team and says, "I need to take four days off to go to a wedding." And the team will say, "OK that's fine with us, we can pick up some slack and succeed without you being there." If someone on the team were to abuse the policy—which has not happened in the 2 years we've been doing it—the team would most certainly let them know that they're not being a team player!

We do, however, have guidelines. For example, our clients have to be taken care of, and important internal tasks must be accounted for. Team members know that if they have your back, you'll have theirs. Allowing people to use their time in a way that satisfies their life, as well as their career, has been a game changer in the business. It frees up the organization to be a lot nimbler and a lot more focused on what is important. It's created a very strong and dedicated group of professionals.

Bill: What is the most important question leaders should ask employees?

Jeff: How can I help? This is a really important question that we don't hear often enough. I try to remember to ask this question every day to at least one person. How can I help you succeed in what you're doing? How can I help you reach your goal? If you look at the model we've developed where people have autonomy to grow in their own area of interest, the most important thing is to help them do that.

How can I help? This is a really important question that we don't hear often enough.

But I also sometimes get more specific with it, "Specifically, what can I do right now to help make you more successful?" I think this notion of servant leadership is overhyped in our market, but I really believe in the principle. Teams want you to make decisions and be a strong leader, but they also want you to serve them and help make them successful. In the book *We Were Soldiers Once … and Young*,[3] the protagonist (legendary Calvary Lt. Colonel Hal Moore) famously promised his young troopers that "when we go into battle, I will be the first to set foot on the field, and I will be the last to step off." That's been my model since I've first read those words.

Bill: What's the most important question employees should ask leaders?

Jeff: I'm writing a book for young technology professionals about how they can take steps early on to be more successful in their career. As part of that book, I've been interviewing CEOs of technology companies to get their perspective. One of the things I'm hearing from them is that, especially with the younger team members, they are not focused on making the company successful. They are not asking, "What can I personally do to make you and your company more successful?"

I think the most important question an employee should be asking management is, "How can I make this organization rock?" "How can I help us win?" When I was coming up in the technology business, I used to ask my immediate manager, "How can I make you successful in your mission?"

I think sometimes people, especially in large companies, don't really see the traceability between their actions and the success of the company. They have a bit of a disconnect between sales and engineering. If you go to a big engineering company like Lockheed Martin, L3, or SAIC, the engineers have very little visibility into what the sales team is doing. There tends to be some friction between the two groups. I tell them, "Look, this is a team. Nothing happens unless your salespeople sell something." And the salespeople don't continue to be rewarded if you don't deliver. We all need each other! If the accounts receivable manager can't get her invoices out, none of us can pay our rent—help make everyone successful! I think people need to do a better job of saying, "What can I do to help this company be more successful?" Then get really specific on it and focus on those things. If they start asking those questions, then everyone is going to be communicating and be on the same page, which should be "let's make this organization rock, so we have great careers, build great products, and have a great time doing it!" Anything else is a waste of talent.

---

[3] Harold G. Moore and Joseph L. Galloway, *We Were Soldiers Once…and Young* (New York: Random House, 1992).

Bill: What's the most important question we should ask ourselves?

Jeff: Ha! Ask me an easy one! But I think one of the most important questions that we can ask ourselves is, "Why not?" As human beings, we are so acclimated to conformance. Even in the United States, which is probably the least conforming nation in the world, a place where engineers are known for extreme innovation through winging it, thinking outside the box, and for challenging authority, we don't often ask, "Why not?" Too many companies run their teams by saying "because I said so." Screw that.

I think one of the most important questions that we can ask ourselves is why not? I've been encouraging my children to ask this question because they'll come home from college and say, "You know, the teacher said I can't do that." I said, "Well, why not?" They'll say, "There's nothing I can do." And I'll say, "Why not?" (laughter). Sometimes I'll be in a contract negotiation with a really large manufacturing client, and they'll say, "Well, we can't go with you unless you have this manufacturing liability insurance" even though it has nothing to do with what we do. And I'll say, "Why not?" Lawyers are called, managers are consulted, and procurement is befuddled. But they eventually come around. Good times!

I think the "Why not?" question is probably the most important thing because we need to get people to explain and verbalize why they take the positions they do.

So many times they're just repeating what they think is an unbreakable rule. Instead of saying, "I won't do that" or "We can't do that," let's say, "Why not, why can't we do that?" Let's start the conversation, let's collaborate on the answer, and let's figure out how everybody can win here, and that starts with those two simple words, "Why not?"

Key Takeaways

- Empower everyone to do the things they need to do to be successful.

- Allow everyone to be responsible for their own meaning and innovation.

- People need coaching more than management because too much oversight can stifle innovation.

- Encourage and motivate people to great performance and be excited about what they're doing.

- A mission and a goal isn't enough. It's People, Mission, and Process.

- Process is nothing more than a definition of expected behavior and is important in growing a powerful culture.

- People want to have time to do the things that are important in their life.

- How can I help? This is a really important question that we don't hear often enough.

- Specifically what can I do right now to help you be more successful?

- How can I make this organization rock?

- Sometimes people don't really see the traceability between their actions and the success of the company, but we all need each other.

- "Why not?" is one of the most important questions we can ask ourselves because we are so acclimated to conformance.

- The "Why not?" question is probably the most important thing because we need to get people to explain and verbalize why they take the positions they do.

Alan Seale

Entrepreneur, Author

How to More Effectively and Authentically Respond

Alan is a transformation catalyst, leadership coach, author of seven books, speaker, and the director of the Center for Transformational Presence.[1] His programs help people develop and expand their capacities for intuitive thinking, navigating complexity, cutting to the essence of situations and circumstances and begin making shifts immediately, partnering with potential, and making breakthrough and transformation an everyday part of your work. Transformational Presence provides the foundational skills and capacities needed for dynamic and effective leadership in today's rapidly changing world.

I got to know Alan Seale and his work after reading his book *Create a World That Works: Tools for Personal and Global Transformation*.[2] I found Alan's story and work were very similar to my own, so it motivated me to get in touch and connect for this interview. Alan's core message is "the more we pay attention—to everything—the more our awareness expands allowing us to more powerfully, effectively, and authentically respond." Alan's latest book, *Transformational Presence: How to Make a Difference In a Rapidly Changing World*,[3] is a great resource for anyone interested in impacting the future of the workplace.

---

[1] https://transformationalpresence.org/
[2] San Francisco: Red Wheel/Weiser, 2011.
[3] Topsfield, MA: Center for Transformational Presence, 2017.

Bill Fox: How can we create workplaces where every voice matters, everyone thrives and find meaning, and change and innovation happen naturally?

Alan Seale: The first answer that comes to me is you just do it! We think we have to have all these models, special approaches. Just do it! Just decide this is what we're doing!

It's about simply making it clear, "You know what, in our workplace, everybody matters."

Invite people into that conversation and just make that choice. You don't need a big model or sophisticated thing or need to hire some expensive consulting firm to help you do that.

Just decide it and do it. Why make this so hard? Just do it.

Bill: What does it take to get an employee's full attention and best performance?

Alan: Find out what they care about and then make sure they're doing something within the company that they care about. There needs to be a connection between the individual's life purpose—I call it soul mission—and the soul mission or purpose of the business or organization.

There can be layers of this, of course. Is the organization truly operating in integrity with themselves and their mission? Are they operating in a way that's congruent with who they say they are and what's important to them? And if they are, then find the connection between that employee's mission and the company's mission. Create an environment where the employee feels like, "Wow, when I come to work every day, I get to live my purpose. I get to be who I fully am and do what I'm here to do in this world by working for this company."

What if creating these kinds of workplaces is simply a choice and you go for it? If not everybody in the company is on board with that, that's OK. The people will fall away who need to fall away for whatever reason. But bring the company into alignment with its own soul mission or purpose and make sure that your employees or company colleagues feel like they can live their own soul missions at work. It might take some time for this to open out through the organization, but it can happen if you make the choice and move with conscious intention in that direction.

Bill: What do people really lack and long for at work?

Alan: It's an interesting question for me because I work with so many people who absolutely love what they do. By the time they come to me, they come not because they're needing to make a change but because they are ready to fly with what they're doing. They're looking for coaching support in taking some really big steps.

So I just want to acknowledge upfront that I'm not the person who is constantly out there in the field with a lot of people who are miserable in what they do.

That said, I think not just in the workplace, but everywhere—what do people want out of life? They want to feel like they matter. They long for that sense of making a difference—that who they are and what they do mean something. That want to be able to say, "It matters that I'm here." It matters to people that what they sense and feel and experience is heard and recognized. It matters to them that they are seen. It matters to them that they are heard.

We all want to feel like we make a difference. It matters that we are here. I think that's not just in the workplace. That's in relationships, that's in families, that's in communities, that's in organizations.

You mention that you've been reading my blog, so you know that I've been writing a series of articles on what I'm calling "The Great Breaking Open." And to me, yes, we can look at all the systems that are, what many would say, breaking down. But to me, they are breaking open.

The human spirit, in general, all over the world at this point is just saying, "No more. No more."

And what is deep underneath all of that is the breaking open of the human spirit. The human spirit, in general, all over the world at this point is just saying, "No more. No more."

Bill: What is the most important question leaders should ask employees?

Alan: What's important to them? We think about interviewing people to make sure they're the right fit for the company, but you also need to know is the company the right fit for the person? What if interviews are really both ways—certainly there are companies that do that. The more enlightened, progressive, forward-thinking companies are recognizing that, but I think still for a lot of companies they're just looking for the person who can do the job that they need to get done. Their main concern is finding the best person to do that because they are primarily focused on results. It's very transactional.

As I sit with your question, I feel it's not about what is the most important question to ask the potential employee; it's even more about how you as the employer choose to show up as you meet that person. And what do you care about with them? And how does the company care about its people? What is the relationship that you start to build with them right from the beginning? As you start to build a relationship with that person, you'll quickly recognize whether or not this person is the right fit for a good working relationship, and not just for a transaction—not just for getting a job done.

There are three fundamental principles behind our Transformational Presence work. They come out of the ancient wisdom teachings and now come from quantum physics. The first is that everything is energy in motion and everything is part of a larger process unfolding. We need to be looking at every single thing that is happening within a much larger context in order to understand it and understand how it fits into a much bigger picture.

The second is that energy cannot be created or destroyed, it can only be transformed. What that principle is saying is that whatever is in front of you right now—the challenge, opportunity, person, or idea—is your next cocreative partner. In Transformational Presence work, we say, "A problem is not something to be solved, it's a message to be listened to." What you have named as a problem is actually just trying to tell you something. Our job is to pay attention. Listen to it and it will tell you something you need to know.

And the third principle is that the world is built on a matrix of relationships. If we talk about companies and employees, what we're really talking about is relationships. If we take good care of the relationships within the company—if we take good care of the space in between us—then the rest is going to take care of itself.

In the bigger picture of where we are in the world right now, I feel like we are, in so many ways, asking the wrong questions.

I actually love that you're asking these questions because, to me, it's really pointing out that, in the bigger picture of where we are in the world right now, I feel like we are, in so many ways, asking the wrong questions. Your question here is pointing that out! It's helping us say to the world, yes these are the questions we are taught to ask, or these are sort of the common questions that everybody thinks are the right ones, but they're really old questions. There's a whole new set of questions we need to be asking now. And those questions are based much more on relationships and honoring the human spirit.

Bill: What's the most important question employees should ask leaders?

Alan: What do they care about? What's important to the management of the company? What's important to the company? Because we have to find out, do we meet here? To me, it's not just the question the employee is asking of the potential employer, but for the employee to have a chance to ask that question of other people who are working for the company as well. What does this company care about? It's one thing to hear that from the management, it's another thing to hear that from the people who are part of the company. What do they really care about? Then the potential employee can discern how that fits for them. They can ask themselves, "Is this a place I want to be?"

Bill: What is the most important question we should ask ourselves?

Alan: That's a really good question. That takes me back to our work at Transformational Presence, which is built on just three basic questions. The first one is maybe the most important question, but I feel like the series of the three is what brings it all together.

The first question is, "What wants to happen?" This is not what I want or what you want or even what we want together. Rather, in the bigger picture, what wants to happen here in service of something much bigger than me or you—in service of something bigger than your company? What wants to happen in the way your company moves in the world? How can your company serve in a bigger way? What wants to happen in terms of my relationship with the company? What is it I have to bring here?

All of these questions are held within that bigger question: What wants to happen? There are many variations on that question: What's waiting to unfold here? What is the breakthrough that is ready to happen? What is the shift? What is the opening? What's the opportunity here?

Our job is to come from that place, that perspective of tapping into the bigger message, the bigger request that's being made right now in our lives.

The second question of our three is, "OK, if that's what wants to happen, who is that asking me to be?" How's it asking me to show up? What are the qualities or characteristics of within me that it's asking to come forward? Maybe it's asking me to be courageous or truthful or playful or creative or whatever. Maybe it's asking me to show up in a certain way or to take on a certain role.

Then the third question is, "What is it asking me to do?" But the third question doesn't come until you've done your work on the first two. So to come back to the biggest question is to ask ourselves: What wants to happen? What's calling out to me now?

Bill: What is your core message?

Alan: To pay attention—to everything. I think that's the essence of the work I do with leaders and coaches all over the world. It's to pay attention, and so we focus on providing skills and tools, frameworks, and approaches that build their capacity to be able to pay attention. Because the more they pay attention, the more their awareness expands, and the more powerfully, effectively, and authentically they can respond to what they sense or hear or feel.

Key Takeaways

- Just decide everybody in your workplace matters and do it.

- Learn what people care about and make sure they're doing something they care about.

- Is the organization operating in integrity?

- Create an environment where people can live their purpose and feel like, "Wow, when I come to work every day, I get to live my purpose."

- What if creating these kinds of workplaces is simply a choice? Go for it.

- People want to feel like they matter not just in the workplace but everywhere.

- The human spirit is breaking open all over the world at this point and is just saying, "No more. No more."

- What's important to them? You also need to make sure the company is the right fit for the person.

- It's not about what is the most important question to ask the potential employee; it's even more about how you as the employer choose to show up as you meet that person.

- Everything is energy in motion and everything is part of a larger process unfolding, so we need to look at everything within a much larger context.

- Are we asking the wrong questions? These are the questions we are taught to ask, or these are sort of the common questions that everybody thinks are the right ones, but they're really old questions.

- What's important to the management of the company? Then the employee can discern how that fits for them.

- In the bigger picture, what wants to happen here in service of something much bigger than me or you—in service of something bigger than your company?

Jim Haudan

Chairman and Cofounder, Root Inc.

Why Are So Many Unwilling to Say What They Think, Feel, and Act On?

Jim Haudan is the chairman of the board and cofounder at Root Inc. He is the author of *The Art of Engagement: Bridging the Gap Between People and Possibilities.*[1] His latest book, coauthored with Root Inc. CEO, Rich Berens, is *What Are Your Blind Spots: Conquering the 5 Misconceptions that Hold Leaders Back.*[2] Jim is a frequent speaker on leadership alignment, strategy execution, employee engagement, business transformation, organizational change management, and accelerated learning; Jim has contributed to numerous industry publications.

I connected with Jim Haudan for this interview after reading his article "9 Lessons from Three Decades of Working with CEOs: What separates the good CEOs from the great ones?"[3] in *Inc.* magazine where he was a contributing writer. Jim offers compelling insights into the world of work and why we seem to be stuck. He raises key issues that few others are brave enough to mention or discuss.

---

[1] NY: McGraw-Hill Education, 2008.
[2] NY: McGraw-Hill Education, 2018.
[3] www.inc.com/jim-haudan/9-lessons-from-three-decades-of-working-with-ceos.html

© Bill Fox 2020
B. Fox, *The Future of the Workplace,*
https://doi.org/10.1007/978-1-4842-5098-3_9

Bill Fox: How can we create workplaces where every voice matters, everyone thrives and finds meaning, and change and innovation happen naturally?

Jim Haudan: I think it's interesting because we are working on another book and one of the constructs of the book is that it has been almost 30 years since Gallup started measuring engagement in the workplace. For the last 30 years, we have continued to see that 70% of the workplace is not engaged. What that means is almost 70% of all the human talent in all the organizations around the world are either scared, guarded, or unwilling to say what they really think and feel and act on every day.

The human talent is not showing up to innovate, change, and create better ways.

The question that is puzzling is that in those same 30 years, there have been major social issues like cancer deaths and traffic fatalities that have had significant improvements but nothing on engagement. You almost step back for a second and ask, "What gives?" I think what we're landing on is that there may be some leadership beliefs that at the very core are dysfunctional to creating workplaces where people are bringing the best version of themselves.

Now the question becomes, "What are those beliefs?" To some extent, how do we begin to create new beliefs as leaders on the role of people on how they come to the workplace? How do we set the environment for our people to make it a place where they do their best work? Not whether they show up with all the right skills and tools.

There was an interesting story I read recently, and it was about the last regrets of the dying. It was about hospice care in Australia. The number one regret was, "I wish I would have lived the life that I was authentically meant to lead rather than the one that I thought others wanted me to lead." We often jokingly say, "No one ever says 'I wished I had spent more time at the office' on their deathbed," but I think there's no reason why you shouldn't say that. I think when we get to this whole issue, the concept of what you say on your deathbed is this: If you live an authentic and integrated life, then what you create at work ought to be as personal and prideful as what you do with your family and the ones you most love.

An interesting thing is millennials are going to force this to happen. They want an integrated life, not a personal and a professional life. All that suggests, what do we have to do to create that type of environment? I think we must challenge and change.

The first thing we should do is begin to see our people as creators and not implementers.

I think way too many times, we see our people as the implementation troops that are going to implement the decisions made by the smart few leaders. What this suggests is that even if it's well intentioned, it's wrong-headed. How do we see not that we need to convince our people how to do a better job, but how do we introduce them to the drama of our business, the challenge of our cause, or the adversity of our nonprofit? How do we ask them to step into it with a new leadership belief that they can create a response to those challenges, dramas, and adversity better than what we could ever tell them? And if you lead that way, then suddenly you begin to create an environment where you're not trying to control or cajole people or pep rally the team to buy in, but you're trying to share the most intimate challenges we face and ask people what they can do to step up to those problems or opportunities. That's a big issue. It's a mindset. It's a belief. It's a way to run a business.

We had several clients that have watched their people go through some challenges in their business, and many leaders have said, "I'm just dumbfounded by the untapped intelligence of our people." They've gone on to say:

"We spent the last ten years trying to teach employees how to do a better job assuming it would improve the business, but we never shared anything about the adventure we're on or the business that we're trying to build and win."

I think those things are a good place to start. I see this not as a business challenge, but a social cause. Whether it's an inconvenient truth in the environment in the United States, or whether it's *Waiting for Superman* and the absolute horrible state of our public schools, especially in our urban areas. Or even the fact that most of our people are disengaged, not fulfilled, or feel unhappy about what they do every day. It's a social issue, not just a business issue. My gosh, why do we continue to accept that 70% of our people sleepwalk through their work life?

One other thing is there's another belief and mindset we must change. I think the mindset we must change is how we view the relationship between leaders and their people. As leaders, I believe we must see our people as customers. We must see people as customers of our strategy and of our direction and coconspirators in what we want to create that doesn't exist.

The best definition of leadership I've ever heard is, "What is it that you want to create that does not now exist for which you're willing to endure personal sacrifice to bring it to life?" I think we got it right in looking at what we do for our customers. We look for insights. We look for ideas. We look for a voice to translate into new products and services. This is all good.

However, we then just presume that our people jump in. We have no ability to try to understand what they see, what they're curious about, what they get, and what they don't get. If we want them to be fully engaged, we need to begin to think about them as customers for what we're creating or the movement we want to create rather than assume they should "just go do it."

The metaphor that I've always been fond of is the one of the orchestra conductor. Years ago, we had a chance to interview several conductors before we developed a performance management tool. What we found was that the very best conductors—when the orchestra didn't play well—always asked, "What am I doing not to conduct well?" The first, second, third, and fourth thing they asked was about their conducting and not about the individual player or the sections not harmonizing with the other sections. That was always their approach. I think in many cases, what we find is that leaders are saying that our people don't get or they don't have any lightbulbs on in there, or they're not capable of understanding—all of which is false. The question is that the conductor just hasn't found a way to truly see them—the players of the orchestra—as talented customers of what we want to do together. We need to try to better understand how to unleash their ability to play at a higher level.

Bill: What does it take to get an employee's full attention and best performance?

Jim: In my book, *The Art of Engagement,* I talk about the four roots of engagement. I think it's a powerful metaphor regarding how to get people's best performance. The number one point is a purpose. You must engage with somebody in an organization on why we are doing it and what we do. The first root of engagement is that we all want to be part of something bigger than ourselves. The goal is not to find yourself; it's to lose yourself in a cause you believe in or a problem that's defied a solution or joining an organization that you believe is on a path to finding a better way. I think the most important point is to be part of something bigger than yourself.

The second point that I increasingly feel particularly strong about is to have a sense of being valued. In times of change, we face uncertainty and uncertainty can make a sense of being valued very fragile. I think many times people are questioning whether they're valued. If you don't feel valued, you'll spend all your time trying to justify it for yourself rather than creating it with others. And so, the absence of that sense of value or even the presumption that you should feel valued, I don't think is adequate. There's a great African word, *ubuntu,* which means "I see you, and you are valued." I think that's important. Maslow talks about a sense of belonging, and this is probably in that same family. But when we look at change, there are so many people that think that just because they have not done this before that they're on a "can't do it" list and they're just waiting to be told that. I think that's the natural part of the fear of being a beginner again after you've had success or when stepping into the discomfort of the unknown. It's important to truly have a sense of value and be valuable to the future.

The third point is about a story. I jokingly say that most of us with our kids or grandkids don't say, "Can I take you upstairs and show you my PowerPoint?" We tell them we want to tell them a story. I think people want to go on a meaningful adventure. They want to be the coauthors of a great story or adventure. The story gets framed by asking questions like: What is it we want to go after? What capabilities do we want to test? What is it that we think we can do to have a breakthrough? What is the size of the prize here? The drama or story is in most of our companies, but we sterilize it. We compartmentalize it. Nobody cares about business-speak PowerPoints. What they care about is, "Can we do something together we couldn't do alone that matters?" I think that's the third point—it's to go on an adventure that matters.

And the last factor is—and I can't tell you how many times we work on this one too—to see how what you do impacts the lives of another human being. We've become so specialized and fragmentized in what we do and how it comes together and then where it ends up. It's hard for people to see how what they do impacts the life of another human being. They tend to see it only as a task.

I'll tell you a quick story about working with a big Pharma company out of Europe. They had their top 400 leaders at a conference, and they were all very seasoned—they had "alligator skin." They knew everything, yet they thought there was some benefit in bringing people together. They did a team building event where they had 40 tables and put a bicycle on each table to assemble. They had done it before, but this time they added a little wrinkle to it. When they were done making the bicycle, they had 40 disadvantaged kids come to each one of the tables. They were going to allow 10 minutes for it. The kids began to interact with these leaders and tell them about their lives and what the bike meant to them. It just shut the place down. Forty-five minutes later, they had to call a timeout because they became so captivated by the connection of the bike they just made to the kid they just met, their story, and what it meant to that child at this stage in his/her life. It was a telltale sign of how we go through the motions and don't take the time to realize—in this case, a drug company's leader's impact on a child by providing a bike. Just think what's possible if they better understood how their drugs positively impacted the lives of patients?

Bill: What do people really lack and long for at work?

Jim: I think there are a lot of ways to answer this question. If I had to pick one, I'd say the thing that people most long for at work is the opportunity to tell the truth. The opportunity to be told the truth and the opportunity to feel free and safe to tell the truth.

But what I think we find is that you can't look at high-performance teams and change if you're not willing to tell the truth. The reason truth telling becomes such a problem is because there are so many interpretations of truth that might condemn somebody, so we just avoid it. We avoid telling the truth. We avoid going after the conflict. We avoid going after the adversity. But when we begin to tell the truth, there's something that happens first and foremost, and that is public vulnerability. And sometimes it's shared public vulnerability. Once you get this shared public vulnerability, a lot of your fears go out the window. It's amazing how things change when you start focusing on what we can do vs. how do I make sure I don't look bad. How do I ensure this doesn't show poorly on me? Whether I'm the CEO or whether I'm the person running a machine, so what I think people long for is the opportunity to talk about what they truly think and feel.

I do an exercise with people where I say there are only three places where we tell the truth in our companies, and they are in the hallway, the bathroom, and the watercooler. Then I pretend I just came out of a meeting. I'm with a friend and we go to the bathroom, but before I say something, I bend over to see if there are any legs in the stall. Then everybody laughs because they've all done that. I ask, "why did you do that?" and they say, "We had to make sure it was safe, and nobody else was in there so we could say what we think." I just pause for a second and say, "You're kidding me."

How successful will we be if we can't say what we think and feel and there's not an environment that cherishes getting the best, candid thoughts from our people vs. what they think we want to hear or what is safe to say?

Bill: What is the most important question leaders should ask employees?

Jim: I think there are many ways to answer this question, but there's one question that popped into my mind the most. If you look at high-performance executives, many times a high-performance executive is somebody who works on the business rather than in the business because you can get caught in all the minutiae. You've got to work at a higher altitude to figure out and ask yourself, "What are the constraints in our business, and if the constraints were removed, could we increase our performance?" Now, how do we remove those constraints?

What are the constraints in our business, and if the constraints were removed, could we increase our performance?

To improve, you often must simplify or remove constraints. But how often do we think about asking, "how do I remove a constraint so my people can excel"?

I think when it comes to our people, I would ask, "Of all that you can contribute to our organization, what percent of your capability do you think you get to contribute?" That question would be tremendously interesting to me because whenever we ask that question, it's a minority of what they think they can do.

Then I would ask the following question, "What are the constraints that are holding you back from contributing even more?" Then I'd be listening like crazy to what is holding them back. Then I'd start focusing on what's holding people back and what can we do to remove those constraints.

Here is a controversial idea—I think it's time to stop measuring engagement in our organizations. It's become a tremendous disservice to all of us. The reason for that is because the tools have become the goal. In too many organizations, leaders are tied to engagement numbers. The employees know if they don't get good numbers, something is going to happen. We've taught all the people how to play the game, just give us a nine or ten.

I was very engaged in the Baldrige quality effort back in the late 1980s. If you go back and look at the Baldrige Award, which was the US Quality Award, Florida Power & Light won the award, and then the year after that they won it, they disbanded it and stopped doing it. The tool became the goal. They became so adamant about the tool that they forgot that the tool was just there to help us run and drive a powerful business.

I think we're there with employee engagement, and I believe we should stop measuring our people and start measuring our leaders. I believe we should ask leaders to measure themselves and ask people to measure them on the four Cs of Care, Curiosity, Constraint Removal, and Collaboration. If we start asking about these four behaviors, we're going to get to build great "people workplaces!"

Bill: What is the most important question employees should ask leaders?

Jim: I think there's a reciprocal nature to this question. When leaders appeal to people's highest level of thinking, they get the highest response. I think as employees, partners, or associates, we all have to be more curious about the business we work in rather than just the job we have.

You mentioned in an earlier conversation about our book the story of the Cleveland Indians. If you go to a baseball game in the United States or a cricket game in the United Kingdom, there's everybody of every age from 4 to 94. For the most part, all of them understand how this game gets played. They understand how to keep score, understand the drivers to success, understand when one thing happens how to respond in a different way, and understand the difficulty of getting to a victory. They also understand the sorrow of not winning. But all together, they understand how it all works.

I think in many cases, we have people that have not become as curious about the great game of business, or the great game of nonprofit, or the great game of public service. They're not trying to see the big picture of how this all comes together and what each of us can do to win. The corollary—at least in the United States because I don't think there's one globally, but I could be wrong—the US economy lost $12B in 2017 from people playing fantasy football and baseball on work time. What that means is that we've got all kinds of people setting up teams, looking at responses, changing players, coming up with strategies, seeing what the results are, and trying to reposition their place in the standings. They're playing strategy every day, just not ours.

I think the challenge as an employee is to say, "I have to be more curious about how this business works." What are the drivers of success? How from where I sit and live can I contribute or detract from that? How can I be a force to make enlightened decisions with my head, hands, and heart? Because if I get it, and I get how this all comes together and where it's headed, I can make a much greater contribution and be more highly engaged.

Bill: What is the most important question we should ask ourselves?

Jim: My first choice would be that I think we're all born with the capability of being creators, so we ought to ask ourselves, "What is it we want to be part of creating that doesn't exist that we're passionate about?"

I think that's an important question. When I ask people this question, they get excited if they have a picture of what that is. If they don't, there's a real pause and blank look on their face. I think this is a question all of us can ask from wherever we sit in an organization.

When it comes to leaders, I think the question we might want to ask is a simpler one, and that is, "How do we help people discover the heroic capabilities within themselves?" And when they do, they realize they're smarter than they thought, more capable than they ever gave themselves credit for, and more valuable to our future than anyone's ever told them. I think as you begin to awaken people to that, you begin to realize incredible possibilities and great things can happen. Clearly the goal is to "awaken the sleeping giant" of human capability and passion in all of our organizations.

Bill: Can you share more information about your new book?

Jim: The new book, *What Are Your Blind Spots? Conquering the 5 Misconceptions that Hold Leaders Back*, came out in October 2018. The original title was going to be The Five Dysfunctional Beliefs of Leadership that Perpetuate Disengagement. We're finding some of those beliefs are around issues that involve leader's views about why people work. I cowrote the book with Rich Berens, Root's CEO.

In leadership, there's way too much belief that people work for the rewards even though there's so much research that doesn't confirm that. When we look at all the places where incentives and awards are used, we sit there and say we're just kind of dumbfounded at how much is missed there.

And I also think close to that belief that profit and purpose can't coexist is costing a lot regarding both outcomes and contributions from people. We've got books on firms of endearment that connect profit and purpose, but I can't tell you how many companies we work with where it's almost as if they have two beakers. One beaker has all the business stuff in it and another beaker has the purpose stuff, but they're separate. However, we need them both, so we cover all the needs of our people.

The fact of the matter is that belief is costing a lot regarding both outcomes and contributions from the people.

Another belief that is so fascinating to me is the belief that human variability must be limited so that we have common standards, common brands, and common experiences for customers. Many leaders we know are working on addressing this issue.

Cheryl Bachelder, the former CEO at Popeyes who wrote the book *Dare to Serve*,[4] is all about servant leadership. Popeyes was trying to build leaders in all the restaurants they create. She's a fabulous leader. But the question becomes, "How do we create a framework for the standards that are key?" And how do we invite the freedom where human variability is the difference maker?

I can't tell you how many times we stamp out variability vs. encouraging it. There's a client we have in the hotel industry that addresses this head on. They believe the world needs more friendly, authentic, caring, and thoughtful experiences, so all their people are asked to do that whether you're funny, witty, compassionate, or empathetic, it doesn't matter. They found a way for a framework and freedom to work together vs. stamping out the freedom, so they have consistent standards.

Or we need to have all freedom, which is chaos. I just don't think we've found how to leverage the human element in our businesses, especially our bigger companies, because we haven't figured out what is it that's common and what is it that is unique to the individual and how to invite them both in.

There's a great story that I remember. A policeman went into a Starbucks in the city of Philadelphia, the City of Brotherly Love, and asked to use the bathroom, but the barista wouldn't let him use it. So, the policeman got upset and blogged about it. The next day Starbucks ran a full-page apology in the newspaper. In response, I wrote a blog asking, "What are they apologizing for?"

What they have said is that we don't believe that our people can have a judgment, discretion, or discernment at the point of engagement to the degree that they are capable of. Thus, we'll create policies for all the anomalies

---

[4] Oakland, CA: Berrett-Koehler Publishers, 2015.

or for all the things where we've been burnt on. I think that creates all kinds of inauthenticity in all our organizations if we script it for our employees rather than call them to be part of it in a unique way we get canned, non-engaged responses.

I think that's a big piece of this belief and that is that human variability needs to conform to our standards vs. invite the uniqueness of that person. Nobody has a good framework or answer for that other than the one hotel I just mentioned. But I think that's key to the future of tapping human capability in all our people.

Key Takeaways

- 70% of human talent are either scared, guarded, or unwilling to say what they really think.

- Build a workplace where people can live authentic and integrated lives.

- See people as creators, not implementers.

- Purpose is the first root of engagement.

- Having a sense of being valued is the second root of engagement.

- The thing that people most long for at work is the opportunity to tell the truth.

- Shared public vulnerability occurs when we tell the truth.

- Recognize the constraints in our business.

- What are the constraints that are holding you back?

- Be more curious about this business.

- Understand how the business works.

- Be aware of what it is we want to be part of creating.

- Help people discover the heroic capabilities within themselves.

Perry Marshall

Entrepreneur and Consultant

How to Get 80/20 to Work for You

Perry Marshall is one of the most sought-after consultants in the world. He is the author of the world's most popular books on advertising, marketing, and sales including *Ultimate Guide to Google AdWords*,[1] *80/20 Sales and Marketing*,[2] and many other books and articles. However, Perry's expertise goes well beyond sales and marketing and spans engineering, art, and psychology. He founded the $10 million Evolution 2.0 Prize to solve one of the leading mysteries in science. He is also the author of *Evolution 2.0*.[3]

I've been a longtime follower and student of Perry Marshall. I asked Perry to join this conversation when he sent out an email describing his interest in using marketing to *shift the culture* and his fascination with the following question:

> "How do you hold conversations that nobody wants to have because of political correctness or stupidity spasms or hidden agendas?"

Shifting the culture and having bigger conversations that break down barriers are at the heart of the interviews we do at Exploring Forward-Thinking

---

[1] Irvine, CA: Entrepreneur Media, 2007.
[2] Irvine, CA: Entrepreneur Press, 2013.
[3] Dallas, TX: BenBella Books, 2017.

© Bill Fox 2020
B. Fox, *The Future of the Workplace*,
https://doi.org/10.1007/978-1-4842-5098-3_10

Workplaces. I'm delighted that Perry agreed to do this interview and share his remarkable insights on 80/20 and much more.

Bill Fox: How can we create workplaces where every voice matters, everyone thrives and finds meaning, and change and innovation happen naturally?

Perry Marshall: You do that by being very selective about who you hire. You do that by being willing to fire people that don't match. I think that people have this idea that it's their job to give everybody else a job and that is not true. That's Marxism. It doesn't work. It's catastrophic. You should hire slow and fire fast.

When you hire people, it should not be an interview. It should be an audition.

People can say anything they want. A lot of times it's not true. Sometimes because they're lying. More often it's not true because they don't understand themselves, or they don't know what they're capable of. Sometimes they're nervous, or they're just trying to find a job, or they're just trying to say what the interviewer thinks they want to hear.

If you wanted a bass player for your band, you would not invite them over to your house and spend 2 hours talking about Primus and Geddy Lee. You would ask them to bring a bass and play. If you were doing a Shakespeare play or any kind of play, you would have them act. You wouldn't sit there and talk about Shakespeare.

One of the mistakes people make when they hire people is they just get everybody together to talk. They hire the person who's most fun to talk to. What you should do is devise a task and give it to them to do. You may even hire them for an hour or for a day to do the task. Or you may bring them on as a temporary person and say here, "Do this." You don't listen to what they say, you watch what they do. Now, when you do that, then you will get A players. If they're an A player, then their voice matters. They thrive, and they find meaning. If they're a B player or a C player—especially if they're a C player—their voice doesn't matter because your business is not a charity. Your business is a high-performance team.

Bill: What does it take to get an employee's full attention and best performance?

Perry: One of the things that I realized the world needed was a way of testing how people communicate, persuade, market, and sell. We have the Myers Briggs test, which tells you if they're an introvert, extrovert, sensing or judging. That's useful. We have the Kolbe test, which lots of entrepreneurs refer to because it tells you how people work. For example, "Are they a quick start?" "Are they high follow-through?" and stuff like that. Very useful.

There wasn't a tool that said this is how people enlist other people's cooperation. The Marketing DNA test tells you how does this person sell and persuade.

Some people do it with numbers, facts, proof, and spreadsheets. Some people do it by telling stories. Some people do it with graphics. Some people do it by inventing something in the moment. Some people do it by proving how incredibly reliable and trustworthy something is. So, I created something called the Marketing DNA test. It comes as part of the *80/20 Sales and Marketing* book, and we also sell it separately. Now I'm talking this test is particularly helpful in customer-facing employees. If they're an engineer working in the back office, then this particular tool doesn't really apply. Well, it doesn't appear to apply, let's put it that way.

If the person is actually talking to customers, then if they are a writer, they should be answering or writing emails. If they're a video person, then they should be live on webinars or Skype or making videos and be putting them on YouTube—or something like that. There are some people I call a hostage negotiator where you just throw them in a situation. They can maneuver their way through anything. You need to match the person to that test—to that profile.

There are some people who will sit in their cave and craft the perfect sales message in Microsoft Word. It will take 3 weeks. There are other people where you just give them a microphone and put them on a stage. They're two completely different kinds of people. All of us know highly articulate people who are very good speakers and negotiators. They always send you these emails with no subject line in two sentences. It's because their brain runs too fast for their fingers to type on the keyboard. That person should never be selling via text or copywriting.

There's another kind of person. Their brains run a little slower. They're extremely thorough, and they're very meticulous about their words. They make a great copywriter. That's a very specific way to get full attention and best performance. Because if they're communicating with customers through their best method, then they will like their job. They will be effective in their job. They'll sell well. They'll be persuasive, so you need to match that up. The bigger the company is, the more different kinds of selling modalities that you need in order to address the full needs of your audience.

Bill: What do people lack and really long for at work?

Perry: There's just this kind of pervasive attitude in our society that life is sort of meaningless. Life only has the meaning that you assign to it and that we're just billiard balls banging around in the universe. Allegedly—supposedly—that's the scientific view. Well, I would submit to you in practice that nobody actually believes that. Nobody acts like they believe that. Perfectly logical rational people who say they believe that will line up around the block with movie tickets to go watch *Star Wars*. The reason *Star Wars* is so popular for so many years is because it's a very well-told Hero's Journey epic story.

What people long for and are also terrified of is living the Hero's Journey.

So what happens in all these epic stories? We could be talking about *Star Wars*. We could be talking about *The Lord of the Rings*. We could be talking about *The Matrix*. Or we could be talking about any of the Disney movies. But in *Star Wars*, Luke is racing spaceships in the desert on a planet and living in his mother's basement. He's just kind of screwing around. Then the hologram from Obi-Wan Kenobi shows up. He says, "Hey, we need you. We have this big giant problem." He doesn't want to do this. But well, OK. He tumbles headlong into this adventure.

I think deep down this is what most people want. Maybe you could say all people. It's certainly what most men want, but they're also terrified because they know they can go splat—and it will really, really hurt. If you start this business, you saved up $50,000 or more. Typically you racked up $50,000 of credit cards, then if the business fails, it's going to be a big, big giant ouch when you're standing there left with the bill. Then there's going to be another ouch when you have to go back and get a job again. You're taking real risks. But people are actually itching for and longing for that in their work. They want to be part of an adventure. They really want to do something that matters. They also want to do something that measurably makes progress.

But they also want to know that they're winning. They want to know that the scoreboard says that they're on the winning team. The score is 21 to 17, and they're the ones with 21. The losers are the guys with 17. That's what people want. I think that trumps a lot of the squishy ideological things that people say that they want. This is why a lot of corporate slogans are kind of meaningless because they're really not speaking to the adventure that everybody wants to be on.

Bill: What is the most important question leaders should ask employees?

Perry: It's really easy to add and sometimes easy to multiply. The really hard stuff in business is division and subtraction. This is part of 80/20.

One of the most valuable questions you could ever ask is: what do we need to subtract?

There's an advanced idea in 80/20 that my friend Len Bertain came up with. It's called the 21/20 rule. It says that 20% of your products or your customers make 120% of your profit. There's part of what you sell and part of who you sell to that makes a disproportionate amount of profit. Then there's a loser part of your customers and a loser part of your product line that loses money. It brings your 120% down to the 100% of what you made last year.

In other words, you made more money than you thought you did last year. But some other customers or some other products lost the money because you're taping dollar bills to every single product that gets shipped out. And by the way, this is almost always true. Rarely is it not true. The truth is you walk into a grocery store and there's like 70,000 items in there. If they cut their inventory down to 60,000 items, they would make more money. They would sell less stuff, and they would make more money. They would stock less stuff. There would be less everything, and they would make more money. But they don't usually know what the 10,000 products are. You'd have to do a really careful cost accounting. And you'd go, "Well, we lose money selling this brand of aspirin, and we lose money selling these potato chips. We lose money having this entire aisle over here." Well, people sort of instinctively know this is true on some level, but they have to be taught how to look for it. People need to be trained to weed it out.

If you have 100 employees, I guarantee 10 of them are losing you money. You could say, "Let's just get rid of this product. Let's just get rid of these customers. Let's just get rid of these employees." Well, that's surgery. If you do surgery and you cut an artery, you bleed to death. It's usually very delicate. Well, we could fire this lady, but she'll sue us. Or we could fire this lady, but there's this one account. I know the sales rep is a train wreck, but there's this one account that she's in charge of that really makes a lot of money. They really like her. You end up with these little dilemmas, and it can be done. You can make those changes, but you have to be very skillful in how you do it. That's the art of business right there. If there's an economic slowdown and your revenue drops 25%, 80/20 says that you could cut 25% of your expenses by reducing only 5% of the things you spend money on. You might actually come out ahead. But it's going to be a very delicate surgery to make those cutbacks. It's going to be painful, and nobody's going to like it. You're going to have to lay people off. There's going to be things that you have to do.

Another thing that you should be asking employees is for honest feedback. Now the culture of the company will determine whether you actually get honest feedback or not. People know whether they can be honest. Or whether they have to make up a story their boss will accept. In my company, I think I have a culture where if the emperor has no clothes, my employees will tell me. But that's not easy. In most companies, you don't actually have a culture of honesty. The honesty needs to go both ways.

Bill: What is the most important question employees should ask leaders?

Perry: I think employees need to know what's the scorecard. How are we doing? Employees really respond when they know. We have a meeting every week where the key employees of the company review all of the product lines we're selling, all of the sales numbers, all of our sales projections—everything.

People want to know whether we're hitting our targets or not. People want to know whether things are working or not. This thing hit the ball out of the park. This other thing was a dud. People need to know. It's just part of a healthy culture and a winning team.

Bill: What is the most important question we should ask ourselves?

Perry: What I think of is in the Beatitudes. Jesus says, "Seek ye first the kingdom of God, and all these things will be added to you." He talks about not worrying today or about the problems that are going to show up tomorrow. People interpret that as kind of a hippie laissez-faire thing, but that's not what it is at all. It's a statement that if you fix your attention on the very highest virtue and the very best that you could possibly achieve and rigorously laser focus on it, then the other stuff will have this funny way of working itself out. It will just flow behind you in your jet stream. I really think that is true. It's another one of these synchronicity things.

You should be asking yourself what is the highest and best good that you can aim for?

I think most of us get caught up in what I call barnacles, which is work that doesn't really achieve much. It just happens to be comfortable and easy to react to. I can sit there and hit refresh on my email inbox 57 times a day. I could go check social media. I could go answer this email from this person, but am I really doing the highest and best thing that I could be doing at this moment?

I like to say the reason that you're checking your email and social media right now is you don't know what to do. You haven't figured out what the highest top 1% or 5% activity is that you could possibly be doing. You're not doing it. You wanted a little brain juice, so you went and got on Twitter. This is how most people actually spend their life. I call it barnacles. It's work. It may have some value. It may have moderate, marginal value to somebody. It feels like productivity, but at the end of a day where that's all you've done, you just feel exhausted and kind of meaningless. That's not how anyone wants to end their day.

Bill: What is the number one takeaway you'd like people to get from your book *80/20 Sales and Marketing*?

Perry: I want people to look out the window—any window, anywhere. I want to be able to say, "Tell me ten 80/20 relationships you see outside that window?" and they would be able to just rattle them off.

I want them to suddenly see that 80/20 is not just a business rule of thumb. It's a fundamental law of cause and effect like gravity and is absolutely everywhere.

Eighty percent of the sap runs through twenty percent of the branches in that tree. Eighty percent of the activity in that house is in twenty percent of the rooms. That's how it actually works. When you can see that, you all of a sudden have this new dimension of problem-solving ability that you didn't have before. You have an ability to ask questions that most people would never think to ask. This is what the real mavens who love *80/20 Sales and Marketing* tell me. They say, "I read that book, and it changed the way I saw the whole entire world. Now I can't not see it anymore." I see those inequalities everywhere. I walk into a room full of people, or I listen to a political talk show, or I watch the election results. All of a sudden I can see all of these 80/20s all over the place that I was never aware of before.

When you have something that's so fundamental like what could be more fundamental than a new law of cause and effect that is nearly universal? What could be more fundamental than that? It affects your time. It affects how you arrange the files on your hard drive. It affects how you drive to work. It affects how you hire and fire, and everything.

It becomes this very Zen-like thing where how good at a punch can a martial arts person be? How good could you get? Well, there's a yellow belt level of a punch and a green belt level of a punch. There's a green belt, a blue belt, a black belt, a third-degree black belt, and a sixth-degree black belt. I guarantee you a ninth-degree black belt punch is different than a fourth-degree black belt punch. It's just a punch, right? No, it's not.

Bill: You say in your book that the primary skill that you master in marketing is thinking backward. Why is thinking backward so important and where else might we use it?

Perry: It goes to Stephen Covey's idea of beginning with the end in mind. It speaks to the fact that human beings are intrinsically purposeful creatures. I'm an engineer. In engineering one of the major, major skills that you acquire is: I want to know in advance how well the bridge is going to work before I build the bridge and before I drive cars on it. I don't want the car to fall into the river because the bridge broke when a big heavy truck goes across my bridge.

If you had a predictive theory of everything, you would never fail. That's thinking backward.

We design the bridge on paper, and we analyze all the weights and load distributions. We figure that this bridge can hold three times the weight of that truck. This is the weight limit sign that we're going to put on the bridge, and everybody's going to be safe. I've never been on a bridge that fell in when I drove my car across it.

In marketing, you're dealing with people, and people are a lot less predictable than bridges. In the context of the book, I said, "Start with traffic, then you convert the traffic, and then you have the economics of the traffic. The whole sequence of marketing is traffic, conversion, economics." But when you design a product, a sales machine, or when you build a company, you have to think backward. You have to think economics, conversion, then traffic because you have to figure out what can I sell? Why are people going to buy it? Where are the people who want to buy it?

I remember when I was a brand-new marketer, it really made my brain hurt to imagine I'm not the sales guy, I'm the customer, and I'm not writing this thing. I'm reading it on somebody else's computer screen. What do I think about that? How do I feel about that? What is my bleeding neck? What are my issues? What problems do I want to solve? Why am I kicking my cat when I go home? It hurt my brain. It was like twisting myself around 180 degrees, and I'm looking at a different computer screen the opposite direction.

But then I learned to do it. It became second nature for me to do it. Now I do it all the time. You start looking at things from all of these different angles. Once you get practiced enough at it, people think this is just like magic. People say, "Oh my goodness, how do you do that? That's amazing!" In fact, they'll pay just to watch you do it because it's so fascinating. I guess that's what I do for a living now to some degree!

We have coaching groups, and a lot of what people are paying for is they want to watch somebody who can just do that complete 180-degree reversal of thinking. You go forward, and you go backward. You go forward, and you go backward again. All of a sudden you end up with this completely different product idea than everybody imagined before the meeting started. Well, OK, we solved that. Why don't you do that, and let us know how it works. Everybody has a big smile on their face.

Bill: A key principle you talk about in your book is "rack the shotgun." What is it and how can we benefit from it?

Perry: Really quickly, the rack the shotgun story is the signature story of the whole book. John Paul Mendocha is a good friend of mine, and he hitch-hiked from Denver to Las Vegas when he was 17. He dropped out of high school and became a professional gambler in Las Vegas. He's living by his wits, and after a few weeks, he's like this is harder than I thought it was going to be! He meets this guy in a bookstore who runs a gambling ring, and his name is Rob. John asks, "Rob, do you think you could help me do a better job playing poker?" Rob, says, "For a percentage of your winnings I can help you play better poker," and so they shook hands on it.

When they were done shaking on it, Rob says, "Jump in the jeep, John. We're going for a ride." They're in the jeep, and they're going down the highway when John says, "Alright Rob, how do I win more poker games?" And Rob says, "You have to play people who are going to lose, and those people are called marks." And John says, "Where do I find marks?" He says, "Here I'll show you."

He pulls into the parking lot of a strip club, and he takes John into the club. There are women dancing. There's booze, bikers, and loud music and everything. A lot of distractions. Rob always carried a sawed-off shotgun with him everywhere he went. They sat down at a table, and Rob pulls a sawed-off shotgun out of his jacket. He opens it up under the table and slams it shut. It goes "click-click" with that racking noise, which is called racking the shotgun. There are a few people in that loud noisy club that turn around, "Like, hey! Who did that? Where did that sound come from?"

They're on high alert. The owner comes over, and he goes, "Hey, what's going on over here?" Rob says, "Don't worry about us. Just teaching the lad a lesson. Not going to cause any problems." Rob says to John, "John, did you see those bikers turn around when they heard that noise?" And John's like, "Yeah!" And Rob goes, "They're not marks. Play poker with everybody else but not them."

Racking the shotgun is doing the thing that polarizes everyone. All great leaders rack the shotgun. That's the essence of it. It takes courage.

Well, that's racking the shotgun. It's doing the thing that polarizes everyone. That's what rack the shotgun is. It's polarizing—separating the wheat from the chaff. The sheep from the goats. The Democrats from the Republicans. The pro-life from the pro-choice. The buyers from the non-buyers. Whatever the issue is.

All great leaders rack the shotgun—courageously. Even bad leaders do it, but leaders do it. Trump racks the shotgun all the time. Hillary racked the shotgun all the time. Gandhi. Jesus. All of them. People are afraid to do it because it creates who are your friends, and who are your enemies? It wears you out a little bit. It gets tiresome. I know. I get it. It's what you have to do. Everything you do in marketing is racking the shotgun. Everything you do in leadership is racking the shotgun, so people are afraid to do it. If you're hiring process is an audition instead of an interview, then that's a rack the shotgun exercise. OK, who can put those screw assemblies together in 15 seconds or less? And who can't? Who can do 600 keystrokes per minute on the adding machine and who can't? That's the essence of it. It takes courage. It takes balls, and you just have to do it.

Key Takeaways

- Be very selective about who you hire.

- Do an audition, not an interview.

- Help people learn how they best enlist other people's cooperation.

- Deep down most people want to live the hero's journey.

- What do we need to subtract?

- How are we doing?

- What is the highest and best good that you can aim for?

- Figure out the top 1% or 5% activity that you could possibly be doing.

- 80/20 is not just a business rule of thumb, it's most powerful when it's an action you take.

- If you had predictive theory of everything, you'd never fail—that's thinking backward.

- Start looking at things from different angles.

- Do the thing that polarizes everyone.

- All great leaders rack the shotgun.

Michael Neill

Transformative Coach, Author

It's Not About Working Harder, or Even Smarter

Michael Neill is an internationally renowned transformative coach and the best-selling author of six books including *The Inside-Out Revolution*,[1] *The Space Within*,[2] and *Creating the Impossible*.[3] His weekly radio show, *Living from the Inside Out*, has been a listener favorite on Hay House Radio for over a decade, and his TEDx talk, *Why Aren't We Awesomer?*,[4] has been viewed by over 250,000 people around the world.

I first met Michael Neill when I viewed his TEDx talk *Why Aren't We Awesomer?*. I was personally so impacted by what I learned that I began a deeper inquiry into his work and books. Michael gave me a new understanding of how my mind works. My mind quieted down, and I became noticeably more productive and creative. In this interview with Michael, he describes how and why this occurs. He also provides an understanding of why and how my interviews frequently result in people sharing their wisdom and saying things they've never said before.

---

[1] London: Hay House UK, 2013.
[2] London: Hay House UK, 2016.
[3] London: Hay House UK, 2018.
[4] Michael Neill, TEDxBend, www.youtube.com/watch?v=xr6VawX2nr4.

B. Fox, *The Future of the Workplace*,
https://doi.org/10.1007/978-1-4842-5098-3_11

Bill Fox: How can we create workplaces where every voice matters, everyone thrives and finds meaning, and change and innovation happen naturally?

Michael Neill: There are two things that I would say to the first part—where every voice matters.

First off, creating a workplace where every voice matters really just depends on meaning it.

In other words, it's a great sounding thing, but you've got to start by seeing—do you actually think every voice matters?

Or do you just think that would be a good thing to do? Because if you just think that would be a good thing to do, you're not going to do it. You're not going to succeed because ultimately people hear what we mean, not what we say.

The heart of that question is, "Why should every voice matter?" And if you genuinely believe everybody has something to contribute at whatever level they can contribute, then actually there are a million ways to create that workplace. That could range from a suggestion box where the ideas are actually considered to meetings where people listen to one another instead of listening to respond.

You know, to me, a bad meeting is like a Facebook discussion where nobody's listening and everybody's making points. A good meeting is a meeting where everyone is listening, and there is space to hear something new beyond what anyone brought into the room with them. But if you don't fundamentally think that every voice matters, then honestly, you could have the best strategy in the world and it wouldn't work.

To create a workplace where everyone thrives and finds meaning, you have to begin by showing people where thriving comes from—and where meaning comes from.

Maybe this is an obvious thing for someone who wrote a book called *The Inside-Out Revolution* to say, but it comes from inside. It does not come from "a workplace." There is no such thing as a workplace that can do that. But you can have a workplace filled with people who are thriving and who know where to look for meaning.

To accomplish that, first there's an education component to it. I would say education more than training—though training is one of the ways you can get at education. Coaching is also one of the ways you can get at education. But an education component where people start to learn, "Oh, that amazing feeling I get when I'm engaged, and I'm challenged but not overwhelmed?" It's a place where creativity is flowing, and I feel great about what I'm doing and how I'm doing it.

That is cultivable from within me. However, there are very clear things that get in the way of that, and when I can take them into account, I will thrive more and more of the time.

So, if I have a workplace where the workers are educated in the inside-out understanding, then they are awake to that capacity to thrive and find meaning in themselves.

I will then have a workplace where people thrive and find meaning. Now I might get lucky, and on a project that people buy into, they'll have that sense organically. But, that's going to be sporadic. That's going to come and go. If I want to make the workplace a place where that consistently happens, then that comes from within the understanding of the people who are working there.

Regarding change and innovation, well the funny thing is that change and innovation do happen naturally when you're not getting in the way. So that's easy—that's the easy one. Stop stopping it! You'll be fine. I think the main thing to see with change and innovation is that these are natural processes that we either facilitate or inhibit.

To introduce a change initiative or innovation initiative is a misunderstanding of change and innovation.

The more we make space for things to unfold—as opposed to trying to make them fit the banks of the river of limited possibility we dug with our habitual thinking—the more they will.

It becomes almost a dance with creative ideas, with fresh ideas, and with innovation rather than a military march. I know there's a bottom line and a military march has an appeal; it's just that the military march by design has very little space for change or innovation.

Bill: What does it take to get an employee's full attention and best performance?

Michael: I think to get an employee's full attention is a *give-to-get-game*. I think fundamentally enough, human beings are pretty simple in that way. If you give them your full attention, you will wind up with their full attention.

Best performance is a function of clarity of intention, buy-in, and state of mind.

If the people working for me know what their job is, they know what they're up to, and they've bought into it, we're more than half way there. If they also understand the natural variance in a state of mind, so they're able to come from the highest and best place that's within them and do less damage when they're off their game, then you're going to get optimal performance.

So, in summary, there need to be three components:

1. Clarity of intention, that is, knowing what they're up to

2. Buy-in, that is, fully embracing the task at hand

3. An understanding of the state of mind such that they can perform at higher and higher levels more and more of the time

Bill: What do you think people really lack and long for at work?

Michael: I can answer that at a couple of different levels. At the highest level, I think what people both lack and long for is connection and a sense of purpose—a feeling of being connected to a larger whole and the sense that what they do matters. At lower levels, you can make the case that they want acknowledgment, they want self-esteem, and they want advancement. Those things are true, but they're lower level. They're never going to be fully satisfied.

I remember years ago working with a weight loss group. I said to them, "There aren't enough cookies in the world to make you feel loved and whole." It's the wrong tool for the job. The things we traditionally think of people wanting, like better salaries, more beanbags, whatever, are sources of "imitation connection," "imitation purpose," and "imitation happiness" at work.

What we're craving is that sense of being part of something bigger than us that matters.

The playwright George Bernard Shaw said:

> "This is the true joy in life, the being used for a purpose recognized by yourself as a mighty one; the being thoroughly worn out before you are thrown on the scrap heap; the being a force of Nature instead of a feverish selfish little clod of ailments and grievances complaining that the world will not devote itself to making you happy."

We all know that at some level. And to get into that mindset of service vs. personal gain is as simple as it being sincere. I was kind of saying this when our conversation started. If you get that "being used for a purpose recognized by yourself as a mighty one" is what matters, you will create a workplace where that's what matters. If you think that's just a good idea or slogan, you're going to struggle like hell.

Bill: What is the most important question leaders should ask employees?

Michael: I'll answer it in an idealistic sense first and then get a little more real. In an idealistic sense, the questions I think they should be asking employees are, "Do you know what you're up to?" and "Do you know what you're really capable of?"

I only call these questions idealistic because for most people, "Do you really know what you're capable of?" sounds like a very loaded question. It's a self-esteem issue. It gets into personal psychology. It's a bit beyond the scope of most leaders or managers to mess with people's psychology.

When I say, "Do you know what you're capable of?" I'm pointing to a deeper dimension of the mind—a deeper dimension of the human potential where creativity, resilience, and resolve come from.

It's that irrepressible part of human nature that bounces back as good as new no matter how many times it gets dropped.

I love the analogy for resilience of a Christmas tree ornament, an orange, or a rubber ball from the book *Bounce* by Keith McFarland. If you're a Christmas ornament, you look great—but don't drop you, because you'll shatter into a thousand pieces. If you're an orange, you look tough on the outside, and you can take a lot of dropping, bouncing, and throwing—but on the inside, you're getting battered and bruised and rotting away. But a rubber ball is made to bounce. We are all "spiritual rubber balls" in that sense. The human design is such that we're made to bounce, but we think we're fragile like Christmas ornaments or tough like oranges. Neither of those self-perceptions gives us the same freedom of movement as knowing the truth that we're made to bounce.

The other question, "Do you know what you're up to?", can be seen at multiple levels as well. There's an old story of Michelangelo walking to the Sistine Chapel while he's doing his painting and passing three stonemasons who were working on the grounds of the Vatican. He stops the first stonemason and asks, "What are you up to?" The stonemason says, "I'm just chiseling away at rock, man. I've got six more hours." He passes another stonemason who seems a little more energized and focused than the first stonemason and says, "What are you up to?" The stonemason says, "I'm a good person. I'm providing for my family. I'm doing meaningful work." Then he passes a third stonemason who's whistling, and he says, "What are you up to?" This stonemason said, "I'm creating a home for people's spirits to soar!"

Well, they're all doing the same job, but they're having three completely different experiences and bringing three different levels of creative engagement to it.

You can hear that story at the level of clever management technique, where you essentially try to convince your employees that what they're up to matters. But when someone sees it for themselves—"this is what I'm up to, this is why it matters, and I'm all in"—that's when the game really changes. Once you're all in, it gets so much easier. Most people don't get that.

If I could drill one thing into people's heads, it's that everything is hard until you're all in.

In some ways, marriage is a good analogy for it, although I know that not everybody's marriage works like this. In a committed relationship, whether it's marriage or not, when you bump into each other and get on each other's nerves, which you will, the question isn't "should we stay together?" or "is he or she the right one?" The question is "how do we make this work?"

Until there's commitment, at least half the energy is going toward questioning the relationship. Once it's resolved, once that's off the table, then both your minds work together to generate creative solutions. As long as you're not sure what you're up to or if you're up to the right thing, more than half of your energy is spent wondering.

Same thing at work. As long as you're not sure what you're up to or if you're up to the right thing, more than half of your energy is spent wondering. You get so preoccupied with that that there's no space for fresh ideas and innovation around what you're up to. Once you're resolved about what you're up to—you're all in—all of that's off the table. That question is out of your head, and you're free to be inspired about what's next.

Bill: What's the most important question employees should ask leaders?

Michael: This may sound a little bit idealistic too, but I think it would be "Could you help me see what I'm not seeing? Help me see what I'm not seeing that would make my job easier, that would make me better at my job. That would allow me to participate fully, express myself fully, give myself over to this more. To get more out of it and put more into it."

Because if you have the choice—and in fairness most people don't see this as a choice—but if you're going to do the job anyways, you want to be fully engaged. You want to be all in. You want to love it.

Help me see what I don't see. People are amazing. When we see a better way, we'll take it.

I use the analogy sometimes of if you've gone to work the same way every day and it's an hour in traffic, and I show you a shortcut that will get you there in 10 minutes through a meandering forest road with no traffic, you only have to see it once. It doesn't matter if you've been doing it the old way for 30 years—as soon as you see a better way, you'll take it.

It's the same with us. We think "Oh habits take a long time to change." Not really, not like that. If we see a better way, we'll immediately start to take it. So if we can help our employees see a better way to work, they'll intuitively and automatically start to take it.

Bill: What is the most important question we should ask ourselves?

Michael: This isn't how I expected myself to answer this question, but the question that's coming to mind is, "Am I here?" What I mean is, am I awake within my body? Am I actually here? When I'm here, I'm incredibly capable. I'm surprisingly wise. I'm oddly compassionate. I'm quirky, but quirky in a way that's perfect.

When I'm not really here, I'm a bundle of psychological impulses and conditioning. My behavior lacks heart and depth, and it doesn't impact on the world in the same way. It's the best of both worlds vs. the worst of both worlds. When I'm here—when I'm awake within myself—I have a much richer experience of life. I'm able to ride the stresses, strains, and variances with a lot more ease and grace. Plus, I'm just more creative and effective.

Not only that, the experience other people have with me and the impact I have at work are completely different. I feel better. I do better. I have a richer experience. I'm able to contribute more. So that is a simple variable: How awake am I within myself? How present am I within myself? Am I here?

Do I always remember to ask myself these questions? No, but it's one of those things that makes a big difference in my life anyways. I rarely notice I'm gone, but I always notice when I'm back. It's like, "Well, hello you! I remember you. Where have you been?" Actually, I know where I've been. I've been in my head thinking.

I talk about it in *The Space Within*, but I talk about it there as *going home*—that experience of being at home in yourself. It's not always easy to notice you're away because you're functional and you're fine. But when you're home, it's obvious.

Bill: In closing, Michael, what question is coming up for you right now after responding to our questions?

Michael: The question that strikes me is "What's the role of coaching and leadership in management? To what extent can an understanding of coaching make you a better leader or better manager, as opposed to the many different styles of management and leadership that take a more top-down approach?"

I see coaching as the art of helping people get more out of themselves and their lives. It's the ability to bring out the best in someone and make the best better—to help people to find capacities in themselves that have been largely untapped. Then you help them to not only tap into those capacities more regularly but to ground in them so deeply that it becomes their primary place to come from instead of an occasional burst of "peak performance."

Peak performance is by definition only occasional, but high performance is sustainable. That distinction comes from an understanding of what we've got going for us and what we're up against. It starts with you. It's a bad news–good news scenario. The bad news is that it's difficult to get the most out of your people when you're having a bad personal experience of work or life. The good news is that you get to be your first "client"—to start with you. It's not selfish to start with yourself because it's your own state of mind and quality of experience that's going to be key to the impact that you have on your people.

In my work, what has become more and more apparent is that what we have going for us is an innate capacity for creativity, well-being, and resilience. What we're up against is that we're very busy minded.

We all walk around preoccupied most of the time. We don't even notice that we're tapping into such a limited part of our creative capacity.

The more I see and experience that insightfully in myself, the easier it is to see in my people, and the more fresh ideas I have to help bring them back into themselves, into the room, and into the game. Once someone is sitting in their full potential, then you can unleash that potential in a direction. If you have a room full of people who are awake to their own potential and are all looking in the same direction, it's amazing how insightful they can be and how quickly things can change.

Bill: How can people learn more about the ideas you shared in this interview?

Michael: We've developed a number of programs over the years designed to wake people up to this innate capacity and to help others to wake up to it as well.

Supercoach Academy is a training program for coaches, teachers, and managers that we've been running since 2010; we've also been running a program since 2009 called *Creating the Impossible*, which is the title of my latest book. The full title is *Creating the Impossible: How to Get Any Project Out of Your Head and Into the World in Less Than 90 Days.*

The program points to the very predictable ways we get stuck and the relative ease with which we can get out of our own way and more forward on what it is we want to create. We do it as a public program but we also bring it into businesses—not necessarily in quite as formal and structured a format because we adapt it to the individual business.

The fundamental notion behind the program is that the reason something looks impossible is because we've already made up in our head how it would happen, and we don't think we can make things happen in that particular way.

When you can go back to the drawing board and start from scratch, it's amazing how quickly different opportunities and possibilities start to appear. What seems impossible at the beginning quickly becomes not only possible but likely. Once people realize that they can take on something deliberately that they don't think they can do but would be worthwhile if they did, it's amazing what gets unleashed.

And that's why it's so relevant to business. It's not about working harder, or even smarter. It's about showing up to any project fully committed and completely open.

There's just this connection to an intuitive creative collective unconscious that begins to emerge. I can't tell you exactly what that is, but it's always available. The way I say it sometimes is, "It's 100% reliable, but 98% unpredictable." Because the ideas and opportunities rarely unfold the way you think they're going to. But they do unfold. And when you know that each time you go to the creative unknown the new ideas will come, that one thing is worth its weight in gold.

Key Takeaways

- Creating a place where every voice matters really just depends on meaning it.
- Create space to hear something new beyond what anyone brought into the room with them.
- We need to give full attention to get full attention.

- Understand the natural variance in the state of mind to come from the highest and best place inside.

- The sense of being part of something bigger is what people are really craving.

- A purpose "recognized by yourself as a mighty one" is the true joy in life.

- Do you really know what you're capable of?

- Everything is hard until you're all in—until then, half the energy is going toward questioning the basic premise.

- Could you help me see what I'm not seeing?

- When we see a better way, we'll take it.

- Am I here?

- Notice when you're not present and you'll begin to have a much richer experience of life.

- Coaching can help you be a better manager or leader.

Sesil Pir

Organizational Psychologist, HR Expert

Why Aren't 21st-Century Employees Thriving?

Sesil Pir is a recognized industrial and organizational psychologist and HR expert with two decades of field experience serving Fortune 100 companies globally. She is currently serving as the founder and consulting lead of Sesil Pir Consulting, focused on building more effective organizations, leaders, and teams.

Sesil has written a wonderful series of articles for *Forbes* magazine. It was her article "Going Back to the Future: Designing Organizational Cultures of Compassion, Wisdom and Well-Being"[1] in *Forbes* that first connected me with her. Sesil brings profound and insightful understanding of the workplace issues of our time. She masterfully helps us navigate and understand the intersection of human physiology, psychology, and spirituality in the world of today and tomorrow.

---

[1] www.forbes.com/sites/sesilpir/2018/11/12/going-back-to-the-future-designing-organizational-cultures-of-compassion-wisdom-and-well-being/#60aecbb96a3c

© Bill Fox 2020
B. Fox, *The Future of the Workplace*,
https://doi.org/10.1007/978-1-4842-5098-3_12

Bill Fox: How can we create workplaces where every voice matters, everyone thrives and finds meaning, and change and innovation happen naturally?

Sesil Pir: That's a lot to inquire in one sentence, so I'd like to divide it into pieces. Where every voice matters. I think of that as everyone having a space to "be" as an individual. I associate that with respect and dignity.

Meaning, change and innovation are different things. And I think someone's thriving is potentially an outcome of many things.

Let's look at "thriving." I find two components that make up the language of someone's thriving. The first component is often associated to vitality. It could be a sense of someone feeling alive, passionate, or even excited. It has a lot to do with having someone's spirits uplifted. The second component relates to learning that comes from having a desire to continuously gain new knowledge and skills. When we think of a thriving workforce, I often think of it as one in which employees are not necessarily just satisfied. They're productive and engaged in creating a better future for themselves and the overall organization. There's somehow an intersection that brings in the beauty and makes people thrive.

An employee who is thriving is productive and engaged in creating a better future for themselves and the overall organization.

I'm not so much for change for the sake of change. I believe in a transformative change, which comes with a valid reason for someone to participate in or to lead change. When it comes to driving successful transformative change, there are a number of things to consider, including

- A purpose that people can feel they can associate to

- Leadership role modeling along the way

- A way for employees to express their opinions and be part of the decision-making

- Outcome metrics that people can measure themselves against

If we look at innovation, what I find is that innovation is an outcome of a number of factors. The most powerful driver is having someone exercise what we would call wonder. It's a sense of awe if you will and that requires a lot of presence from people.

In some ways, it's not surprising that many organizations struggle with the concept of innovation because they're so busy. They're busy with many things (and sometimes not related to their vision), and that's a counterproductive thing for people to go through in the process of creation.

Creativity requires information taking, but then a lot of reflective time for people to digest and experience that sense of awe. That's where creativity kicks in.

When people are going from one meeting to another or from one task to another with no time for breathers, they aren't digesting the information. They're not having enough reflective time to find themselves in that state of awe.

One thing we have to ask ourselves as leaders of 21st-century organizations and as organizational specialists: Why is that despite the vast amount of investment that's been done over the years, organizations continue to struggle with levels of productivity and well-being in the workplace? According to the Organisation for Economic Cooperation and Development (OECD), productivity and well-being in the workplace have been trending down tremendously. We continue to invest more capital into our organizations. We're investing in technology. In some cases, we are growing our organizations by getting in more resources. But why aren't we getting any more productivity or any more health out of our workforce?

It's a fact that 21st-century organizations are struggling for their existence, and I genuinely believe it's not for a lack of a good idea or a product to manufacture. They have many ideas to remain competitive in the market. It's because they don't understand how to think of their structure, role, networks, and routines in the context of human evolution. They don't understand human physiology, psychology, and spirituality well enough to be able to provide the environment and experience for them to thrive. That's where the click is.

Bill: What does it take to get an employee's full attention and best performance?

Sesil: First, I'll give you my personal view; then we can have a professional answer around the performance.

As a psychologist and as a human being, I genuinely believe we all want to be seen, heard, and cared for. When you take those factors into the workplace, we also want recognition for our contribution.

To get someone's full attention, you need to genuinely desire and be there for them. I know no other way.

For example, if I am in a restaurant with my husband when a service person comes to take our order, I try to look at them in the eye and connect before I respond. I want to recognize they are another living soul. They deserve every bit of respect and care and everything else that I seem to think I deserve for myself. I see us as equals. That's very hard to do in our modern lives. I'm sure there are cases where I was also looking at my phone when someone came to the table to take our order. I don't mean to say I'm a perfect human being. That's not the point. It is a genuine struggle we share in our modern lives. If we commit to remaining mindful and conscious of our interaction with others, I think that's the inspiration.

At an organizational level, there are several indicators of performance, and I see many struggle in this area. When we go into businesses, it could be a small organization of 100 people or it could be a multinational of 400,000 people; we associate performance with productivity. If you look at the dictionary for what performance is, it is something that's associated to our ability to act on a particular function or task. It's arguably correlated to productivity. Therefore, we assume if we have the knowledge, skills, and reward mechanisms in place, then we should be able to generate the desired outcomes. Unfortunately, linking productivity that closely to performance is a false association, and it falters from a scientific point of view. It undermines the inner and outer support factors required for someone to not only complete a task and potentially overreach it.

To reach a specific outcome, we have to be in a particular state of mind, body, and spirit.

That state differs from one person to another. Being busy doesn't equate to effectiveness in the workplace. If you take it to the broader scheme, profits don't equate to social impact either. There is another issue there that we need to tackle.

It invites in a challenge for leaders, too. They want a pill. They want a formula. Take this pill and suddenly we all become more productive. I wish it was that easy. What I can say is that there's both an individual and an organization at play in achieving desired performance.

Individually, a mindset shift may help. First, to understand we are human. Second, to understand we are enough. And third, to feel at the core we are worth it. If you are in a mindset where you recognize your humanity, you know you're enough. You feel you can belong and that you're worthy. You feel recognition and appreciation for the value you bring. Then you can already put yourself in a thrive state where you can reach productivity.

Organizationally, there are several things we can do, including having a clear purpose for why someone has to do something. Giving people autonomy is also important—providing the space to do it and then coaching them to mastery. If they have to learn something new or different, or if they've done something well, to note that they have done so, so they can repeat it. In summary, having that purpose, autonomy, and mastery focus really helps. That's my take on performance.

I also think we should remember that performance management from an organization perspective is not to eliminate error or people. But rather the idea is to understand the situations in which we thrive individually and collectively. Then if there's an unseen that has occurred, learn and grow from it from that point forward.

Bill: What are people really lacking and longing for at work?

Sesil: A lot of us are struggling to find meaning in our lives. Our lives are so different from what they used to be. I grew up in a house where we had no TV or telephone. Our toilets were outside of the house. So as children, we had to invent ways to keep ourselves entertained. Now I look at how my cousins or my friends' children and how they are spending their time. They too are very busy.

If I default the signs, what makes up meaning for individuals in the workplace, it's a sense of belonging and it's a sense of leveraging your skills, combined. There are two things at play there: "Who am I?" and "What am I doing?" or "What am I contributing?" So the way I like to think of when I think of meaning or when I talk to leaders, I ask them to think of it in a way of giving to employees an experience that honors who they are and whether that experience can enhance their form of identity.

It's a beautiful question to ask: How can you design workplaces and work experiences that will provide meaning for people?

In our work, we try to bring in four things: inspiration, meaning, safety, and joy for the workplaces.

Bill: What's the most important question leaders should ask employees?

Sesil: I think it's important for any leader to ask their employees what drives you most? What are you here for? That motivation is going to be different for everyone, and actually that motivation will change for the person over a course of their career too. It's important to understand what drives them most at that very particular point in their life.

Then I'd ask, what do you need to be successful?

Thirdly, how can I best support you? That last question I'm super passionate about. I don't hear enough people leaders ask it, or what can I do to unblock certain things for you?

Those are the three questions I think are the most important.

Bill: What is the most important question employees should ask leaders?

Sesil: I would start by asking, what am I looking to achieve? I am contextual and need to connect to purpose. Because of that, I tend to assume people want that, too.

Then, what are the values I need to honor along the way? I see a lot of organizations sort of trip because they either have a misunderstanding of the values that they have agreed to play by or a misalignment on the values itself.

The last question is, how can I best contribute? When someone is brought to a job or a particular task or project, there's usually a good reason or why. So, what are the strengths they're looking for me to play with? I would like to understand that and then build on that.

Bill: What is the most important question we should ask ourselves?

Sesil: There's one question that I keep asking myself. I tend to ask, what am I over- or underlooking? You could take it both ways. What am I overlooking? What am I overvaluing? What am I overusing? You could say undervaluing or underusing too, but I somehow use that question to keep myself in check.

When I don't, it's because I'm too busy to have that reflective state of mind. Then I definitely get myself into trouble, so I learned to make time for it and hold others accountable to hold me accountable.

Bill: Who's had the biggest influence on who you are and the work that you're doing today?

Sesil: This is such an important question for me because there have been several people who have not only been supportive but super inspirational for me. I will start by saying that my grandmother has been an immense role model for me. She lost her mother and father early in life and married at 14. She bore children at 15. She had no opportunity to go to school and self-educated herself to read and write. She's different, not comfortable going to restaurants and being with people who she considers fancy, for example. She's your typical village woman, yet, there's just so much resilience and strength in that character. I have looked up to her all my life.

My mother has been another great role model for me. I think as a young person, you often have a difficult time understanding the circumstances and appreciating people for who they are. It comes to you later in age. Until my late 20s, I was frustrated and questioned why I was born into such a poor family. Why did I grow up in a village and work twice as hard as other people to get to where I am today? I really had my journey. However, with age and maturity, you recognize what the role models in your life give you, so my grandmother and my mother are big role models for me.

Then there are several other people who have touched my career. There is Danielle Monaghan, currently an executive at Amazon. She was one of my early managers and had an immense impact on me. The help she gave was really more about who she was than anything else. For example, I was so cautious of hierarchy because I came from Turkey, which is very patriarchal and hierarchical. Turkey is a totalitarian country. When you grow up in that state, you are shaped by certain behaviors. Therefore, earlier in my years, even though I was working at multinationals, I would wait until my managers left the office before I would leave the office. I thought it was expected that I would stay as long as they were there. One day she knocked on my door and said, "Do you have a few minutes?" She then went to explain that in the Western World, staying until my managers left was unnecessary. She would literally spend 30 to 45 minutes to educate me about what was required.

Carol Bubar, who is at the moment my company's COO, was at some point my manager at Microsoft. I hired her because she has had such an impact on me over the years. She has become more of a friend, someone I look up to personally and professionally very much. She's a world-recognized strategy execution expert and an amazing human being.

Lisa Brummel, who was a former Chief HR Officer at Microsoft, was a great character who impacted my development. John Younger, who has been a mentor for the last 3 to 4 years. Sean Kelley, who by a way of feedback supports inspiration and confidence for me.

There are several people I haven't met that I really love and admire, too. There is Melinda Gates (whom I have met) who inspires me every day. Krista Tippett, who is a journalist that does humanitarian work and has a podcast called On Being. I am pretty religious about listening to her. Then there are several business leaders I look up to. People like Jeff Bezos and others that have amazing minds. I don't know them personally to speak to their values, but I admire their business intelligence.

Bill: What question is at the heart of Sesil Pir?

Sesil: There are probably three things that I'm really tackling or working with at the moment. The biggest one for me is how do I become a source of light for others? I'm on my way to my calling, I think, so, it is an ongoing question for me.

In my profession, the question I'm tackling is, how can we redesign leadership and people practices? That is what I do day in, day out. That's the question that I'm living with.

Then, there is a deeper question that I think I will come to later in time. I am not there to work with this question yet. The question is, how can we better grow the next generation of HR (a term I am unsatisfied with) professionals? Spiritually and financially, I'm not in a place to be able to think about the next generation or shape things for them. But I think once I'm done with tackling the first and second question, that would be the next question that I would really want to spend quite a bit of time with.

Bill: What can any person at any level in the workplace do or be every day to bring more humanity to the workplace?

Sesil: That's an interesting question. Let's start with the term "being." What can they "be"?

I think for anyone of us to carry an aspiration is to discover and bring forward who we really are. That's a good place to "be."

This is not something we reach overnight. It's not something we reach once it's done because we are complex and evolving creatures. Consciously and unconsciously, we change by the minute. By every breath we take in, we're evolving. I will say that's not a spiritual statement. That's a physical, scientific statement. That's a fact we are evolving by the breath that we take—our cells replenish itself. At any moment, carrying an inspiration in our heart to connect to who we are and who we are becoming is a good place to "be."

In terms of "doing," I think the little things make the biggest difference. Generosity is a big value for me. Aside from that, I really observe life is generous with people generous with life. We think of generosity as grant-giving like donating money to someone or someplace, but it's so much more than that. Take smiling. I think smiling is a great act of generosity. When we are walking by someone's desk to say, "How are you today?" Of course, meaning it, too! Not just for the sake of it.

Compassion is another key value for me. If we see someone in a place of pain or suffering or having a challenge. If we are fortunate enough to recognize the pain, at least asking of, "Is there anything I can do for you?" I think that's a great act of compassion. If you want to share your knowledge or skill to help others, that's wonderful too. The point is your "doing" doesn't have to be so grandiose, but hopefully, it can become a vehicle to lift up self and others.

Bill: I've really enjoyed our conversation, Sesil. Is there something you'd like to say to close this interview?

Sesil: I liked your questions so much. I'd like to share that when it comes to leadership, it's important for us to remember that it is a lifelong journey. That's what I would end with. Just like the question you asked of employees, I think a leader can always recollect themselves and reconnect to who they are.

A leader can always ask themselves, "What am I here for?" I think that's a really good grounding question.

It is a lifelong journey. There are no pills for it and we are not as alone as we think we are. We are in it together. Each one of us as human beings is a pseudo artist and maker of our lives. I hope we can enjoy the ride together. That's certainly what I wish for myself and for those around me.

Key Takeaways

- An employee who is thriving is productive and engaged in creating a better future for themselves and the overall organization.

- Innovation is an outcome of a number of factors, but the most powerful driver is having a sense of awe and that requires presence.

- Creativity requires information taking, but then a lot of reflective time for people to digest and experience that sense of awe for creativity to kick in.

- 21st-century employees aren't thriving because organizations don't understand human physiology, psychology, and spirituality well enough to be able to provide the environment and experience for them to thrive.

- To get someone's full attention, you need to genuinely desire and be there for them.

- To reach a specific outcome, we have to be in a particular state of mind, body, and spirit.

- How can you design workplaces and work experiences that will provide meaning for people?

- It's important for any leader to ask their employees what drives you most?

- An important question to ask yourself is, "What am I over- or underlooking?"

- People can bring more humanity to the workplace by carrying an aspiration to discover and bring forward who they really are.

- A good grounding question for a leader to ask themselves is, "What am I here for?"

David Marquet

Author, Leadership Expert

Give People More Control

David Marquet is an author, a top-ranked keynote speaker, and the president of the Intent-Based Leadership Institute. His bestselling book *Turn the Ship Around!*[1] is regarded as the best how-to book on driving flawless execution and for creating leaders at every level. After being assigned to command a nuclear-powered submarine, then ranked last in retention and operational standing, he "turned his ship around" by treating the crew as leaders, not followers, and giving control, not taking control.

I first learned of David Marquet and his work in 2012 when I read his article "A Submarine Captain on the Power of Leadership Language"[2] in *Fast Company* magazine. After reading his book, I wrote a blog post[3] for the Lead Change Group about what I had learned. Shortly thereafter, I met David Marquet when he visited the Washington, DC area. I organized and hosted along with several businesses a leadership event with David where he was enthusiastically welcomed by a packed auditorium of government leaders and business executives.

---

[1] New York: Penguin Group, 2012.
[2] L. David Marquet, "A Submarine Captain on the Power of Leadership Language," Fast Company, July 23, 2012, www.fastcompany.com/1843334/submarine-captain-power-leadership-language.
[3] Fox, Bill. Lead Change Group (https://leadchangegroup.com/what-can-a-us-navy-fast-attack-submarine-captain-teach-you-about-leadership/).

© Bill Fox 2020
B. Fox, *The Future of the Workplace*,
https://doi.org/10.1007/978-1-4842-5098-3_13

Bill Fox: How can we create workplaces where every voice matters, everyone thrives and finds meaning, and change and innovation happen naturally?

David Marquet: My short answer is that we give people more control. It's all about giving control. Anytime you give control, it's giving control within structure and giving control within bounds. But fundamentally it's all about giving people control. Control over how they work, where they work, and what they work on.

Give people more control. Control over how they work, where they work, and what they work on.

Bill: Do you believe the experience you had aboard the USS Santa Fe that was featured in your book *Turn the Ship Around!* accomplished the question we are asking here?

David: Yes, but we were driven there not from a desire to change things but out of survival. There was this idea that it really sucks to work here, and we need to make things better just from an ethical point of view. But it was really more about survival.

We were driven there out of survival instinct. I just physically couldn't run around and manage people on a machine as complex as a nuclear submarine. If people are just going to give orders (including me), some of them will work and some of them won't work. People will try to follow orders and we're going to make a mistake.

We all know the situation where the leader gave an order and there's this foreboding sense of this is perhaps not right or maybe we'll get away with it. Then the organization does it and then it turns out that people die. It's a legitimate fear. I tell people you don't need to be pushed into it out of fear, I hope you are not. I'd much rather you see this as "the light on the hill" and move in that direction not from a place of fear but from a place of aspiration.

Bill: How do we give people more control?

David: The way we talk about giving people more control is there are two things. One is giving people the control part and the other one is the change that's wrapped up in a change management structure. But basically, the way we give people control is by changing the language.

The way we give people control is by changing the language.

For example, we use a device called the Ladder of Leadership. Basically, there are seven layers and the safest path of least resistance is when someone comes to you and says, "Tell me what to do," and when there's an applied tell me what to do, you just tell them what to do. It takes psychological strength to resist telling them what to do and to say instead, "Well, what's your take on the situation or what do you see here or what would you do if you were me?" You need to jump a track to get to the next higher level.

We say push authority to information as opposed to information to authority.

We have a very language-based approach to it. We say philosophically you want to push authority to information as opposed to information to authority, but the mechanisms are the interactions that happen all day long. You can have a hundred of them all day long with all your people. They happen on email. They happen in meetings. They happen on the phone. They happen face to face. And in all those interactions, just be attuned to where the other person is and resist falling into the trap of telling them what to do.

It also requires knowing who owns what. Ownership is very important. Instead of focusing on past achievement, leaders focus on task ownership. In a traditional organization, we say, "Bill you're responsible for this and on Tuesday I'm going to come down to your office with my little checklist and see how are you doing on steps 1, 2, and 3." In that situation, we call it stealing ownership.

Even though I said it's yours, my actions are really stealing the ownership, creativity, and authority over it in the end because now you're feeling, "Oh crap, now I need to answer a bunch of questions."

So the onus is on ownership. "Go, this is yours. Let me know what you need." But this is also a message that many times the workers and followers in the organization love to hear. Then I say, "But it puts a greater onus on you, a responsibility on you being transparent and visible to your boss about what you're doing." You say, "Oh great, I'm in charge of it," then we go disappear into our cubby hole and come out in 2 months. No, no, that's not going to work. You are going to lose the right to be in control of your life. Transparency is what gives you the right to be in control of your life.

Bill: What does it take to get an employee's full attention and best performance?

David: I would ask the question a little bit differently.

> I would say under what conditions do employees give their full attention and best performance?

Because the question is from a mindset that I'm manipulating my employees. I'm getting them to give me my best attention and performance, as opposed to you know what, I really can't control that. I can really only control myself, but if I set the environment right, I can move in the direction of getting their full attention and best performance.

It's like farming. I plant the seeds in fertile land and fertilize and water them. I don't order seeds to grow, but they are going to grow. We think there is a duality, which is that the leader focuses on and is responsible for the environment. The employee focuses on and is responsible for their behavior.

For example, let's say it's Friday afternoon and the team is working late, and one employee sneaks out the back door. In a healthy organization when we talk about that on Monday, the leader is asking, "What is it about the environment that is making it easy for that person to sneak out the back door as opposed to staying and helping the team?" The person who snuck out early says, "What about my behavior was unhelpful there?" There may be a good reason. Maybe their child was sick and he had to run out. Who knows. But in an unhealthy organization, it's the opposite. The leader blames the person and says you don't understand our core value of empathy, and the person blames the environment. You have a toxic work environment. So that's the worst situation. The best situation is when the people take responsibility for their behavior knowing that our behavior is powerfully shaped by the environment and vice versa. The leader takes responsibility for the environment knowing that even in the best of environments, some peoples' behavior will be bad behavior.

Bill: What do people really lack and long for at work?

David: I believe it's control, value, and purpose. When I think about the unpleasant times of my work, they were things like plenty of abuse and then you feel trapped because you feel like there's no one to talk to. If you speak up, you're going to get fired. You're not a team player. You risk social ostracism and so it's not safe to vent at work, so you come home and you vent at home. Maybe it's safety, a sense of security.

I think 30 years ago our parents would have said, "I feel secure here." They would have described workplace security as a feeling that they're going to continue earning income. As opposed to now it's more, "I feel like I can't be my true self here and if you piss me off (even if you're my boss) I'm going to let you know you pissed me off here."

Bill: What is the most important question leaders should ask employees?

David: I think there are several important questions. "How can I help you?" "What are you trying to achieve?" "How can I help you achieve that?" "Is this company acting in a way that's consistent with your principles?" "Do we have integrity between what we say and what we do with what we do with our clients, and what we do internally?"

Is this company acting in a way that's consistent with your principles?

Management is typically more secure in their job; they have a better perspective of what the organization is trying to do; they can muster more resources. They can say, "Well you want to take night school classes, then we can help pay for those." "You want to take every Tuesday morning off so that you can take a pottery class?" "Great, we can figure out how to change your work schedule." Management has a lot of ways of helping people and they should.

Bill: What's the most important question employees should ask leaders?

David: "Is there anything I'm doing that is making it hard for you?" Employees need to understand the bounds of what they're responsible for and what decisions they can make. "What are we trying to achieve here?"

I did an exercise called "sliders and sorts" the other day. We publish a periodic article called "The Weekly Leadership Nudge." The idea is that too many times workers can hide behind death by 1001 questions. Leaders can kill initiative by asking too many questions, but workers can kill leaders' attempts to give them any initiative by asking too many questions.

Do you remember we used to say, bring me a rock? The problem is management isn't honest enough to say I don't even know what this looks like, but I'm going to go talk to the secretary about this, and I need a framework for the discussion. Go work on it. Well, the employee says, "What are you trying to achieve?" You say, "Just go work on it." I'm sympathetic to that because I want the team to put some brainpower into it. Then we ask ourselves if we were the boss, "What message would we want to get to the secretary?"

Well, a response might be, "Here are three key questions to ask." Now when you come back to the boss rather than having open-ended questions while laying on your belly with your legs in the air saying, "Help me here." Come in say, "Well, we thought about it, and we believe there are three key points you need to bring up. The question is, how provocative do you want to be? Do you want to tell him this is what we need to do or open a conversation?" Now it's a much more helpful conversation.

Bill: What is the most important question we should ask ourselves?

David: I'm hopeful that for more of humanity that work will become discretionary, something that we voluntarily do. So I think the question "How do I want to spend my time?" is the most practical sense of that question. Questions like, "What's meaningful for me?" and "What's my dream?", those questions to me are a little bit to pie in the sky. I really don't know what to do with them.

When I ask myself what do I want to do with my time, it makes it more concrete.

For example, "What do you want to do tonight?" "What do you want to do tomorrow?" "What do you want to do next year?" "What do you want to do for the next decade?" Those are the type of questions I end up asking myself all the time. "Do I want to go do this talk or do I want to go hike the Alps?" "Do I want to go work out or do I want to do another 10 emails?" "Do I want to read this book or do I want to sit on an airplane?"

Key Takeaways

- Give people more control.

- Change the language to give control.

- Lead from a place of aspiration—not fear.

- You can really only control yourself.

- Leaders focus on environment—followers focus on their behavior.

- People feel trapped when there's no sense of security.

- Today people want to be their true self.

- Do we have integrity between what we say we do and what we do?

- Management has lots of ways of helping and they should.

- Employees need to understand their boundaries.

- Add brainpower to move beyond open-ended questions.

- How do I want to spend my time?

- Asking yourself makes it more concrete.

14

John Toussaint

Lean Healthcare Leader

Insights from Leading a Lean Healthcare Revolution

Dr. John Toussaint is the executive chairman of Catalysis Inc. and is one of the foremost figures in the adoption of lean principles in healthcare. John has written three books, all of which have received the prestigious Shingo Research and Publication Award. His books include *On the Mend: Revolutionizing Healthcare to Save Lives and Transform the Industry*,[1] *Potent Medicine: The Collaborative Cure for Healthcare*,[2] and *Management on the Mend: The Healthcare Executive Guide to System Transformation*.[3]

I was introduced to John by Norman Bodek, owner of PCS Press and a pioneer in introducing lean techniques and thinking to the western world. Although John's experience and work are focused in the healthcare industry, what he brings to the conversation is very much applicable to any workplace.

Bill Fox: How can we create workplaces where every voice matters, everyone thrives and finds meaning, and change and innovation happen naturally?

John Toussaint: I think it's a combination of things. I always go back to John Shook's, CEO of the Lean Enterprise Institute, description of how we truly get to excellence, which is it's about processes, and it's about people. We have

---

[1] MA: Lean Enterprise Institute, 2010.
[2] WI: ThedaCare Center for Healthcare Value, 2012.
[3] WI: ThedaCare Center for Healthcare Value, 2015.

© Bill Fox 2020
B. Fox, *The Future of the Workplace*,
https://doi.org/10.1007/978-1-4842-5098-3_14

to equally recognize that we need to have an environment in which people are allowed to do work that gives their life meaning, so that's the people part.

The leader's role is to make sure that the people that work in the organization are allowed to do work that gives their life meaning.

But then we also have to have systems or processes. I like to call them systems in which people can thrive. If there aren't any systems (or processes) that are standardized and reproducible every day, then people end up doing a lot of non-value added work. If they're doing non-value added work, this then gets back to this point of they're not necessarily doing work that gives their life meaning.

I think it's a combination of these concepts of building systems that allow people to do work that gives their life meaning, and the leader's role is to make sure that there's a balance between these two activities.

Bill: How do we get an employee's full attention and best performance?

John: I think there has to be a recognition of why people come to work every day. We've been doing a lot of work in our company with something called Strengthsfinder, which focuses on what your strengths are rather than your weaknesses. In the classic performance review that you get once a year, you have all these things you're supposed to get better at, but nobody really talks about what you're really good at doing. This concept flips the equation to let us focus on what you're good at and how can we take what you're good at and make you even better at it?

Focusing on your strengths is one way to try to help figure out how you as an employee can best help your organization.

From the standpoint of understanding the human dynamics of why and how people work, focusing on your strengths is one way to try to help figure out how you as an employee can best help your organization. We've found that to be very helpful because first of all, everybody has different strengths. From a team perspective, you can leverage each team member's strength if you understand what it is. Then when we put each team member's strengths together, we can really do some pretty amazing things that we wouldn't be able to do if it was just one person at a time who has a certain role.

I think it's very important to tease out where people's strengths are and how their personality traits can reinforce effective teams by understanding the diversity of who they are and what their strengths are. If we start there, then we can look at what is the work to be done and really try to understand what is the value that's being created and what every person in the team's role is to help create that value. That's how I think we begin to get these high functioning teams.

Now at the same time, we also need to be focusing on the processes of that value creation. We need to understand how to most efficiently and effectively with the highest quality produce that value. We need to understand what the value stream is. We need to understand where the non-value added activity is and try to remove that every day. Then we need to build a system of rapid learning so that as we identify new customer needs, we can "skate to where the puck's going to be" with either a new value stream or a refurbished value stream to deliver that value that the customer is seeking.

I think it gets back to this balance of let's make sure we leverage the strengths of the people we have in our organization, which can then make them excited to come to work. But let's also build the systems to understand how we create the maximum value for the customer that we serve.

Bill: What do people really lack and long for at work?

John: I think the most important thing is respect. You read every day about some multinational corporation laying off thousands of workers. To me, that is just the ultimate lack of respect for people.

One of my mentors in the leadership work that I do is Paul O'Neill, past CEO and Chairman at Alcoa. He made Alcoa the safest company to work for in the world back when it wasn't cool to do that. He did it based on a fundamental respect for people. His point was the ultimate respect for people is to not have them get injured at work. In a manufacturing environment back in the 1980s, a lot of people were being injured. If we fast forward today, safety is job #1 in most manufacturing companies. I think today it's respecting the work that people do and celebrating that work, which is another way of showing respect.

What people fundamentally are looking for is respect for my opinion, my ideas, and some kind of celebratory function saying "you're doing a great job, thanks for being here."

But I think what people fundamentally are looking for is respect for my opinion, my ideas, and some kind of celebratory function saying "you're doing a great job, thanks for being here." You get to the bottom line by building these fundamental human systems in which you create an employee that's willing to go to the mat for you.

Bill: What is the most important question leaders should ask employees?

John: Have I made sure that our employees have the tools, training, and environment to do work that gives their life meaning? I think that's the fundamental question.

We often throw people into situations where they don't have any knowledge, and we expect them to figure it out themselves. That's unfair. I do most of my work in hospitals and clinics. The work environment in most of those places is caustic. They're full of fear, and the autocracy of the traditional healthcare management systems makes people not want to take any risks or try anything new or improve anything. That environment is just extremely negative.

I think it's the leader's role to ensure we are trained at what we need to do, that we have tools at our disposal to do it the best we can, and that we have an environment that's conducive to doing good work and improving that work.

Bill: What is the most important question employees should ask leaders?

John: If the environment's been created to flourish, the employees then need to ask, "What is it I can do that's going to contribute to the success of the organization? How can I contribute? What do you need from me in order to be successful and effective?"

But the first condition is leaders have to create that environment. Then once that's created, the employees have a responsibility to respond to that environment with their best work.

My experience has been after being CEO for three different companies that if the leaders do create the environment, most of the time the employees will respond because, frankly, people do want to get up and go to work and do a good job. I fundamentally believe that people given the right environments are going to make good choices. The reason they don't make good choices is that the environment stinks, and so they have to go into survival mode. But if you have an organization that's really trying to achieve the top of Maslow's triangle, and if the leader has been able to create that environment, then that brings out the best in people.

Occasionally that's not true. Occasionally you have an employee who is not willing to or able to do what's necessary. But by far and away the lion's share of people that I've worked with over the years—if you give them what they need to do their work—will do great work for you.

Bill: What is the most important question we should ask ourselves?

John: I think it's a question of self-reflection. I work with a lot of CEOs around the world, and one of the things we find is they take very little time for self-reflection.

I think the question is: "Do you have a process to reflect on how effective you've been as a leader and is that happening on a regular basis?"

Some leaders that I work with schedule 15 minutes once a week on their calendar. It's a specific time where they reflect on questions such as, "What did I do this week that unleashed the creativity of the people that work for me?" Or, "What did I do that shut people down?"

We published an article with the CEO of the San Francisco General Hospital and in *The New England Journal of Medicine* online journal where we identified five core behavioral traits that are really important to build this culture of continuous improvement.[4]

We created a radar chart around those five traits, and we asked people to rate themselves on a scale of one to five. One being not practicing it to five being proficient. Then you end up with this radar chart that shows several places where you really need to improve. We've asked them to use this process as a way of self-reflection, so they can use those questions of what did I do this week that really worked well, and what did I do that didn't work well and then work on those key behavioral traits to begin to change some of those actions.

I think the biggest thing for leaders is this making time for self-reflection.

Bill: How did you make the leap from the medical profession to being the CEO of an organization that brings lean thinking to the healthcare industry?

John: I worked as a medical doctor for about 20 years. I stopped practicing when I became the CEO of an integrated healthcare delivery system in Wisconsin, which is where we experimented with the principles of lean. I spent a lot of time in manufacturing companies trying to understand quality processes, and that's where we stumbled across lean thinking.

We were one of the first places to apply it in healthcare, which is why I do what I do now because we found that it was so powerful. We wanted to bring

---

[4] See "Five Changes Great Leaders Make to Develop an Improvement Culture," http://catalyst.nejm.org/five-changes-great-leaders-improvement-culture/.

it to the rest of the industry, so I started a not-for-profit education institute in 2008 after I stepped down as CEO to work with the many different hospitals around the world.

We facilitate a peer-to-peer learning network of many organizations around North America, and we do a summit every year called the Lean Healthcare Transformation Summit. I've written three books, published multiple articles, and peer-reviewed journals including the *Harvard Business Review*. We also do executive coaching from the perspective of the CEO and senior executive team to try to help guide them on the content knowledge and behavioral change that's required to build lean principles into their organizations.

It's been an interesting journey to try to transform the healthcare industry. We have some really great examples now of organizations that have been doing unbelievably better work than when they started this learning journey. We know it works. It's a challenge because it's not anchored in the DNA. What's anchored in the DNA of healthcare people is fear and trembling from the massive autocracy that exists within the industry including starting with the medical education system. But some of that is starting to crumble in certain places, and we're part of the wrecking ball that's trying to change it.

Key Takeaways

- It's about processes, and it's about people.
- Without systems, people end up doing non-value added work.
- Focus on what you're good at and get better at it.
- Leverage people's strengths and build systems that create value.
- Respect people's opinions and ideas and celebrate them.
- Have I made sure our employees have what they need?
- It's unfair to expect people to figure it out themselves.
- Leaders must create an environment where people can respond.
- People make good choices when given the right environment.
- Do you have a process to self-reflect regularly?
- What did I do this week to unleash creativity?
- Recognize that fear is anchored in the DNA of many organizations.

Hrund Gunnsteinsdottir

Managing Director and Film Director

Shifting the Center of Gravity

Hrund Gunnsteinsdottir is the managing director at Festa, a not-for-profit center focusing on a broad-based peer-to-peer and public-private partnerships and excellence in social responsibility, and is chair of the Technology Development Fund for Innovation in Iceland. Hrund is an experienced entrepreneur, thought leader, and speaker in creative and critical thinking in education, global trends, and the workplace of the 21st century.

She is also the scriptwriter and codirector of the documentary film *InnSæi—The Power of Intuition*[1] (or "The Sea Within"), which explores our ability to be creative, compassionate, and connected in a world of distraction and stress.

I first learned of Hrund Gunnsteinsdottir after discovering her extraordinary documentary film. In the film, Hrund takes us on a global journey to uncover the art of connecting within in today's world of distraction and stress. Hrund brings and shares that same wisdom in this interview.

---

[1] New York: Zeitgeist Films, 2016.

B. Fox, *The Future of the Workplace*,
https://doi.org/10.1007/978-1-4842-5098-3_15

Bill Fox: How can we create workplaces where every voice matters, everyone thrives and finds meaning, and change and innovation happen naturally?

Hrund Gunnsteinsdottir: One of the things that come to mind is the word constellation. If you think about a workplace in the sense that you can create a constellation, which represents a clear framework, then there are some borders to what we do. But inside the constellation, there is a lot of trust. I trust my colleagues and my supervisors in a way that I can speak openly, ask silly questions, or be genuine about what I'm thinking. I'm free to think outside the box and open my mind. Then there's encouragement and affirmation, so I'm encouraged to be who I am. I feel that what I say and how I see things really matter. I think that is important to people.

Inside a constellation, there's a lot of trust. I feel that what I say and how I see things really matter.

Innovation is very much about risks. What I mean by risks is that you take a risk in suggesting something, so it's the way you talk to people. You're not afraid to take risks to come up with ideas. We often talk about economic risks and financial risks when we talk about innovation, but I really think it's minimal when you both allow space for something that's a known risk and something that's an unknown risk. But in order to create that creative workplace, you need to have that constellation that makes people feel secure in their space where they are genuinely listened to. People appreciate what they have to offer because of who they are—not only what they studied. It's also a workplace that encourages you to use tools that you're not necessarily specialized in. And when I say tools, I mean knowledge. It can be a concept, theory, or just a bit of information from somewhere that is not your specialty but you have feeling it may help a thought process, strategy, way of seeing things, something that is worth exploring.

I also think in essence it's about leadership within that workplace that understands the incredible value of intrinsic motivation. You're willing to do so many things when you are intrinsically motivated. My friend Gordon Torr, who wrote *Managing Creative People*,[2] said if you have a room with five highly creative individuals and you want them to come up with a very original creative idea, then you don't say to them, "You know, if you do this in a week then you'll get a free parking space for a year or I'll give you a pay raise." It's not really going to motivate them in a creative or innovative sense. But if you see who they are and you see them for who they are and you want more of them, they can feel that. Then they feel like you respect what they have to offer—that's a whole

---

[2] West Sussex, UK: John Wiley & Sons Ltd., 2008.

different way of approaching things. They will feel safe, unafraid to take risks by coming up with ideas and explore because you are willing to take that risk with them—and you trust the process. This way, they will trust that their exploration and ideas will have value, that they matter in the bigger context. They will not be afraid to ask challenging or critical questions, which ultimately lead to something that will give that company or organization the lead, small or big. That is what intrinsic motivation does. When matched with extrinsic motivation, which defines the framework, you've created that alchemy we are all looking for.

Bill: What does it take to get an employee's full attention and best performance?

Hrund: I think you need to set an example yourself. You need to practice what you preach. One of the barriers we sometimes have in the workplace is basically the lack of people showing that they're imperfect. Let's say I'm a leader in the workplace, and I want people to excel in an area. If I have the self-confidence to show that I make mistakes, and I sometimes say silly things, and I don't know everything, then people are more likely to do that too and they relax. I think that's one of the things that we can do.

But then there's also this recognition that I see you for who you are, and I want more of you. If you're in a workplace where the people around you and your supervisors want more of you and they can't get enough of you, then they help you to be the best version of yourself. But they also recognize your days vary. Some days you peak. Some days you're really low on energy and grumpy. We give space for that, but it is also clear that we want the best of you. I think it's again this kind of nourishing environment where we want you for who you are, but we also give you responsibility to show what you are made up of.

If you're in a workplace where the people around you want more of you and they can't get enough of you, then they help you to be the best version of yourself.

Responsibility is very important in this context. You're being held accountable for what you're responsible for, which is another clear framework. But it also gives you the freedom to do the things you need to do the way that you want to do them.

The antidote to the question you asked is micromanagement and lack of trust. A leader who would say "Don't you say or share anything without asking me first" would shut you down. It's a statement that embodies a lack of trust. You become risk averse and that limits your agency. So, I think it's about the kind of things you can do to draw the best out in people, but there's always a question of peer frameworks. We do have to have rules because I think that in order to play, we also need a clear framework, which is kind of a security net.

I trust that you will catch me if I fall. But if I don't stand up to my responsibility, I will also have to address that or possibly leave at some point. I also think that makes us be a little more on our toes in order to perform the best we can but not in a frightening way. I trust you to do your job. If you don't find your place here, then we will have to move on. Having said that, we all need the peer support to find our place; it's not about being put alone out on the ice.

As an example, let's say you have a workplace that's been around for decades. You've been doing things that are traditional and now you need to be innovative. You need to do things differently, so that's shifting the center of gravity in the way that we approach work—and I think that's what we're all going through in one way or another. It means we are exploring, learning, and asking questions together. In a team.

You've been doing things that are traditional and now you need to be innovative. You need to do things differently, so that's shifting the center of gravity in the way that we approach work.

One of the things we've sometimes used in the programs I've worked on is shaking up the language around things. In Iceland, we had Prisma, which was a university diploma program, based on creative and critical thinking and a cross-disciplinary approach. It was all about finding one's voice and going into the unknown. Sharpening your creative compass, with a sense of meaning for the bigger context. The module was designed for students to "learn and do" in the face of uncertainty. Conventional education has focused on certainty, but today, the world is characterized by uncertainty. Prisma embraced that. How best to flourish and enhance your agency in times of uncertainty. Prisma was recognized by the Nordic Council for being one of the education programs that best responded to the 21st-century work market. Rather than using the word teachers, we used the word facilitators. In Icelandic, it translates into "he or she that makes things easier." It's kind of funny but when you work with it, it's very freeing because it is not hierarchical or too serious. The teachers really loved it. It broke down the barriers between the teachers and the students. It's more like "I'm here to make things easier for you my friends." Just playing with words like that can take the seriousness away from it. It's part of the constellation.

We have work processes, hierarchies, and bureaucracies, and sometimes the reason why we don't change things—for example, in education—is because we have contracts in place that dictate how people's career will end 30 years from now. Or we have a bookkeeping system that has different keys that don't allow a disruptive approach to anything because everything is totally pinned down to different silos. I think it's important to just ask how can we change that? How silly of us to not allow progress because of things like that. Sometimes we have to create a new word and then tie things up to that word in a different way. Words translate into action. Then it's a whole new constellation around the way we do stuff.

Bill: What do people really lack and long for at work?

Hrund: I think it does depend on where you work and what you're doing. I'm probably very influenced by the work I've been doing through the film and other projects, but I think that people today would like to find more harmony between their private life and work life. By harmony I mean I feel like I can cope. It's not just at work, it's also at home. And not only can I cope, I can thrive.

I've talked about intrinsic motivation and bringing out the best in people, and this idea of enabling people to live out their fullest potential is amazing. But you can't just focus on that at work. We need to respect that people have different roles and responsibilities, so I think that it's key to recognize that and approach every individual from that perspective. Not everybody makes that distinction. Some people are what they do. Some people come home and take care of their kids, and they can't stop thinking about what they're doing at work. It really benefits them and what they do at work to be present with their kids or otherwise in their private lives. So I think it's learning to allow all these components to work together.

They say that when Gandhi was out in the countryside, government officials came to see him because there was trouble going on somewhere. He would just ask them to wait while he was feeding the goat or talking to the kids. He'd then take all the time that he needed to think through the answer to their requests to synchronize his intuition, experience, and knowledge of the situation. Then he'd come back to them with maybe three sentences or something well thought through. So I think giving people the ways and tools in order to find this harmony is very important. We all need time to reflect, let go of control, and allow solutions to come to us.

In 2020, creativity, critical thinking, and the ability to solve complex problems are going to be the top three skills sought after.

We also talk about creativity and innovation. That's the big thing today in the world of work. In 2020, creativity, critical thinking, and the ability to solve complex problems are going to be the top three skills sought after in the work market, according to the World Economic Forum.[3] At the same time, the World Health Organization (WHO) is telling us that depression is increasing and is the leading cause of disability in the world today. I remember 18 years ago to be precise, I was looking into what were the five main health

---

[3] www.weforum.org/agenda/2016/01/the-10-skills-you-need-to-thrive-in-the-fourth-industrial-revolution/

threats to people globally, and I realized for the first time that depression was actually one of the five highest-ranking things that are debilitating us health wise in the world. So, you have depression, stress, and anxiety peaking, and you have a need for creativity, resilience, and open-mindedness at the same time. This does not go well together. These are things we need to think about. Then there's this third middle factor that we can add in, and that's a MacArthur Foundation report about education and technology in the 21st century—it states that 65% of school kids today will be doing jobs in the future that have not been invented. So how are we preparing them for the unknown future? By offering them tools that were meant for a world that no longer exists?

Bill: What is the most important question leaders should ask employees?

Hrund: How can I support you? How can I make your work more challenging and rewarding depending on what's relevant? What information do you need that can help you? Can I connect you with people who can help you in terms of meeting like-minded people or getting information that you need? Or can I elevate you somehow?

How can I support you in becoming professionally strong in the work market in general, but you will still choose to work here?

It's a matter of being there to support people to grow, evolve, bearing in mind that people need different things. Like I'm very protective of introverts, in our world that elevates extroverts. They need to be allowed to be introverts. Extroverted people may need something else than introverted people need.

I also think that there needs to be a strong vision. Leaders need to have a strong vision, and it needs to be inspiring. People look up to and want to be around visionaries. They want to work with the individual, but that individual is really there to support them in reaching that vision.

And in order to be supportive of your people, you can't be dominated by your fear of them taking your job away. I love it when I hear leaders say, "I'm so honored to be here." "The people I'm surrounded with here are so much more intelligent, clever, and efficient than I am ever." "But I'm here to be the facilitator of great things."

Bill: What is the most important question employees should ask leaders?

Hrund: What will you do to make me thrive in your environment? How can I best support the objectives, visions, and my colleagues?

In order for me to do the best job that I can do, what are you offering me so that I will thrive and build my skills, and I will become so good that I still decide to work for you, but not somebody else?

I think that's a question I'd like to see more of because it's totally dynamic. It's not arrogant when you think about automation and how jobs are becoming more technical and many jobs will be disappearing or changing. Many people hear the message: More than half of you aren't going to have any jobs. We already have that in the banking industry, for example. Managers and leaders are not finding the response to that question because they also worry about their own jobs.

It may sound counterintuitive but could it be genuinely economically feasible that employers build the skills of employees that do not directly relate to the jobs that they're in? But they make them feel like they will be sought after in the workplace in the future? Because that could lead to some extraordinary innovation inside that same corporation. It's again about trust and self-confidence. Discovering the creative potential that we can have. One of my favorite sentences now is "The only thing that's certain about the world we live in today, is uncertainty." So how do we build skills that enable us to best navigate uncertainty?

Bill: What is the most important question we should ask ourselves?

Hrund: I think on a collective scale and in the context of the Fourth Industrial Revolution, which involves immensely fast technological and scientific developments, globalization, political, social, and economic turbulence, it would be, "Do we want to want this?", as the historian and author of *Sapiens* and *Homo Deus*, Yuval Noah Harari, coined it. What is the meaning, end goal, of these technological and scientific developments?

We need to remember, perhaps now more than ever before, that technology, science, and systems are a means to an end.

They are not, or should not, be an end in themselves. They should serve to improve the lives of people and a thriving ecosystem on our planet.

Maybe the most important question to ask individually and collectively is "What is the meaning of life?" I think we're back to the old philosopher's questions. Just really ask ourselves, "What is meaningful to me and my community and how can I allow that to be the basis of everything I do?" By that, I don't mean that we're not challenging ourselves, but I think that's the most basic thing we can ask because this disconnection from ourselves, which we explore in our documentary film *InnSæi—the Power of Intuition*, disconnection from nature and each other, and the work that we're doing is a big phenomenon today. And it's not sustainable.

When I ask my students—who are usually managers and leaders—what are the two things that education should be based on, they always mention elusive things. They say things like students should learn to be good people and have good values. Empathy, good people's skills, emotional intelligence. They mention things that have very much to do with the good qualities of a human being. Sometimes I worry that we're just totally relying on artificial intelligence and all these amazing technologies, at the cost of our own values, intuition, creativity, experience, and knowledge. We shouldn't place more trust on things that lie externally to ourselves than we trust our own inner compass, our very essence of humanity. There needs to be a balance between the two.

Bill: There was a fascinating theme that runs through your film InnSæi. I'd like to ask you, what would it mean if we lived more connected between the head and the heart?

Hrund: If we lived more connected between the head and the heart, it would mean that we would be more empathetic. We would be more courageous to be who we are. We would be better able to put ourselves in other people's shoes. This way we would be more creative and responsible. Our agency would be much stronger.

If we lived more connected between the head and the heart, it would mean that we would be more empathetic.

When it comes to nature and climate change, we would approach that totally differently. You know, most of us are most afraid in the places where we are most sincere. We are more vulnerable in our hearts than in our heads, so to speak. Cynicism is the best shield against sincerity. Where we are most sincere is the source of all our creative ideas and that's where empathy comes from. The reason why people are afraid to express their creative ideas is that this is where they're most vulnerable. It goes together.

Even scientists and professors that teach intuition at some of the best universities don't teach how to use it. They only recite, summarize, analyze, and teach research that has been done. In a sense, they teach it in an abstract way. They don't make the connection for people on how to actually apply it. It's a field that we are very hesitant to go into because things can come out of it that we can't control. Your first question, on why I resigned from a permanent position at the UN. It's partly because I have a strong initiative and entrepreneurial spirit. The very hierarchical and bureaucratic work environment didn't fit for me, it confined me too much, and maybe that has changed over the years at the UN, at least I hope so to some extent.

When I see a sparkle in people's eyes, I know something wonderful is happening... I realized that that was an energy I wanted to see and feel and be a part of.

I remember walking the hallways of the Palace of Nations in Geneva one day, and I would look for a sparkle in people's eyes. I very seldom found it. When I see a sparkle in people's eyes, I know something wonderful is happening, at least partly—because of course life is never perfect. I realized that that was an energy I wanted to see and feel and be a part of. I think that's important. I think that has to do with the connection too.

Key Takeaways

- Create a constellation, which represents a clear framework where what I say and how I see things matter.

- In order to create that creative workplace, people need to feel secure and genuinely listened to.

- In essence it's about leadership that understands the incredible value of intrinsic motivation.

- One of the barriers we sometimes have in the workplace is the lack of people showing they're imperfect.

- You've been doing things that are traditional and now you need to be innovative. That's shifting the center of gravity—exploring learning and asking questions together.

- You can't focus just on work. Give people the ways and tools to find harmony between work and home.

- Depression, stress, and anxiety are peaking while the need for creativity, resilience, and open-mindedness is becoming greater.

- How can I support you in becoming professionally strong in general?

- Leaders need to have a strong vision, and it needs to be visionary.

- What will you do to make me thrive in your environment?

- How do we build skills that enable us to navigate uncertainty?

- Do we want this?

- If we lived more connected between the head and the heart, we would be more empathetic.

Robert Fuchs

Culture Architect

What If Corporate Culture Is Perfect, But I'm Not?

Robert Fuchs is a culture architect and creative design leader with a background in systemic psychotherapy. He leads the research of the HappinessGroup.eu on highly effective teams and corporate culture transformation. The HappinessGroup.eu develops meta-frameworks, methods, and tools for decision-making and problem-solving by integrating the latest insights from consciousness science and quantum mechanics with philosophical schools of thought.

I connected with Robert after he commented on one of my posts on LinkedIn. A conversation followed where we discovered the fascinating and groundbreaking research he was leading at the Happiness Group, in Munich, Germany. Robert's work is a far-reaching project that is collecting, evaluating, and integrating state-of-the-art models from natural and social sciences to provide more people access to this collected knowledge.

Bill Fox: How can we create workplaces where every voice matters, everyone thrives and finds meaning, and change and innovation happen naturally?

Robert Fuchs: Change and innovation happen naturally in environments that foster learning and growth, which naturally leads to transformation and is the same as innovation.

© Bill Fox 2020
B. Fox, *The Future of the Workplace*,
https://doi.org/10.1007/978-1-4842-5098-3_16

Now comes the tricky part because the environment or the corporate culture is only partly visible through explicit values and value priorities. And at the same time partly invisible through our own constructions of this reality. This means that a culture can be perfect, but because of flaws in my consciousness, perception, and mindfulness of this reality, I can't see the possibilities I have within this culture.

A culture can be perfect, but because of flaws in my consciousness, perception, and mindfulness of this reality, I can't see the possibilities I have within this culture.

From a leadership perspective, I have to ensure that every voice is heard and relevance is seen in the diverse voices. From an individual perspective, I have to find a function within the organization that I can give meaning to. Meaning is not something external, but only I can give meaning to the things that happen in my life. Life by itself is meaningless unless I give it meaning. Function in combination with meaning results in purpose, so this is the personal task of every employee, which happens best in collaboration with the rest of the team. Only in interaction and collaboration with others can I find the sweet spot where purpose for the team and purpose for me personally intersect.

Because today roles and responsibilities change as fast as the business models they are grounded on, we have to regularly evaluate these tasks and refactor or reintegrate ourselves as we do with software.

Bill: What does it take to get an employee's full attention and best performance?

Robert: The conditions for best performance are peace, love, and happiness. However, since these conditions are usually at least partially fake in hierarchical structures of organizations, we therefore need a truthful way to assess the state of attention or mindfulness.

High-performance information processing lies at the intersection of integrated knowledge (Phi) and balanced experience (Psi) at the point of wisdom (0 distortion of reality). The point of wisdom requires three preconditions:

1. Self-determination.
2. Psychological safety.
3. Certainty about an information.

These preconditions can be easily identified with the following four questions:

1. Is the employee experiencing pressure to act or is it possible to act freely?

2. Is the employee not able or not willing to perform at best?

3. Is the employee mentally and emotionally present (or still in the past or already in the future)?

4. Is the employee ready to learn something new?

Only if all four answers are "yes" we can assume the best conditions for successful information transformation. This applies of course to both agents in an interacting system. All other answers indicate a distorted reality construct and require change first.

To make this more tangible, we have to look at two aspects.

An employee's attention depends on internal and external factors, so let's look at the external factors first. Our brain works perfectly when we have to process the right amount of information with the right level of abstraction and complexity. If there is too much information, our brain produces misunderstandings. If there is too little information, our brain produces false assumptions. Both produce human error and are the sign of the absence of attention.

In other words, lack of attention can be a direct result of useless information input. Our internal resources are limited by our capacity, utilization, and availability to process new information. The smaller our capacity and the higher the utilization, the smaller is the availability—in this case, our attention to process new information. We have to be aware that our brain is in constant problem-solving mode as long as we have problems to solve. The more problems we concurrently have to process, the less we are able to focus on the problems at hand. In other words, the more private or personal problems we have, the more of our capacity is utilized, which results in less availability for new problems. In this case, the employee is not able to perform better until other problems, which rank higher, are solved. For example, if a child is sick or the employee has to look for a new apartment, then the new branding guideline of corporate marketing ranks a lot lower on my internal priority list.

The second dimension of attention lies with our talent and fitness or with our skills and abilities. The more skill in pattern recognition the employee has, the easier it is to make sense out of information and to derive meaning. In addition, the greater one's fitness or level of pattern integration, the easier it is for employees to stay attentive. In other words, I would say that performance is based about 1/3 on the pattern recognition ability, 1/3 on the integration ability of new with existing knowledge, and 1/3 with physical fitness. Everybody has firsthand experience with attention when we have sleep deficits. Some companies even pay their workforce bonuses for sleeping 8 hours at night. Just look around during your next meeting and check how many of your coworkers are well rested. Then imagine the impact on their decision-making and problem-solving abilities.

Enough sleep, healthy diet, and regular exercise probably reduce most attention problems. The rest can be dealt with through clear and meaningful communication and with more consciousness in reflecting on personal issues—that keep us from paying full attention to a situation.

Bill: What do people really lack and long for at work?

Robert: From a philosophical perspective, people lack function, meaning, and purpose; and they long for peace, love, and happiness. If employees believe that the role and responsibilities they have serve a good purpose, they are happy at work. This leads to theoretical and practical implications.

The theoretical aspects can be derived from our understanding of living beings. The function, meaning, and purpose of living beings are learning, growth, and transformation (to who we truly are). This means that in order to learn, grow, and transform, we need liberty to explore new solutions, equality to perceive and communicate information on the same eye level, and fraternity for collaboration.

The practical aspects of performance can be derived from our understanding of decision-making and problem-solving processes. People perform at their best level if they are at peace with themselves and if they work in a peaceful environment. They also perform at their best when they can share love and empathy and feel loved themselves. Interactions with coworkers that make them feel happy are important too. The absence of any of those three aspects results in mental, emotional, and/or behavioral stress. When this occurs, performance drops sharply.

Now we come to the problem. We have to differentiate between what people "want" and what they "need" because those two are regularly different. People themselves have a hard time distinguishing those two from each other. The "wants" that people have are the short-term happiness factors. What people need are the long-term happiness factors. The problem with fulfilling short-term wants is that people need more and more to get the same positive experience. Whereas if a company focuses on the long-term needs, employees will become satisfied sustainably.

Having said all this, let's take a look at a more global perspective and then think about the consequences for individual companies and employees. We know that we use up 1.5 times the resources of our planet within 1 year. This means that we are producing 50% more stuff than would be good for humanity as a whole. This means that the output of every second employee is harmful to humanity and therefore cannot be meaningful per se. The logical consequence is that no leadership or coaching initiative can seriously support employees in their journey to find meaning in what they are currently doing—unless it changes the business model of the company as well.

If employees complain about a lack of meaning in their work, chances are that their work is, in fact, meaningless, and they should quickly start looking for alternatives before they are replaced with an algorithm.

My advice would be to look for companies that focus on social change because only products and services that support social change will be sustainable in the future.

Bill: What is the most important question leaders should ask employees?

Robert: For me the key issues here are engagement and fulfillment, because they are root causes of happiness. Considering that 85% of the global workforce is disengaged (66% in the United States)[1] and 50% would quit their job if they had a slightly better offer,[2] they are together with the overall employee experience the most critical questions for any organization.

Disengaged means not integrated and unfulfilled means disbalanced. No system can function if its parts are not integrated and balanced with each other.

The most important question management should be asking employees is, "Are you happy?" Now this question, however, opens a huge can of worms because unhappiness can come from personal issues, organizational issues, or both. It is hard for management to differentiate those from each other due to their interconnected nature. However, it reflects the paradigm shift in leadership we see happening. Leaders will only have value in future organizations if they transform into coaches for their teams. Only if management is able to help and train employees to become better at understanding themselves and become better at decision-making and problem-solving. Hence, when employees are learning and growing, they will stay engaged, fulfilled, and happy.

What we see in employees a lot is "learned helplessness" behavior, which leads to burnout or bore-out.

Employees start at a company engaged and motivated only to realize some weeks later that whatever they suggest to make the company better or more effective—either structures or processes or both—isn't acted upon. After about three times of fruitless engagement, people resort to the mode of "Just

[1] Jim Harter, "Employee Engagement on the Rise in the U.S.". Gallup, August 26th, 2018. https://news.gallup.com/poll/241649/employee-engagement-rise.aspx.
[2] Deloitte. (2018). Global Human Capital Trends 2018. Deloitte, London.

tell me what to do," or "I don't question anymore whether it makes sense or not." This mental, emotional, and behavioral checkout is the worst that can happen to management because you can't manage a dysfunctional and therefore unpredictable system.

Bill: What is the most important question employees should ask leaders?

Robert: I think the current view on employee engagement is too shortsighted. The future of work will change dramatically, so the focus of employees should not be on the present and how a company can fulfill my dreams and wishes today but in the future. Fifty percent of jobs will disappear due to digitalization and automatization within the next 20 years, and so will many business models and companies. The most important questions for employees should, therefore, be "What do I need to learn? How can I grow to still be more valuable than an algorithm in 5 years?" The point is that humans are in a race against algorithms. Only if we can do things bots can't do will we have a job in the future. Only if we are more effective in learning, change, and transformation than AI, we as humanity will have a future.

■ The current view on employee engagement is too shortsighted. The future of work will change dramatically.

On a personal level, employees should, therefore, be asking management how they ensure continuous learning and growth, so they are prepared when they have to leave the company.

On a corporate level, employees should be asking management how they are ensuring adaptability and resilience of the company's business model, structures, processes, products, and services to be sustainable, so they won't have to leave the company sooner or later.

Bill: What is the most important question we should ask ourselves?

Robert: The most important question we can ask ourselves relates to our identity and is: Who am I? Only if we know who we are, can we accurately determine the possibilities and probabilities of our life.

Who we are consists of the three questions: What am I, how am I, and why am I? On the one hand, these questions either limit or open up possibilities and probabilities. On the other hand, these answers also show us our level of integration. Only if we can answer all three questions for every facet of our life are we integrated or have integrity. Only integrated systems can function properly. In other words, misunderstandings and false assumptions are the result of errors in our reality construct.

Fragmentation and disbalance give us the illusion of knowing when in fact we only believe to know.

On a personal level, the goal is always sustainable happiness which requires the integration and balance of our fragmented self. Like a fragmented hard disk, our brain, heart, and body become fragmented and disbalanced simply through usage. Fragmentation is a natural consequence when we are quicker to learn new information than we are able to integrate this new knowledge with our existing knowledge. Disbalance is the natural result if we get more of what we want up to a point when something good becomes bad. Fragmented and disbalanced knowledge cannot be applied to other areas and becomes not only useless, but it can cause consciousness, perception, and attention problems. Fragmentation and disbalance give us the illusion of knowing when in fact we only believe to know. Hence the common term of "dangerous half knowledge."

No matter how good a company culture is, no matter how good leadership is

- If there are gaps and contradictions inside of me, I cannot create true peace outside of me and cannot perceive goodwill toward me.

- If I don't like myself, I cannot be empathic toward others and cannot perceive good deeds toward me.

- If I am unhappy inside, no amount of fun culture around me can sustainably change that.

The only effective way to increase performance is therefore to start with understanding ourselves first, before judging other's performance. Indicators of the fragmented and disbalanced self or cultures are "blame and alienation" which cause shame and guilt, arrogance and ignorance, pride and prejudice toward self and others. These distortions of the reality construct are the barriers to high performance. These barriers can be overcome with "forgiveness" and "reconciliation," which lead to identity and intimacy, dignity and worth, humbleness and gratitude toward self and others.

The next step is to learn and train the following skills and abilities:

1. Adaptability and resilience
2. Alignment and resonance

These skills and abilities automatically transform us to be engaged and fulfilled, prevent burnout and bore-out, and result in sustainable happiness—regardless of the cultural conditions around.

Key Takeaways

- Change and innovation happen naturally when learning, growth, and transformation are fostered.

- Flaws in personal perceptions of reality limit possibilities.

- It's the job of every employee to discover what has meaning for them.

- Lack of attention can be a direct result of useless information.

- Restful sleep, healthy diet, regular exercise, clear and meaningful communication, and conscious reflection are all important.

- We need liberty to explore, equality to perceive, and fraternity for collaboration.

- Companies should focus on long-term needs.

- Leaders should ask their employees, "Are you happy?"

- Employee ideas must be acted upon to avoid "learned helplessness."

- What do I need to learn to remain relevant to this company's future?

- We must know who we are to determine the possibilities and probabilities of our life.

- Integration of our fragmented self gives us the illusion of knowing when in fact we only believe to know.

- Indicators of the dysfunctional and disabled self are "blame" and "alienation," which cause shame and guilt, arrogance and ignorance, pride and prejudice. In the presence of those distortions of the reality construct, high performance is not possible.

- Indicators of the functional and enabled self are "forgiveness" and "reconciliation," which lead to identity and intimacy, dignity and worth, humbleness and gratitude.

- Learn and train the following skills and abilities: adaptability and resilience, alignment and resonance. The result is engagement and fulfillment or happiness under any condition.

Sandra Krot

Human Dimension Consultant, Insight Principles

Do You See the True Paradigm or Not?

Sandra Krot is a human dimension consultant at Insight Principles and a coauthor of *Invisible Power: Insight Principles at Work.*[1] Sandra works with individuals as well as working groups and leadership teams. Her work is based on fundamental principles about how the human mind and human thought work. An understanding of these principles provides people with a glimpse into their potential for creative thought, well-being, and relationship effectiveness.

I reached out to connect with Sandra after reading her book. I was so impacted by what I learned that I felt it was very important to bring this knowledge and understanding to my own work and the collection of interviews that are part of this book. Sandra brings an understanding that helps us look beyond mindset to something different that unlocks the wisdom and greater intelligence of the human mind.

Bill Fox: How can we create workplaces where every voice matters, everyone thrives and finds meaning, and change and innovation happen naturally?

---

[1] Ken Manning, Robin Charbit, and Sandra Krot, Invisible Power (Lexington, MA: Insight Principles, Inc., 2015).

Sandra Krot: I'd like to answer that question from three different perspectives: the perspective of the individual person in an organization or business, the perspective of the leader in an organization or business, and the perspective of people like you and me who are wanting to be of service to businesses. I'll start with the individual because what I have to say is the foundation for all three categories.

 The critical problem for all human beings in all businesses across the globe is the pervasive misunderstanding of where our experience and feelings come from.

It's a misunderstanding that's comparable to the misunderstandings throughout our history that blocked our evolution. For example, take the misunderstanding that the earth was the center of the solar system and not the sun, or the misunderstanding of where infection came from. These were pervasive misunderstandings, and they had consequences.

There's a misunderstanding today that somehow our experiences and our feelings can get put upon us or be caused by something outside of our own minds, and this misunderstanding has profound consequences in business.

There is a principle-based paradigm at work. A paradigm is, of course, a set of assumptions or a set of facts, or a way to look at something that is very definitive. It's very black and white. You're either in the paradigm or you're not. We are living in what you might call a false paradigm. Just like we were when we misunderstood the earth was the center of the solar system. It was a false paradigm.

 The false paradigm that we live under in this world is the paradigm that something other than thought—or other than our own internal psychological process—can bring us an experience or a feeling.

I call it a false paradigm, not to judge it in any way, but the earth was never the center of our solar system and infection was never caused by evil spirits and bad air. These paradigms were false, but not in a judgmental way. They simply were not true. The outside-in thinking paradigm we believe as human beings is not true.

When people who work in an organization get awakened to what's actually true about how the mind works, they can see for themselves how the mind doesn't work or can't work. It puts them in a position to be everything we want people to be, and everything we want ourselves to be when we're working in an organization.

When you don't feel victimized by your circumstances, when you have a feeling of choice, when you have options, you really do settle down as a human being. You settle down as a worker. You settle down as a contributor. You become a better listener. You see what to prioritize in your work. You see what purpose you really serve, and what's important. And you become very creative because you're not at the mercy of thinking that fills up your head, taking you away from your own ability to be creative and to have new thinking at any moment. For individuals to see past this false paradigm—to see that the mind really works only one way, that it works from the inside-out, that our experience is being created within. To see this is a game changer.

Leaders and people managers, in my mind, have a little bit more responsibility than the individual contributor. To some degree, leaders and managers have influence over others. That's why when we work with businesses, my company, Insight Principles, starts with the leadership. We feel that leaders need to see for themselves what is going on inside. Once leaders see for themselves that there is nothing—not the economy, not the deadlines, not the customer, none of those things are the source of their feelings and their stress. Once they truly see this, they can make the kinds of decisions they need to make for their businesses to thrive. And of course, just like individuals, they become better listeners. When you're a good listener, you get more and better information. This really has an impact on the company and on the bottom line.

And from the perspective of those of us who are trying to help organizations, I think we stop focusing on changing behavior. Behavior to me is the caboose on the train. People behave how they feel, and people feel how they think. If we don't address thought, we really have no hope of changing behavior—not consistently or sustainably. If we don't address the source of thought, then the behavior will be something we constantly have to be on top of. That's a workload for any corporation. It's a workload for any human being. So, we need, as practitioners, to stop focusing there and to begin to see what the true source of behavior is.

I know that plenty of programs look at thought, but they look at it as thinking styles. Or they look at it as trying to change what people think to get them to think better.

What is far more valuable is to teach people that they think—to teach and show people that they are gifted at birth with this incredible power called the power of thought.

This power is bringing to us every feeling, every experience, and every glimpse of reality we have ever had since the moment we were born until the moment we die.

The power of thought is truly the most powerful force in the universe. It's sitting under our noses, and we don't know it. We don't see it. We don't realize it. As a result, we don't get to use this gift the way it was designed to be used. I feel like my first and sometimes only job when I'm helping a business is to help people see the power of thought.

Bill: What does it take to get an employee's best performance and full attention?

Sandra: When I walk around the corporations I work with, what strikes me is how busy people's minds are. It is very difficult to get people's full attention. What is needed is for all of us to realize how the human mind actually works.

When I saw that my experience can only come from thought in the moment, this realization took so much thinking off my mind.

I stopped fretting about things. I stopped thinking about whose fault it was. I stopped having these long dialogues in my head about why this was unfair and who's to blame and what I needed to do to feel good about myself. There's so much extra thinking that people do. It keeps them preoccupied.

One of the results we hear from our clients when they realize how their minds actually work is they say to us, "Wow, I can't believe how much more present I am!" They discover that when they become present, a whole set of capacities and abilities shows up. They feel more insightful. They feel more creative. They feel that they can see the bigger picture, so they get perspective. It's not like they're not already doing this, it's that these capacities show up more often when their minds are free of unnecessary and unproductive thought.

You can tell people, "You just need to quiet your mind or clear your head or be mindful." But that's like telling people you just need to lose weight or stop smoking. It's great information, but to be able to pull it off, you have to see in the moment what actually is filling your head up. It was a surprise to me how much extra thinking I was doing that served no purpose other than to perpetuate an outside-in illusion. To get people's full attention and best performance, we need to teach them and help them see for themselves how their minds actually work.

It's interesting when you see how your mind works because at the same time you see how it doesn't work. That's the nature of seeing something as a paradigm. When you see something as a paradigm, it's like putting a box around it. It's definitive. It's black and white. When I realized my experience was coming from thought in the moment and no place else, it eliminated all other possibilities. That realization rendered so much thinking useless.

My mind quieted down, and my mind cleared and I could pay attention. I see this happening with the companies that we work with. It's making a big difference.

Bill: What do people really lack and long for at work?

Sandra: I recently read a study that concluded people are feeling more stressed today than ever. I certainly do observe this when I go out into companies. People are feeling a tremendous amount of stress, which of course they attribute to the job and/or their life in general. They're stressed about their inability to balance their life at home with their job. People are feeling the stress of that, and people feel rushed. They feel they don't have enough time.

When I ask people if they had a magic wand, what would they want? Many of them will say, "I want more time." Then I'll ask them, "What would more time do for you?" They'll say, "It will allow me to get all my work done." Then I'll say, "What would that do for you?" They'll say, "I would be able to relax." Then I'll ask again, "What would that do for you?" Finally, you get to the fact that people want this sense of peace, this sense that they are fine. All is going to be OK. They'll find the answers that they need.

Because we live in the misunderstanding about how the mind works, we don't see that there is only one paradigm that's actually true. We think that the peace we're looking for is going to come at the end of all our work being done. The to-do list is completed. But that's not where peace comes from. Peace is a natural state. It's the state we would be in if we understood how our minds worked. It's the state we're in when thinking comes off our minds and we are present.

We instinctively know that the state of peace is actually a very productive state. In that state, we have tremendous capability and capacity that seems to be present without working at it or making it happen. When people see for themselves that this peace that they're looking for is actually within and only a thought away, they settle down. Lack of peace is being created in their own minds and in their own thinking. When people understand this, they stop looking for peace by getting everything done or by being all things to all people. They may even say no to things.

I worked with a young executive who was on the fast track at his company. He goes through a difficult divorce and ends up getting custody of his two young children. I remember talking to him about it, because he said, "You know Sandy if I hadn't learned about how my mind worked, I would have been tied in knots. But I could see the extra thinking I was doing about my career path and about my role as a dad." And he said, "It became so clear to me that I had to tell my bosses that I wanted off the fast track. I had to dedicate these next few years to my children. I was going to be the one who drove them to school and picked them up. I was going to be the one to go to their soccer practices, dance recitals, etc." He said it did not feel like a sacrifice. "It felt like that's what

I'm going to do. I know I could not have done it with such ease and grace had I not realized the true source of all my stress, upset, and future worry."

I see more and more people saying no to all the activities that are available in the world that end up taking our time. They're so much happier for it. But I can't tell people, "You know, you really should stop being on social media so often!" Or you should stop taking your kids to every single activity on the face of the planet! I don't tell people what to do with their lives. I don't try to change behavior, but I think when people see where peace really lives, they make decisions accordingly and again they are not hard decisions, they're obvious. And they don't feel like a burden or a sacrifice. They feel like it's the wisest way to go.

Bill: What is the most important question leaders should ask employees?

Sandra: I can't say there is a most important question. I just think management should be asking questions. I don't think we ask enough questions.

We make a tremendous amount of assumptions. We forget that we live in a thought-created reality and nobody thinks exactly the same thing at exactly the same time, so we are going to live in different realities.

Truly we live in separate realities. But we forget this. It's easy to forget it because our reality looks so clear and obvious to us.

Management lives in their own reality and they forget to talk to their people. I can't tell you how many times I've worked with an executive, and they'll be so perplexed or so confused about their team's behavior. I'll say, "Have you asked them?" And they'll say, "No." It's just a surprise to me. I don't know that there's a magic question, but I really think that being curious, asking questions, and having an open dialogue are critical factors for a team's success.

Bill: What is the most important question employees should ask leaders?

Sandra: The only thing that I would add to what I said above is that employees should be asking a lot of questions, too. I think we get the idea that asking questions is a bad thing. Oh, I should know, or I don't want to let them know that I don't know. It's just ego. It's that image of self-importance that we all suffer from.

I think that as people gain more respect for how brilliant the mind is and how much intelligence and wisdom there is in every human mind, we become more comfortable asking questions.

Questions are truly the gateway to finding new information. We don't look for new thought if we think we've got everything nailed. We think we know everything already. Why would we look?

Because I have such a respect for what's behind the mind, I'm always asking, and I'm always looking. As an employee, I encourage them to ask questions, to be persistent but not in a bad way. Some things employees are asked to do are a waste of time. We should make sure that the boss or manager has thought through the implications of what he or she is asking us to do. Sometimes they haven't.

Bill: What is the most important question we should ask ourselves?

Sandra: This question made me chuckle because many of my friends and colleagues know that I often say, "I'm going to have a tattoo put on the inside of my wrist, and the tattoo is going to say, 'Do you know where this feeling is coming from?'" It's such a show-stopper question for me. When this question comes to mind, it helps me remember how the mind actually works.

The other question I ask myself is, Have I looked for an insight? An insight is really what I need when I'm in a dilemma, have a problem, or can't make a decision.

It really does throw everything into another level, and I'm able to have the mental clarity needed to see what to do next. When the unnecessary thinking has dropped away from my mind, there's this open, empty space. Then the insight shows up and helps point me in the direction I need to go.

Bill: You seem to have a little different perspective on the Three Principles. Can you help distinguish that for us?

Sandra: For me, when I saw the principles as a paradigm, that the mind works only one way and can't work any other way, it took so many of the discriminators or conditions that I had innocently and inadvertently put on connecting to our deeper intelligence. That's the piece I wanted to hone in on responding to your questions. I believe it helped me simplify the whole message.

I used to talk about states of mind a lot, but I don't talk about them anymore. The reason I don't is because when I did talk about different states of mind, people inevitably heard there are good states of mind, and bad states of mind. They wanted to know how do I get into the good state of mind? I kept scratching my head and wondering why are people asking me how-to questions? I'm not trying to prescribe a behavior or a state of being. I'm trying to explain how the mind works!

Then I realized, I'm setting up this dichotomy of good thinking, bad thinking, good state of mind, bad state of mind, and so on.

What I want people to see is—the mind works one way. Period. It works from the inside-out.

When you think it works from the outside-in, you're going to have a battle. You are going to get split—me against what's causing my feelings or experience. It's this misunderstanding that splits us from our wisdom and deeper intelligence. That's what does it. It's not a state of mind issue, it's a misunderstanding issue of how the mind works.

When people see for themselves in the moment, "Wow, I've just gone outside here." We come back to how things really work. When we come back to how things really work, we get the benefit of the built-in design of the human mind to help us and to show us the way.

Key Takeaways

- What we experience and feel doesn't come from anywhere but thought in the moment.

- Awakening to how the mind works is a game changer for business when you don't feel victimized by your circumstances.

- With a new understanding of how the mind works, you become a better listener, which enables you to get more and better information.

- Recognize the true power of thought and how it impacts how people think and feel.

- Understanding how the mind works quiets the noise and reduces the amount of thinking on people's minds.

- Peace is a natural state when thinking comes off our minds.

- The state of peace is a very productive state where we have tremendous capacities.

- We don't ask enough questions and make many assumptions when we forget that we live in a thought-created reality.

- Management lives in their own reality and often forgets to get their information from the people who know.

- Asking questions is not a bad thing. Let go of self-importance and ask more questions.

- "Do you know where this feeling is coming from?" is one of the most important questions we can ask ourselves.

- "Have I looked for an insight?" is one question we can ask ourselves to help us drop unnecessary thinking and free up space for new answers to show up.

- An understanding that the mind works only one way—from the inside-out—gets us in closer touch with our wisdom and deeper intelligence.

Andrew Bennett

Leadership Coach and Professional Magician

The Surprising Secret of Magic in Business

Andrew Bennett is a leadership consultant and executive coach partnering with leaders building cultures where people can thrive. Andrew began his career as Ross Perot's personal assistant. For almost 50 years, Andrew has been a magician and is a member of London's Magic Circle, the highest honor in magic. Founder of EDS and former US Presidential Candidate Ross Perot encouraged Andrew to use magic in his business presentations. Magic is the art of transformation, and Andrew uses it to teach people how to rethink possibilities and obstacles, opening the door to new ways of thinking and acting.

I connected with Andrew through his fascinating TEDx talk, *The magic of words—what we speak is what we create.*[1] Above and beyond using magic to help us see how the impossible is possible in all areas of our lives, Andrew calls attention to the idea we all overlook: the power of our words to create. I designed and created the Exploring Forward-Thinking Workplaces conversation to enact the belief that "we see the world we describe."[2] When we include and listen to every voice in one conversation, we create a better workplace and world together.

---

[1] www.youtube.com/watch?v=BVK4mWaS3F8
[2] Jaworski, Joseph in Synchronicity (San Francisco: Berrett-Koehler Publishers, 2011).

© Bill Fox 2020
B. Fox, *The Future of the Workplace*,
https://doi.org/10.1007/978-1-4842-5098-3_18

Bill Fox: How can we create workplaces where every voice matters, everyone thrives and finds meaning, and change and innovation happen naturally?

Andrew Bennett: First, what you described in your question has to be valued by leaders as a basic starting point. We credit Milton Friedman with saying the sole purpose of business is profitability and return on investment to shareholders. In his opinion, that's the only obligation that a business has. I think his idea has been a prevailing focus for most businesses, but there's a growing number of people and leaders who believe business can be so much more than that. It's a shame when it's not.

It begins with a leader who values people and the human spirit.

I'm very encouraged by the growing number of leaders and organizations that are creating the environment you're describing. But it begins with a leader who values people and the human spirit. A leader who feels that it's not enough just to have a profitable business. Someone who believes that business can be a place where people can become more of who they fully are. A place where people can bring their gifts and pursue what they care about—fulfilling that fundamental drive to make your life matter and to have meaning.

Igniting the Spirit

On a more tactical level, I've been doing consulting, coaching, and speaking on leadership and culture for 25 years. I believe there are three parts to your question. The first part is igniting the spirit or the heart. That means unleashing the energy available to all of us when we deeply care about something that gives us joy and fulfillment. Not just for us personally, but to make a difference in the world, serving our fellow human beings and knowing our life matters.

So how do we create those kinds of environments? From a leadership perspective, it's looking at your organization for how it makes the world a better place and putting that first. Like all of our decisions about what we do and how we do it, is it in service of that deeper purpose? I come from Michigan, which is a big auto country. There are people who are making stuff. They're making gaskets, mufflers and assembling cars. It all started with Henry Ford, but if you look at his vision, it wasn't articulated as a vision statement. He talked about the automobile becoming a way of life. It was not about profit. It was about families enjoying God's Great Open Spaces. Those are literally the words he used. He realized the deeper purpose of his work. No matter what your organization does, if you take the time to look, you can discover it. Finding your deeper purpose gives people something to connect with. If they don't, then there's some place else for them to do that.

Freeing the Mind

Another part is about freeing the mind. I think so much of what unconsciously is at play day in and day out is fear. No one wants to talk about fear. We're afraid of talking about fear, but it shows up in the work environment. The workplace is fertile ground for fear to grow because of all the different power structures. Freeing your mind is about being aware of the role that fear plays in your life, but particularly as a leader in understanding how fear and anxiety influence how one leads. Becoming curious about that is super important. Being willing to have the humility and courage to lean into that and ask, where might I be unconscious of how fear is getting in my way? What can I do to not make it go away, but how can I work with it in a way that allows me to transcend it? And how do we address that as an organization?

Building the Culture

And that leads to the third part, which is building the culture. Building a culture where people lift each other up. Where we see the best in each other. Where the default assumption is that people do things because they mean well, not because they've got a sinister plot. So those three things have become the foundation in my practice for how you create the kind of environment you describe in your question. First, it's inspire the heart and the spirit, second is free the mind, and third is build the culture.

Bill: How do we get an employee's full attention and best performance?

Andrew: You need to care about them as people. Be genuinely interested in getting to know them. That old saying came to mind just now of people don't care how much you know until they know how much you care.

I think about work in a way that it's not a separate world, it's all life.

There's not a personal life and a work life, there's life. We're whole people but too many organizations treat people like they're resources. The latest one I cringe every time I hear it is human assets or talent management. All these ways we are objectifying people as cogs in a wheel to be moved around and disposed of. It's caring about people. Finding out what they care about and what are their hopes and dreams. What do they want for their family? What are they afraid of?

The environment I seek to create is a place where people can talk about their fears. They know they're not at risk of exposing themselves to someone using their fears against them because when we do that, then we can support each other in rising above those fears. We can even take those fears and use them to inform creative thinking.

I think the leader-employee relationship really isn't any different from any other relationship. Good relationships are those where you trust the other person. You trust the other person has your best interests in mind. You know you're safe with them. If we did a study, we'd probably find that most employees do not feel safe with their leaders. The way to get people to engage in the business is to engage with them sincerely. You can't fake it. It's not a technique. Either you care or you don't.

Bill: What do people really lack and long for at work?

Andrew: It's feeling valued, and that comes in many forms. Rewards and recognition are fine, but being valued and appreciated is the experience of being seen as a person. We need to get paid and health insurance is important. I don't belittle that at all, but I think that's a minimum way of living. I don't want to come across as judgmental because we need to make a living. I think human beings have so much more that we're capable of than just taking that 40 hours a week to go do something we don't feel really matters above the pay we get for it.

I believe if we can use all of our abilities to serve people to make the world a better place, that's really not a huge expectation to want that. But for a variety of reasons, that's not the case for most people. Many people feel their 40 hours a week really doesn't create something that gives them joy and satisfaction.

But respect and appreciation from leaders and peers is such an uplifting experience. The simple act of saying, "Bill, you know what I really admire about you is the way you listen so deeply. I know that you are really with me and that we're really connected because you ask questions that reveal that you're hearing something even deeper. I feel valued by the way you listen." To have someone give you feedback like that where they see something in you and they name it and share their admiration, it's not just a generic pat on the back. It's not a certificate of achievement. It's not a gift card for dinner at a restaurant. Those things are nice, but you don't have to spend money. It's just being seen, recognized, and appreciated genuinely and sincerely. I think most people at work lack that. Many leaders are afraid to do that because they don't want to make you too full of yourself. Or they want you to have a little fear about whether you're safe around here, so you don't slack off.

Bill: What is the most important question leaders should ask employees?

Andrew: I think on one level it's how can I help you? How can I support you to use your gifts at work and help you share your ideas? How can I create an environment where people aren't afraid? How can we make the world a better place is also a good question because it facilitates a connection between the employee and the purpose of the organization. Leaders can learn a lot about how people view their work and how it's impacting the world.

I worked for Ross Perot for 10 years, and for my first 6 months, I was his personal assistant. He would call six people each morning. He had 20 minutes blocked out on his calendar to call six people each morning. He sat down and dialed the phone. He randomly selected people from all over the world. He would just ask people, "What are you working on right now? How does it help our customers?" He wasn't looking for the employee handbook or a canned answer. He could tell when people weren't being authentic with him. There would be times when I was in his office for some of those calls. He was a straightforward guy and would say, "No, what are you really working on?"

People felt safe with him. He was a very demanding man, but you also knew he had your back. So I think that question of what is this we are all creating together? What good is this? What good are we doing? What's the legacy that we're leaving in this world? Those are all good questions for a leader to ask.

Bill: What is the most important question employees should ask leaders?

Andrew: I think it's a question reflecting reverse servant leadership, "What can I do to support you?" What are your biggest challenges as a leader? I always think the vision question between employees and leaders is important. There was a survey by an organization several years ago that asked employees all around the world, do you know the strategy for your organization? Eighty-six percent of them said, no they couldn't. Then they had a corresponding question with five different strategy statements. One of which was their own company's strategy, and you were supposed to pick which one belonged to your company. It was the combination of those two questions and still 86% didn't know. It's such a basic observation to say well, how can we really do that well if only 14% of people know where we're going?

When an employee is with a leader, a good question to ask is, where do you see us going? Even if there's a vision statement or if it's talked about in Town Hall meetings, I still believe it's important for employees to ask, where do you see us going and what's important to you?

Bill: What is the most important question we should ask ourselves?

Andrew: Fear has become a big topic for me in the last few years as I see the influence it has on everyone. As a result, I think one of the most important questions to ask ourselves is, how can I learn more about how fear is influencing me?

I'm reminded of the work of Kurt Lewin. He was considered the father of social psychology—behavioral science. He had this concept called force field analysis, which was the simple model or observation that there are forces pushing things forward and there are opposing forces. As forces push against each other, it creates resistance. What behavioral scientists took from this was that we focus on how to push harder instead of looking at those opposing forces and reducing them.

I believe fear is one of those huge opposing forces. For example, you can work longer hours or learn more to develop yourself. Fear is insidious because its influence is invisible, it's unconscious. We're not aware of how fear is showing up and how it's holding us back and influencing other people.

So, how is fear influencing me? Where is it getting in my way? What makes it particularly challenging is that many times our fear reactions show up as strengths. I have a tremendous fear of rejection because of how I grew up and because of that I have become great at pleasing people. I'm a pleaser. I'm great at getting people to like me and make them happy. You know, "Andrew is a great guy. He'll go the extra mile for you. He's always there." So what's wrong with pleasing people? It makes me a good husband and good friend, but in a leadership role, it got in my way.

I had an experience when I was working for Ross Perot that's a good example of how fear can get in the way. I was managing a business for Ross in Australia. I said yes to everything the customer wanted. I wanted to please them and make them happy. But the list just kept growing of things they wanted from us. We were so busy managing the list. Even though I had a team of 24 people, we couldn't get any of the work done! They were growing more and more angry, and finally Ross had to meet with them. He came out, and he said, "You trying to make these people happy is making them very unhappy!" Then he said that the minute you can say "No" to them because it's in their best interest, we'll stop being a vendor and start being partners with them. So that's what I did, and we then grew that account from $5 to $65 million a year in 2 years because of that shift! But I was not conscious of how my fear was getting in my way. When Ross pointed it out, then I could work differently. I think everybody has an issue with fear. Actually, I don't think, I know. I know everybody has an issue with fear.

Bill: You recently posted a fascinating quote on social media about the meaning of the word Abracadabra. You said almost all magicians use it but don't really know what it means?

Andrew: It's true. My nonscientific observation is 99.9% of magicians do not know Abracadabra is an Aramaic word that means what I speak is what I create. I was journaling one morning about 10 years ago and for whatever reason this question just popped in my head, what does Abracadabra mean?

Abracadabra is an Aramaic word that means what I speak is what I create.

This past Christmas Day, I celebrated 50 years of practicing, studying, and performing magic. Even though I've practiced magic for that length of time, I never used Abracadabra in my act. I thought it was a goofy word and was so cliché. But this one morning, I thought what does Abracadabra mean? I did some research and didn't really find much other than it's an incantation. I eventually found my way to the MIT Linguistics Department and sent them an email asking for help.

Within the hour it surprised me to get a phone call from Noam Chomsky. Now, Noam Chomsky is an intellectual force. I've read his books and have seen documentaries featuring him; however, I didn't know he worked at MIT in linguistics. He told me it was almost like a newsroom environment where something comes off the ticker tape and people ask who wants to run with this story! An administrator received my email and asked, "Does anybody know what Abracadabra means?" Noam said it really caught his attention because he didn't know its meaning. He called me and said I will research it but just wanted you to know we're on it. So a couple days later he calls, and he says, "Are you sitting down?" He then said Abracadabra's history is Aramaic, which is pre-Hebrew. They say Jesus spoke Aramaic, and he said it means, "I create that of which I speak." There was a really long pause on the phone and he said, "Can you believe it?"

That's how I discovered the meaning of Abracadabra, but I rephrased it so it would be easier to understand and more accessible. I changed it to "what I speak is what I create." I actually have a trademark on it. But that's the way I discovered it. It's part of a much bigger story about my search for meaning in magic that's coming into the spotlight now. A year ago, I formed a group of magicians from all over who are using magic for deeper purposes beyond entertainment. We meet twice a month online to support each other. We don't talk a lot about tricks. We talk about the purpose we're using our magic for and help each other think about ways to use magic to help people think in different ways. We have our first 3-day event in Chicago in October. The Magic on Purpose Group will work with the Association for Managers of Innovation leading a 3-day meeting.

Unfortunately, magic has been trivialized over the centuries. Its roots are in ancient tribal communities where shamans and medicine women and men would use simple magic tricks to give people a "Wow"—a sacred moment. It was a moment where you're in touch with the Divine. It's the experience of seeing something you thought was impossible being made possible. It's this invisible force that is greater than your understanding of the material world.

Key Takeaways

- It begins with a leader who values people and the human spirit.

- Look at your organization for how it makes the world a better place and putting that first.

- Much of what is unconsciously at play day in and day out in the workplace is fear, so it's important to ask, "Where might I be unconscious of how fear is getting in my way?"

- Build a culture where people lift each other up and see the best in each other.

- There is not a personal life and work life, it's all life.

- Help people feel valued by the way you listen.

- We can facilitate a connection between the employee and the purpose of the organization by asking, "How can we make the world a better place?"

- Force field analysis is a useful concept that helps us look at reducing opposing forces rather than pushing harder.

- Be mindful that our words have great power—what we speak is what we create.

- Magic helps us experience something you thought was impossible being made possible, giving us a taste of an invisible force that is greater than our understanding of the material world.

Dicken Bettinger

Founder, Three Principles Mentoring

What Is the Most Important but Least Recognized Variable in Business?

Dicken Bettinger is the founder of Three Principles Mentoring, which exists to guide individuals, groups, and organizations in deepening their understanding of the Three Principles. He spent 16 years of his career developing and leading corporate leadership training, team development, and executive coaching. He is the coauthor of *Coming Home: Uncovering the Foundations of Psychological Well-Being.*[1]

I connected with Dicken Bettinger after reading his book *Coming Home*. This is a book that speaks beyond the written words in ways that will deepen your understanding of the human spirit and mind. My life and work were forever changed by reading Dicken's book not once but three times. Dicken does a wonderful job of bringing out the salient points of the book in this interview.

Bill Fox: How can we create workplaces where every voice matters, everyone thrives and finds meaning, and change and innovation happen naturally?

---

[1] Dicken Bettinger and Natasha Swerdloff, *Coming Home: Uncovering the Foundations of Psychological Well-Being* (La Conner, WA: 2016).

© Bill Fox 2020
B. Fox, *The Future of the Workplace*,
https://doi.org/10.1007/978-1-4842-5098-3_19

Dicken Bettinger: The first point I think that's relevant here is that everybody already has built into them everything they need to thrive. A lot of people think they lack the qualities that are necessary to thrive, so they work hard to try to develop those qualities. It's a different starting assumption when a group of people already has what they need to thrive, be creative, productive, inspired, and motivated. It's built-in to all of us. It's built-in to human beings to have that capacity. There are things that people can learn that help bring out those innate capacities and abilities.

The next point I think that's important to talk about is state of mind. I worked for 16 years doing executive leadership, staff development, and cultural change programs.

Repeatedly, we began to see the most important variable—and the least recognized variable regarding importance in a business setting—is the state of mind of people within the workplace.

It's critical. It's the biggest determinant of how productive people are, how well they listen, how well they communicate, the quality of the decisions they make, the ease with which a group can make decisions, and their ability to solve problems in a collaborative fashion. All these qualities are determined by state of mind.

When I worked in companies, the first thing I would do is help people become more aware of state of mind and why it is so critical. And furthermore, why that variable is necessary to be addressed for people to suddenly access this innate capacity for thriving, being productive, and collaboration—all the things people are looking for in the workplace. For example, if you have two work groups working on the same task, and one is burdened with stress and the other is stress-free, it's pretty evident which group would be able to do better with a certain task, especially in the long run.

A person's understanding of state of mind determines how resilient they'll be, which means there's no problem with experiencing stress in the workplace. But if you live in stress for longer periods of time, it begins to affect all the key variables. Helping and teaching people what they need to learn, so that they can become more resilient and accountable for their own state of mind, is an incredible way to leverage any person or any group in the business setting.

This all becomes possible when people discover their potential for new thinking.

Without new thinking, things don't move forward in a business context. Things don't evolve. Problems don't get solved easily.

The only things in the way of new thinking are the habits and patterns of thinking that people get caught up in without being aware that their own thinking is the problem. Most people have not learned that the stress they feel is being created from their own thinking. Most people have erroneously been taught that stress is created by circumstance.

We're finding out by all kinds of scientific studies that circumstances can't determine a person's state of mind. If you took a very stressful situation and put 100 people in it, some people would experience great stress, but a lot of people would be extremely calm. At the same time, a lot of people would be thriving, inspired, and productive despite this circumstance.

However, there's also another variable that people have been missing, and that's the role that thought plays in creating an experience. In my business trainings, it would be the most important key factor to teach people.

Each one of us is always thinking and whatever we think we will experience. That's where our experience comes from; it's created from the power of thought. It's not created by circumstance.

It's very interesting, you go into a company, and you find people who are not being productive, who are feeling stressed, and who are in unproductive states of mind. Then you ask them, why do you think you're feeling stressed? Why are you unproductive? Why are you having difficulty communicating, and why are you so preoccupied that you don't listen? They will always point to something in their circumstance that they think causes them to be the way they are. And that's the misunderstanding. That's the human misunderstanding that's gone on for centuries that creates so much stress and unhappiness in people anywhere in the world. It's a misunderstanding, and there are now new discoveries about the actual way in which experience is being created. Now we can account for the state of mind and why we go in and out of different states of mind. And why sometimes we get stuck in states of mind that are not very helpful or productive. We now understand that very scientifically, so we can teach people about the importance of the state of mind and that state of mind is determined 100% from thought—as opposed to circumstance.

The key factor in business is state of mind, and the key determinant of a state of mind is a person's understanding of the role of thought.

You'd be surprised, that one missing link—the role the power of thought plays in creating experience—that one piece people are not very aware of, makes all the difference. It can help people wake up to the fact that they're a thinker. How they think about things creates how they feel about things. People begin to realize that thinking is the source of their tension, stress, reactivity, and dissatisfaction. When people begin to realize that those are feelings created from thought as opposed to circumstances, they will back off from the thinking that's perpetuating that stress or upset. As soon as they do, their head clears of that thinking fairly soon. Their head clears of that thinking without any effort, without any technique. And with greater clarity, people always do better. Out of greater clarity, people automatically begin to get new thinking, which is uplifting and helpful. The key factor in business is state of mind, and the key determinant of a state of mind is a person's understanding of the role of thought.

Bill: What does it take to get an employee's full attention and best performance?

Dicken: There are two main approaches. One is you try to get their attention externally, which is a constant effort where the responsibility for getting someone's attention is on the leader.

The other approach, which is the one I obviously subscribe to, is that the leader helps the person gain an understanding that leads them naturally to states of mind that are more productive, more attentive, and more present-centered. That work is extremely rewarding because when people begin to take responsibility for their state of mind, it's very different than if people try to create that from the outside. It is much, much more effective to help people access their capacity for being fully present and engaged.

Bill: What do people really lack and long for at work?

Dicken: There is a research study that was done with 600 business executives where they really pressed them on what they most want. The highest answer was peace of mind, because when people are at peace internally, they function the best.

Leaders can help other people access their own clear and creatively responsive state of mind, and then collectively together they can solve anything—literally anything.

A leader is often described as someone who has learned how to bring out the best in themselves and others, which is a calm, clear, peaceful, and creatively responsive state of mind. Leaders can help other people access their own clear and creatively responsive state of mind, and then collectively together they can solve anything—literally anything.

One of the leadership staffs I worked with would get repeatedly stumped with problems and end up in disagreements and arguments. Their meetings were positional and oppositional. They learned the role of thought, and over time they began to collaborate at such a high level they would beg the company to give them a hard problem! They would lock themselves in a room and have pizza sent in. Then they would stay there and work collaboratively to creatively generate new ideas and thoughts. They would build on each other's contributions, with zero conflict, zero arguments, and zero positioning.

I'm reminded of what they say at the negotiation project developed at Harvard University. They say the hardest thing in any negotiation when people have differences is to get them off their positions, so that something new can happen. When people are wedded to their opinions and ideas, it's the end of new thinking. It's a stalemate, and nothing moves forward.

Bill: What is the most important question leaders should ask employees?

Dicken: I think everybody—if they have an opportunity to participate and to reflect—has a sense of what would make things better, but often they're not asked. I've heard that repeatedly over the years. No one ever asks me what I think we should do. No one ever asks me what I think would make a big difference. Now that's not always true, and there are certainly very healthy teams and companies, but often people are just not asked, "What makes sense to you? I'm interested in your common sense. I'm interested in what your wisdom says would be helpful."

I think everybody—if they have an opportunity to participate and to reflect—has a sense of what would make things better, but often they're not asked.

Bill: What is the most important question employees should be asking management?

Dicken: They can ask management how they can help management. When I worked for someone else, I asked my boss that question all the time. How can I help you? And he'd stop and reflect. It would be a show-stopper. How can I help you be of more service? What would be most helpful for you? How can I take things off your plate, so that you have more time for reflection?

The higher up you are in the company, the more important it is to have time to be reflective. Many leaders have so much on their plates they never stop and pause. They don't have time to reflect on what's most important and helpful.

It's been my experience in unhealthy companies that the attention all gets focused on what people are dissatisfied with within the company, rather than continually focusing on how can we be more of service to the customer. When the flow of attention goes toward the conflicts in the company, as opposed to toward the customer, you know there are going to be difficulties.

Bill: What's the most important question we should ask ourselves?

Dicken: Do I know where my feelings are coming from? Where does my new thinking come from? And what state of mind is most conducive to new thinking?

Bill: What's a good starting point for people to learn more about the power of thought in business?

Dicken: There are lots of resources for people in business. There's a book written by colleagues of mine called *Invisible Power*. If people are interested in the relationship between state of mind and business results as well as learning more about the power of thought, this is a good book. It's my favorite book for sharing the importance of the power of thought in creating experience in the business context. It's filled with very practical examples. Learning about the role of thought is the most practical thing I think a person can learn if they want to enjoy life more, have greater job satisfaction, be more creatively responsive, feel more empowered, and be less burdened by their own thinking.

Key Takeaways

- State of mind is the biggest determinant of how productive people are and how well they listen and communicate.

- When people realize their own thinking is the problem, they can take responsibility for their own state of mind.

- Our state of mind is determined 100% by thought—not circumstance.

- Lead people to states of mind that are more productive, attentive, and present.

- People with a clear and creatively responsive state of mind can collectively together solve anything.

- When people aren't wedded to their own ideas, magic can happen.

- Everybody has a sense of what would make things better, so asking people what they think makes a big difference.

- Employees can help management be more reflective by asking better questions.

- Healthy companies focus on the customer, not problems.

- Do I know where my feelings are coming from is one of the most important questions we can ask ourselves.

- Ultimately, collaboration is not just an interaction between two people but is a listening for shared wisdom.

Dianne Collins

Author, *Do You QuantumThink?*

How to Be a Powerful Agent in the World to Create the Forward-Thinking Workplace

Dianne Collins is a media personality, an award-winning author, and the creator of QuantumThink. In her book, *Do You QuantumThink?*,[1] she teaches a groundbreaking methodology—21 specific, advanced principles that blend scientific insight and universal knowledge into practical modern wisdom—to create real solutions for our modern lives.

I discovered the book *Do You QuantumThink?* in 2012. Dianne's book gave me an understanding of how we can live and work in new ways and helped me move more fully into my intention and work that became "Exploring Forward-Thinking Workplaces." I was so gripped with what I learned that I had to talk to her. An email resulted in a fascinating phone call and conversation. Dianne and I kept in touch, so when I started this interview series, she graciously and enthusiastically agreed to take part.

Bill Fox: How can we create workplaces where every voice matters, everyone thrives and finds meaning, and change and innovation happen naturally?

---

[1] New York: SelectBooks, 2011.

© Bill Fox 2020
B. Fox, *The Future of the Workplace*,
https://doi.org/10.1007/978-1-4842-5098-3_20

Dianne Collins: I love you're asking that question, Bill, because in today's world, it is more important than ever.

People more than ever desire self-expression, authentic connection, and I think also, we want to experience mastery.

We are in this age where because of our wonderful technologies, people can communicate in so many ways. We want to engage and there's a level of engagement people yearn for. What I see with executives and leaders in major corporations is that everyone wants to be recognized for their unique contribution. And it really should be that way!

Step into Our Own Leadership

Imagine that every one of us is being called upon to step into our own leadership—whether you are formally in a leadership position or not. Every single person is on the team, part of the group, and part of the organization and has something to contribute. Each one can contribute his or her unique perspective. Gifts they were born with. Talents they've developed. That person is you and only you. And I think if we become enlightened and aware of this in one another, we truly see every one of us as a leader. When we recognize this, then we are all listening to one another.

Being in One Conversation

One of the distinctions of the QuantumThink system is called Being In One Conversation. We realize we're many voices in a conversation of creative dialogue. Or what I refer to as a relational field of communication and relationship. When we're in this one conversation, we can all be conscious of what each one of us is contributing to the workplace, to our team, our organization, and to this project we're all working on together.

From Industrial Age to Quantum Age

We're also seeing our systems and structures undergoing a great transformation. Restructuring is one of the energies of the time because we're making a leap from the Industrial Age to the Quantum Age. This is the overarching premise of QuantumThink—that we're in a Quantum Age still using Industrial Age thinking, and that's limiting us. When you look at how our organizations were formed, it was based on Industrial Age thinking that relied on "command and control" management styles and silos—separation-into-parts type of thinking. We've moved beyond that now because of our technologies. What if our thinking was as up to date as our technology? That's the leap. When you QuantumThink, you think from the perspective of wholeness—interconnected whole systems. That's what makes it natural. That's the leap. It's time for us to recognize the value each one of us brings as integral to the whole—regardless of position or stature in the organization.

In an earlier conversation you and I had before this interview, you talked about how the events of 9/11 led you to learning how to fly, and you discovered an appreciation of a higher perspective. I believe that higher perspective is one of the essential aspects of what would be an enlightened and forward-thinking workplace.

Context vs. Content

It's important that we distinguish between context and content here. When you step back to look from another QuantumThink principle we call the Perspective of All Perspectives, this is the context that enables you to think from possibility. Most of the time, we're in content-oriented conversations, meaning we are looking at the options in our immediate view. Conversations may start with a vision, then devolve into the either/or sticking points. We get into the content that brings up my way or your way. I like it, I don't like it. I agree, I disagree. It is in these situations where we can get trapped in stalemate communications. At the same time, yes, the content of what we're doing is vital. We live in content daily—in life and in business. The idea is when you can make this distinction between the context of the conversation and the content of the conversation, then you can step back and you will create a space for new possibilities. From a quantum worldview, reality is context dependent, so we know context will shape the field of actions and the field of communications. And the results.

It's also important to distinguish here that the question you're in is also creating a context and giving a trajectory of where we will go. It's going to influence what line of thinking and actions we will take.

As a simple, quick example, let's say your team is trying to decide on a business model to implement. You can see two options in front of you. Yet, neither of those business models will lead to the accomplishment of the desired goal. You can pose a new question and something new will open up.

Past-Based Formulas May Limit the Future

Right now we're in three undeniable conditions of the world. First, the pace of change is speeding up. We have rapid rampant change. It keeps getting faster and faster. That's a scientific fact and we experience that. The second condition is the increasing complexity and number of choices we have. And the third condition is, because of the changes, for the most part unprecedented change, we have daily uncertainties. Some of them are unfathomable. We never know what to expect, and I think that has been the case since 9/11.

Now we find ourselves in these three undeniable conditions where we can no longer rely upon whatever formulas we used from the past—in business and in our lives. We can't even rely on knowledge because it changes so quickly.

Isn't that very interesting? And so, what do we do? How can we be effective in these three undeniable conditions? We can move into the mastery perspective.

Think of yourself as a martial arts master. You don't know what will be coming at you. But what you do know within your own being is that you've trained yourself. You know you can be so present now. You are open to possibility. You know whatever circumstances arise in the world or come your way, you have the wherewithal and the confidence to be in right or masterful action.

I think that's what people want right now—to know within yourself you have the wherewithal to be effective in this changing world. We're in a time right now where everyone you speak to and I speak to—we're all looking. We all want that 30,000-ft perspective where you look at your life and think about, what do I want now? How do I want my life to go moving forward in this environment? How do I make my contribution? How do I live my purpose? How do I live in the state of being joyful everyday living my life? We all want that. I think those three conditions in the world—change, complexity, and uncertainty—are causing people to step back and reflect on it.

Bill: What does it take to get an employee's full attention and best performance?

Dianne: One of the things we find that people, employees, are looking for is a vision—for themselves, what they're accountable for in their work, and for the company or business unit they're working in. That vision needs to be expressed and valued.

Yet, we tend to think of the company leaders as "the visionaries." They're the ones who are creating the vision and trying to get that vision heard among the employees, aligned on and embraced. The unfortunate word for it—"buy-in." That sets up an "us and them" situation where "they" try to convince "us" to buy in to their vision. This is really an old worldview approach. It's not the most effective, as we know!

In QuantumThink we do an exercise called Your Holographic Vision. We ask people to look at their vision for all the areas that express the whole of their life. The areas include having a vision for Self, Significant Other, Family, Work, Community, Country, the World, and for Ideas That Shape The World. QuantumThink, for example, is an "idea that shapes the world." You don't have to have your own trademark to have an idea that shapes the world because everyone has an idea about it. You have an idea that shapes the world. Exploring Forward-Thinking Workplaces. It's an idea that shapes the world.

Every one of us has a vision in each of these areas of life although we may not even be aware of it. Ask an employee, what is your vision for your work here, and you start to see everyone has one unique aspect of the vision. When you put it all together and employees feel they're participating in that overall vision, that's when the vision comes alive. That's when the top-level leader doesn't even have to worry about whether their vision is getting embraced. Because when each person sees how their personal vision is getting fulfilled in the collaborative vision—that's when it starts humming and buzzing. People become passionate about what they're doing. I think that's a very big part of it. You're recognized and you're valued.

The Observer Effect—What You Bring Is What You Get

You know how they have all these employee surveys? What determines the outcomes of those surveys? To a great extent, how the questions are posed. Remember, reality is context dependent and a question is a context that shapes how things go. In quantum science, this is known as "the observer effect." In essence, when you look at life as whole systems interconnecting—there is no objective reality "out there" apart from you and me. We each have an influence on what we experience. In QuantumThink this is a core principle, Observer-created Reality. I say it simply, what you bring is what you get. How you pose a question on employee surveys—whether it's a Gallup poll or political poll or anything else in the world—the response is going to be shaped and slanted by how the question is posed and framed.

How do you get the best performance from employees? That is the question you asked. When you look at the results from employee surveys, one thing always comes up when you ask, "What do the employees really want?" They want to be valued. That is significant for everyone. Imagine that, as we've been discussing, when a person is valued, they give their best. Then you say, well that's nice, now what?

Everyone knows what to do; everyone knows people want to be valued. But what is going to give a person the experience of being valued?

My work and my passion is about having us go from knowing what to do, "knowing" the wisdom—to actually living it—to being the walking, talking, embodiment of these values, these virtues.

That's where conscious intent comes in—for everyone—whether you're the manager or the person reporting to that manager. You relate to people with the intent that they experience being valued. Of course, it takes conscious action as well.

What should managers be asking employees? How about, "What do *you* think?" When you are asked, What do you think? What's your vision? What's the direction you think we should be going?—it is understood, in the subtext as they say in the movie business, that the person experiences being valued because you are asking them to contribute their thinking, their point of view.

Move Beyond Least-Action Pathways

Let's talk about for a moment what can limit us in the day-to-day culture of work environments. It is what I call "Least-action Pathways." Because of the automatic habits engendered by a formula-driven, mechanical, Industrial Age way of thinking, thought can tend to become a Least-action Pathway. A Least-action Pathway is the route the thought takes simply because it's been that route before. It's the most mechanical, automatic way or action—the least conscious way of thinking about something. We have cultural Least-action Pathways, family Least-action Pathways—just about in any area of life. For example, the Least-action Pathway in our current news reporting is to tell us what went wrong, is wrong, or will go wrong (smile). That's the automaticity of current news media.

The importance of noticing Least-action Pathways is so we can move beyond them, so they don't have to limit us. Please don't give them any meaning—good or bad. They're simply automatic habits. We don't even know how they got here—and truly, the "why" and "how" of them are irrelevant.

What is relevant is that when you start to live consciously, when you can see your automatic habits, in that moment, you can make another choice!

If a Least-action Pathway is limiting you, or your team, or what you want to accomplish, you can recognize it immediately. Then you can interrupt it just by recognizing it and saying, "Okay, how can we think about this differently?"

When you look at Least-action Pathways, there are Least-action Pathways of individuals, corporate cultures, media, government, politics, gender, whatever. There's also a Least-action Pathway of leadership. Leaders feel like they have the weight of what happens on their shoulders. If you're a leader, you have to know it all. You have to figure it all out. Yet, that is simply not "the truth." We are in a time of authentic collaboration. The leader does play a directive role, for sure. Yet, he or she doesn't have to figure it all out. They just need to guide the action and allow for everyone's genius to come through. It's not an either/or world. It's a both/and world.

This is a forward-thinking workplace. It engenders participation. It engenders the experience of being valued. It's a team. It's not like, let me show you the way to go. It's a collaborative context.

The top-level leadership, it's their job to create direction. If you're an enlightened leader, you're doing it with input. You're doing it because you're valuing people—not because you're telling them "You're valued," which isn't bad either to let somebody know that. But, it's in the way you are relating to them. You're asking them what do they think? What do they see? How would they do this? What's your vision for this aspect of our business? That's the big difference.

Let's Talk Trust

People talk about trust a lot. This idea of trust—I think we're born with trust. Trust is an aspect of who we are. When you look at babies or children, they have trust. There's a certain trust in little children, and I think it's because it's a part of who we are. It's in our being.

When you start to ask, "Do I trust this?" or "You have to gain my trust" or "You have to earn my trust"—this to me is a very ineffective level of unconscious intent. What we would call "unaware intent" because it's part of separation thinking. It separates. If you don't have to earn my trust, we're already on the same side. We're moving forward—together.

A lot of times we suggest the use of this creative dynamic of intent for our clients, with their customers or employee partners. I ask a client, how about creating the intent that you're already partners—with the person you are about to meet with. This kind of intent is powerful. It literally alters the relationship, for the better, of course.

Intent is something you hold in your being. People can start to intend we are in this together. You create an intent for the relational field—for how you want both of you to experience being related. You can do this with people you report to, with someone who is your peer, or someone who reports to you.

We can do it with customers. We're partners in this. How can this work for everyone? And of course that's one of the key contextual questions of my own work: How can this work for everyone? When you stand in that question, what happens is we start to get ideas that come from this intelligent mind field we're all sharing and living in. When that happens, you just start to create partnership. Trust is not a factor. Do we have to talk about trust? Or do we just work together, beautifully?

Bill: What do people really lack and long for at work?

Dianne: One of the things that people long for at work is being excited and passionate about what they're doing. People want to experience their passion. They want to feel that their work is an expression of their purpose, too.

I like to look at the energetic trends that impact all of us, regardless of what industry we're in or what we're doing in our lives. I refer to them as the "energies of the time." There is a certain "feeling tone" in every era, as life unfolds on our magnificent sparkling blue planet. In this moment and for years to come, we are in a time of restructuring, of expressing a new "identity," of a yearning for authenticity, of living our passion, and of creating a new period of harmonious relationships. These energy trends are transforming us. We're starting to think from a more expanded, higher, and more consciously awakened perspective.

Energy Trends in Action

We witness the restructuring of our societal institutions, including our companies, industries, government, healthcare, education, and judicial systems. Think of it this way. The current forms of our institutions were born from Industrial Age thinking. Now we are in a Quantum Age—and it's time to update our institutions to be in sync with the times. The example of the educational system is striking—because it is so antiquated when you look at what's possible utilizing current technologies. Then again, the "new education" is taking place as well outside of the conventional structure. YouTube, distance learning, and so much more is available, and people are enjoying and engaging in it.

What about the predominant energy trend of "authenticity"? Criticisms of social media notwithstanding, the fact is we can get closer to the people we know, and we can know so many more people because of the Internet and social media. Privacy may have been eroded, yet we don't want to live behind a mask. We want *authenticity*.

We're in a time of "the new you." When you step back and reflect, you start to make choices that are simpatico with who you are in your heart, soul, mind, and spirit.

You want to be able to step forward with a new expression of who you are. "The new you." Whoever I was in the last 5, 10, 20 years isn't who I want to be now. I can now go to a new place. New questions start to arise like: How can I get to the next octave of my self-expression? How do I want to be known to myself and in the world now?

And what about this idea of *passion* as an energy trend? As you ask, what's important to me now—we want to be doing what we love. It's not at all selfish or superficial because when each one of us tunes in to what we're passionate about, we are at the same time tuning in to the clues, gifts, talents, and experiences that we've been given by our destiny—what we've been expecting and hoping for throughout our lives.

The Power of Happy

When we each start to be excited, happy, and passionate about what we're working on and how we're expressing ourselves in the workplace—that is probably the greatest contribution to our world at large.

It's easy to see why—because happier people are more productive, healthier, and have a greater uplifting influence on others when you're in that elevated joyful state. You have a clearer connection to source—the infinite field of mind, Infinite Intelligence. That's where genius gets ignited. That's where we spark new ideas.

That's where we can keep opening our minds to ideas that we may not, at first glance, be connecting, resonating, or agreeing with. We begin to open our minds because we're in a joyful state ourselves. We can start to work together and collaborate on how we can create this to work. We transcend the either/or options that divide us. You have the freedom to express your passion in the work you do and appreciate and honor that passion in others.

Which leads us to a very important energy trend right now, and that is one of creating harmonious relationship. You can use plain, ordinary logic in the world to see the divisiveness that people have been disappointed in—even in despair about—and you wonder how does it ever end. How do we ever come together? Connect to the desire for harmony. When you create the intent for it in your relationships, that starts to emanate out.

It comes down to are we living a conscious life or not? It means living consciously knowing how to use the faculties of mind—what I call the Five Natural Faculties of Mind. Intent, which allows us to create; Intuition, which allows us to connect; Subtle Energy, which allows us to tune in; Resonance, which allows us to manifest; and Meditation, which allows us to focus.

Because of the big paradigm shift in science, which has filtered into our technology, industries, and the way that we live today, the world is shifting from a physical-based reality to a mind-based reality.

Then when you say everybody wants to create results, the question becomes how does that happen? How do we create the results that we want? When you're looking from a physical-based reality, it's all about the existing circumstances. It looks like I have to take the right actions and then I'll get the results I want. That has validity; that is true. However, when you look at what is at the *source* of creating the right action, then you have to look at thinking. We know that our patterns and habits of thinking give rise to our ideas and our actions and, therefore, to our results.

My question that led me to create the QuantumThink® system of thinking was: If thinking creates results, then what is creating our thinking?

And my revelation was that since everything in the universe is a system, we think in a system. The thinking system is based on the assumptions and ideas and beliefs of the overarching worldview. Very simply, the worldview is whatever we believe to be true about the nature of reality and how it works.

When you worked in the Industrial Age, thinking was organized around the physical five senses. What did we study in school? The brain, the physical. We didn't learn about the five Natural Faculties of Mind—Intent, Intuition, Subtle Energy, Resonance, and Meditation, which I consider not just a "practice" but a natural faculty of mind.

From Matter to Mind

In our Quantum Age, cutting-edge scientists are saying the Universe is less like a giant machine and more like a giant mind. We're living in a mind-based reality.

We have to look at these invisible fields of energy intelligence because that's where the power of intent is working. It's where intuition and connections through our intuitive faculties are working. It's where we can tune in to the subtle energies, for example, the energetic trends I mentioned we're in, and what we're resonating with.

When you start to look at our mind-based reality, then you start to say, what does it mean? It means that we can connect to the creative dynamics that we have been endowed with by virtue of being blessed with human birth. That means that we can create consciously from intent because when you look at life, sometimes it drifts good and sometimes it drifts not so good. So, how do we make an intervention, right? We take command of creating from intent. Intent is not a cause and effect, push-pull dynamic. Intent generates a field of energy, and the quality of that energy generates many results consistent with the specific nature of the intent.

Let's take, for example, how do you create harmonious relationships? Well, the first place is to have a conscious intent for that. This is where it all begins. The dynamic of intent is the creative dynamic we've been born with. When we start to use this consciously, everything shifts and it's instant. It's an amazing thing to start to recognize that we are born with these capabilities, and when used consciously, can shift our lives and the world.

Sometimes people get hung up on, "Well, I had an intent and it didn't work." That's because in the physical, things obviously move slower. But in a relational field, in the field of our own state, our state of mind, our own state of being, our own peace of mind, and in our own relational field with another—that is an instantaneous shift.

When you shift your state, everything shifts with it because we do exist in fields. We operate in fields. I read once that Einstein said "The field is more important than the particle because the field conditions the particle."

Bill: What is the most important question leaders should ask employees?

Dianne: I believe one of the most important questions leaders should be asking employees is "What do you really want to be doing?" It's a question that very few leaders ask to people who report to them, probably because it's not in the organization's culture to ask that particular question. It's another one of those Least-action Pathways of corporate culture (remember, neither good nor bad—just habit)—for leaders to manage from the idea that you are going to have to do what I need you to do. That is of course also essential, to make sure that the job gets done. However, when you want to engender the highest performance, the happiest, most passionate, and enthusiastic work force, you want to think in a both/and frame of mind. The business needs a certain type of task accomplished, and the question is, who is the best person for that particular function? For example, "Okay, Joe can do that, right?" But maybe Joe doesn't want to do that—or maybe that's not his key talent.

So I think asking this question, *what do they really want to be doing* on this team, to understand how they see things, is very important. You may not get every dream come true as the employee, but at least you'll have a starting point. As the manager or the leader, your business is going to be that much more masterful and effective when you have people doing what they want to do. What they love to do. It goes back to that happiness and joy and being excited about the work factor.

Bill: What is the most important question employees should ask leaders?

Dianne: I think the employee should be asking, "What's your vision for where we're going?" This is an important question for several reasons. The first one is that leaders are expected to have a vision, but they may not be making it known. Employees may be unaware of it. Or perhaps they may not be asking about it. Yet, the vision is tantamount to a "living intent." The vision generates the energy-intelligent field that gives rise to actions and results.

From a QuantumThink perspective, a vision is a living possibility that consistently generates outcomes—it's not a someday-maybe future event. I think when we ask a question like that, "What's your vision for where we're going?" it gives the leader an opportunity to express it in a conversation. It gives the leader a platform to present the vision and bring it alive for everyone. It's one of the most satisfying experiences for both leaders and employees. It's a cocreative dynamic. New possibilities open up in the dialogue. That question is a force that creates the future.

It gives the employees a clear space to step into, to become part of it. If you're just operating in the day-to-day, unaware of a vision, work can become quite monotonous. However, when you're present to a great vision, you can see everything you're doing, even the small stuff, as a valuable contribution to the manifestation of that vision. It's the context. It's generating a new reality. And it's exhilarating for everyone.

When someone asks you a question something like, "Okay Bill, what's your vision for this Forward-Thinking Workplaces project?" what would you say? That question would cause you to pause and think about it. Well, you may say, "I want it to be a global conversation that spreads around the world!" And it also might cause you to think about it in a new way just by having been asked the question.

That question then leads to a natural next question for the employee to ask the leader, "How do you see me contributing to that vision?" Then you get an idea of how the leader sees you and where you stand. This type of communication creates quality relationships because you're getting to know one another at a deeper and more authentic level.

Thus, when people ask, what do you think or what is your vision, it's a very interesting phenomenon in terms of creating quality relationships in the workplace.

Bill: What is the most important question we should ask ourselves?

Dianne: I believe we can look at this question in at least two ways. One would be very simply to ask oneself, "What do I really want—now, and going forward?" When I'm doing what I want, it genuinely supports the world and the people around me.

And the other way to look at this is with this very important question, "How can we have this work for everyone?" This question is powerful. In the subtext, in the unspoken, it acknowledges that, in fact, we *can* have it work for everyone. And it also evokes what each and every person wants.

A lot of people will repeat this question back to me and say, "How do we *make* it work for everyone?" No, that's not the same question. It's a very carefully worded question.

When we ask how can we have this work for everyone, it's a place to stand to see what shows up.

There is an *allowing*. There is a calling forth of "intel" from the energy-intelligent quantum field of mind. It's not how can we make it work—because that would be back to command and control. There's no forcing in "how can we have it work."

"How are we going to make this work" isn't a bad question because it brings up a little passion, which is good. However, it also brings up static. With more static in the system, our genius might not be arising because you're blocking the energy field when you get too tense about it.

Consensus Decision-Making

When you say it this way, "How can we have this work for everyone?" it creates operating from consensus, rather than compromise or majority rules.

This is so important, so please let me share an example. We've always operated like this in our business. My partner in everything in life is my husband and business partner for more than 15 years, Alan K. Collins, who is a Master QuantumThink Coach. You can imagine that also being married we could be very familiar with each other. However, we do operate from this very important question of *how can we have this work for everyone?*

We make decisions from this question, not just between the two of us, but also with the various partners we work with. Let's say there are three of us and we need to decide on a project. Well, it's not going to be two against one, for example, "Too bad Mr. Third person who didn't get your way." We don't operate that way. What happens when you're in that question of how can we have this work for everyone is you have an intent for consensus decision-making where everyone is aligned and happy about the decision. You may not agree with every little aspect of it, but what happens is that question as a context opens possibilities and you keep seeing possible solutions in new ways. Eventually, you arrive at a possibility for that third person, the "Mrs. I-Don't-Agree-with-This" person, until she finally sees, "Wait a minute, if we did it this way, yes, that would work for me!"

It does work like that. If you have an intent for how can we have this work for everyone, then we can always come up with another tweak, another angle, or another revision until everyone is satisfied. That is a superior performance in an organization. When everyone is psyched about what you're doing, there's no drag on the energy field. Everyone is moving forward, coming up with ideas, feeling like their ideas are recognized. They're participating fully. It may sound like an overidealized way of being, yet it doesn't mean you're not going to have snags, conflicts, or challenges along the way. What it does mean is that you know you're going to work it out. Why? Because that's your intent.

It's also interesting because I believe this idea of how can we have this work for everyone is implied in your opening question for this interview: "How can we create workplaces where every voice matters, everyone thrives and finds meaning, and change and innovation happen naturally?"

I couldn't decide how I was going to answer that question, and I considered, "What question should management be in?" As you know from reading my book, *Do You QuantumThink?*, in the QuantumThink distinction #8 entitled Transformation As Distinct From Change, the practice for re-creating that principle in real time in your life is called "Being in the Right Question."

And my recommendation for an example as an all-encompassing question to be in is this very question we've been discussing: How can we have this work for everyone?

Of course, there are many "right questions" we can pose. As you were recognizing this, you said that it made you think, are we in the right questions on these interviews? And I say yes! Very much so, you're asking very good questions, Bill.

Let's take your example a little further for everyone.

When you're trying to produce a business result, that's a perfect question for a manager to ask an employee: Are we in the right question?

For example, let's say you needed to close 50 deals this year to meet your forecast. What question would be asked in this situation? You might say, "How are we going to get these deals closed?" Or maybe you'd be in this question, "What should we do to close these 50 deals?"

However, a new twist, a question that will redirect your thinking could be, "What enables a deal to be closed?" Or, "What has people say yes?"

The difference is that in the first question, "How are we going to close these deals?" you might come up with logical answers. "Well, let's go to the list of clients we've worked with before." That might be good, too.

Yet, in closing the deal, you might want to look at, what is it that has people say yes? It could take you in an entirely different direction. I'm giving a simple example because we don't have an actual situation in this moment. And I know you get the idea of how asking a different question will take you somewhere else. Somewhere you really want to go. And that is so exciting. It's exhilarating. That's the genius. That's forward-thinking!

Key Takeaways

- People more than ever desire self-expression, authentic connection, and mastery.

- Every one of us is being called upon to step into our own leadership—whether you are formally in a leadership position or not.

- When we're in one conversation of creative dialogue, we can all be conscious of what each one of us is contributing to the workplace, to our team, our organization, and to this project we're all working on together.

- We're making a leap from the Industrial Age to the Quantum Age, but we're in a Quantum Age still using Industrial Age thinking, and that's limiting us.

- Most of the time, we're in content-oriented conversations, meaning we are looking at the options in our immediate view.

- The question you're in is also creating a context and giving a trajectory of where we will go, which is going to influence what line of thinking and actions we will take.

- We can no longer rely upon whatever formulas we used from the past—in business and in our lives. We can't even rely on knowledge because it changes so quickly.

- Everyone has one unique aspect of the vision. When you put it all together and employees feel they're participating in that overall vision, that's when the vision comes alive.

- When you start to live consciously, when you can see your automatic habits, in that moment, you can make another choice.

- When you step back and reflect, you start to make choices that are simpatico with who you are in your heart, soul, mind, and spirit.

- "What do you really want to be doing?" is an important question leaders can ask employees.

- Expressing a vision is tantamount to a "living intent." The vision generates the energy-intelligent field that gives rise to actions and results.

- When we ask how can we have this work for everyone, it's a place to stand to see what shows up.

Brian Gardner

Minimalist Designer, Entrepreneur

How to Be Intentional to Design an Authentic Life and Better World

Brian is the founder of Authentik and StudioPress and a Partner at Rainmaker Digital. Brian is a champion of community, and he loves minimalist design and believes in white space. He is a well-known and influential leader and minimalist designer in the WordPress community and marketplace.

My connection to Brian Gardner began when I decided to take the Forward-Thinking Workplaces web site to the next level. That search led me to Brian Gardner and his work, which I soon embraced. But I also came to know that Brian was mastering the art of creating his own workplace where he could thrive and work independently and with others. While most of the Forward-Thinking Workplaces interviews address the traditional workplace, Brian brings innovation and clarity to creating our own workplaces where more and more of us are now moving to in greater numbers.

Bill Fox: How can we create a workplace where every voice matters, everyone thrives and finds meaning, and change and innovation happen naturally?

Brian Gardner: First off, it depends on whether you're referring to your own workplace at home—for those who are solo entrepreneurs like myself—or those who work in buildings and offices with other people.

© Bill Fox 2020
B. Fox, *The Future of the Workplace*,
https://doi.org/10.1007/978-1-4842-5098-3_21

For me, the best way to create a workplace that works is to surround myself with the things that make me feel comfortable.

As a creative, it's very important for me to have a palette that allows me to paint the pictures I want to paint. If I have a busy atmosphere, then I cannot clear my mental clutter and create the things I want to create. I think a lot of it is just the general space you're in. Whether it's pictures, or furniture, or even music in the background. For me, those are all key elements to creating something that helps me thrive.

I just wrote a blog post on Authentik on creating more and consuming less. First, you need to give yourself the opportunity to step outside of the office if you will. I do a lot of my best creative thinking either on the trail or in the shower. The idea is to create enough of that time so you can come up with those things. But then follow it up with time where you're back at the desk or back in front of the computer, so you can expand those thoughts you had into something that's more meaningful.

Bill: What is the most important question we should ask ourselves?

Brian: The most important question we can ask ourselves is twofold: (1) What is it I want to do and (2) What's keeping me from doing it?

Really, the second question is the one I focus on because I think it's easy for us to have wants, but am I willing to do it? Am I willing to sacrifice whatever it is to pursue that whether it's a dream, a particular job, or even moving?

Identifying what you want to do and do you have the courage or tenacity to make that jump and a leap of faith?

Sitting here as somebody who loves the mountains, the easiest way for me to explain that is being at the bottom of a mountain and looking at the top of the summit and saying I want to be there. I want to ski down that hill. Am I willing to get on that lift? Am I willing to remove the barriers and go there? As you go down that hill, it's a pretty good feeling. That's what it really comes down to. Are you willing to take the step?

Bill: What's the most important question we should be asking each other in the workplace?

Brian: While I don't work in a traditional office building, I do consider myself a leader because I have a team I lead. The question I always want to make sure I'm asking the people I work with and for is, are you doing things that make you happy and are you doing the things you love?

That's the most important part because if I know that they're not happy, then I know their work isn't as good as it could be. Maybe they're not in the right spot or the right position, and I want to know if they're not feeling like they're in the right spot. I want to put them in the right spot as it makes sense in our business. Really what it comes down to is, are you fulfilled? Are you happy with what you're doing? Because if you're not first, you may already detect that, so I'd like to put you in a place that makes you happy.

Bill: Your latest project and passion is called Authentik. What can you tell us about it?

Brian: Authentik is something I've had on my heart for many years. Over the last 2 years, it's come specifically as a domain name and the written-out project. I've always been a fan of authenticity and transparency in life. And life as the person and as the way you do your business.

Through all the experiences and the difficulties, the one thing I learned is that being true to yourself and surrounding yourself with the things that bring you joy and make you happy have always been important.

For 10 years now, I've been an online creative entrepreneur, and I'm a partner at the content marketing firm, Copyblogger. I've learned through this experience many things about people who are trying to do the same thing I have, which is create a business, do it online, and work from home.

I've grown an affinity for the people who I am—a sort of creative entrepreneur. For me, Authentik was about creating a movement and way of doing life and business because I believe they're symbiotic. Just being intentional about things, open, and honest. And consequently, attracting people who might become readers or customers or followers or members of your community that are like-minded.

Bill: What question is at the heart of Authentik?

Brian: The questions at the core of Authentik are what do you want to do, how do you want to do it, and who do you want to do it for?

Authentik is a lifestyle ideology. It's a business ideology. It's really about being intentional. That's the word I like to put at the foundation of it all.

It's making sure that what you're doing has meaning. That there's a heart-centered message built around what you do.

I feel so many people in life and in business really have a tendency to do things because other people are doing them—not because they want to be doing them. That leads them down a path of nonsustainability, boredom, and resistance to success.

If people can get honest with who they are, what they want to do, and who they want to do it for, it opens the doors to an opportunity to be successful.

I'm a huge believer that the journey is the reward. The things you learn and identify along the way are so much more important than the things you think you're seeking. I know for me that's been the case on several projects where I started in one thing, but I've been open to change or being agile and realizing where I think I'm going isn't necessarily where my heart wants to go when I started that journey. Being open to fluctuating with your circumstances and the encounters along the way really helps bring you to a place of peace.

Bill: What does it take to build an authentic brand and digital platform?

Brian: A lot of it is a very obvious thing, but I think it takes some guts. Sometimes the business world can be very scary and ominous. The ability to go against the norm or even what is expected of you really is at the core.

Authentik will take a lot of courage. The courage to stick with the plan and stick with the things I feel strongly about and not to get swayed by social media or other influencers and the way they're doing business. Just be true to that and hold that mission as straight as possible.

Bill: Would you like Authentik to become a movement?

Brian: One thing I've learned as a business owner and as a consumer is that the brands I love just aren't brands. They're really lifestyle choices. My friend Jeff Sheldon runs a company called Ugmonk. It's a small organization but to him, it's his passion. He's been able to build a lifestyle brand, and those are kinds of environments where tribes are built. People are connected to that type of community.

I wanted Authentik to be the same thing. I didn't want it to just be a blog or a business. I wanted it to be a way of life. A way of doing things from a personal and business perspective.

I have a huge affinity toward building audiences and communities. Life is best done with other people. Life is better together is what a friend of mine used to say. I feel like there is so much we can do together from a business perspective on our personal journeys to help and encourage one another. The success I want to build and the success I hope others who follow Authentik want to build, those are the foundations built on stone. When they're built on courage and honesty and doing things with one another rather than gimmicks and marketing plays and witty word choices.

Bill: The following quote on your blog caught my attention, "Where your passion meets their need, that is your calling." Who said it and what does it mean to you?

Brian: I met Allison Fallon a few years ago as a happenstance. She was on the cusp of finishing her book *Passion Life*. As I was reading through it, a lot of things she wrote about resonated with me specifically about letting go of things that hold you back or you don't have any need for. But when I came across those ten words in the book, it forever changed my life.

Where your passion meets their need, that is your calling.—Allison Fallon

---

However, it took a couple of years to get to a point where those words became clear. I loved what she wrote, and it made so much sense. But over the years as I've tried to identify what it is I want to do and who I want to do it for, it's taken a little time beyond when I first read those words.

Within the last 6 months, things have become crystal clear in terms of the creative entrepreneurial space where folks need to be. Not taught but just encouraged and shared with the things I've learned along the way—both good and bad. I realized that my passion is for creative entrepreneurs—those who write, design, take pictures, create videos, and so on. I just realized there's the group of people I want to work for. They need to have tools especially as it pertains to being online whether it be a web site or even as granular as social media graphics. Supplying a toolbox if you will of items that might apply to them such as WordPress themes, design aspects, and other things that can help them create the business they want to build.

I have a specific design aesthetic I like—a minimalistic, monochromatic design. I feel from a web perspective that enables people to focus on the things that matter, which is primarily the content and photography. When I realized this is a group of people I want to work with and for and this is how I want to do it with them, then I realized I am on the cusp of my calling. That synced up with the availability of the Authentik domain, which I had been after for several years. I realized my next life journey in my entrepreneurial career is this Authentik thing. I don't know yet where it will go. I have an idea and I'm willing to adjust as I see fit but really identifying the passion and the need and realizing this is my calling. I'm so excited about this path I appreciate being on here with you and finding avenues in which I can talk about this, especially as Authentik starts off.

Bill: What is the "Authentik Equation?"

Brian: What it really came down to was identifying that I wanted to create something I can talk and write about that makes sense on paper. It came down to identifying the three things that got in the way of my own journey with fear and limitations—a lot which are self-induced. I wanted people to see if you take these factors and remove all of them, then taking the concept of adding them together, then you're able to create freely.

One of the unofficial taglines of Authentik is to create honestly. Filters are great when you want to put the spotlight on something, but I believe so much of at least my art comes from the core experiences I've gone through. It's being able to remove the things that get in the way of being able to hone in on that honestly and creating from that. That turns into an end product that I think is so much better both on an honest standpoint and from a production or creative standpoint. I feel my best work comes when I'm able to move all the other things that get in the way, and I can just do my thing.

Bill: One lesson you talk about on your blog that I really liked is you said that the more you focus on how many people your work will reach, the less impact it has. Can you talk more about that?

Here's one thing I've learned over the years as a creative: The more I focus on how many people it will reach, the less impact it has. The more I focus on how deep it will reach, the more impact it has.—Brian Gardner

---

Brian: My Internet story starts when I was a project manager at an architectural firm. I loved my job. It was a smaller company, and I loved the people I worked with. I learned a lot about business and computers, but I realized that's all it was for me. That was the job I went to. I cared for the people that were there, but that's all it really was. I would go home and then start the other life.

Early in my career, I had the good fortune of being able to sell some products online that have taken off and enabled me to leave that situation to pursue a career on my own terms. I realize that not everyone gets that lucky and not everyone has that opportunity.

During the 10 years I've been doing the online work, there have been seasons of where I was still living to work. This was still a job and still something I was trying to figure out. But over the last 4 or 5 years, as we've grown as a company and brought in mid-level management, I've been able to pursue outside projects and also more things I'm passionate about. I know it's something people say all the time, and a lot of times people don't believe it's ever possible, but I get to wake up and do what I love every single day. At some points and most times, I can't even define the differences between living and working because as they say when you love what you do, it's not work. For me, I get to create and that's my job. That for sure is living a dream.

Bill: You shared something interesting on your blog that you learned from Sally Hogshead. What does "different is better than better" mean to you?

Different is better than better. That being the best isn't enough, if nobody notices or cares. Stop trying to be THE best. Start being YOUR best.—Sally Hogshead

---

Brian: I was attending a conference and had no plans on seeing Sally's session that morning. I was busy, and I was just going to go hide in the corner and do my thing. I couldn't find a corner, so I sat in the auditorium's corner. I opened my laptop to get some things done when Sally walks on stage. She starts her talk by asking if anybody in the audience had never done a shot of Jägermeister before?

I immediately said to myself, "What is going on here?" She brings a person on stage and they do shots of Jägermeister! She goes on to talk about Jägermeister and what that company is about, and how they differentiate themselves. Some things she said made sense.

The punch line of her talk was it's not enough to just try to be better than the next person, it's trying to be different. "I always like to use the analogy of Hollywood stars and celebrities who put on makeup but the Instagram shots that go the most viral are the ones without makeup because they're showing their naturalness."

So many people look up to these celebrities, but when they take off their makeup and they just show themselves as real people that's where they're resonating. That's where people come out of the woodwork and they say, "Hey, yeah, that's me." I have blemishes. I have pimples. I have all the things that normal people have, but it's just great to know.

The greatest gift you can give someone is the reassurance they're not the only one. That's what Authentik is all about. It's channeling your inner uniqueness and being comfortable with that and living off of that. There are things about me that my CEO, Brian Clark, likes to tease me about. One of which is my affection for the singer Sarah McGlauglin. It's me. It's who I am. It's what I love. I can pretend to be something different. That won't make me feel good. It will convince you I'm something I'm not. What's the point in all of that? There's a lot to be said about being different and how setting apart that can be.

Bill: What are your thoughts on building a legacy?

"The more we focus on being great, the less we succeed at being good."—Brian Gardner

---

Brian: I wrote a blog post about what we want the perception of our work to be. Usually, the authentic material written in the context of business people. I was trying to sift through and figure out what are the things I want to be known as 20 years from now when Brian Gardner is up in the mountains, not online, doing his own thing.

One thing that came up while writing that blog post was the news of the death of The Cranberries' lead singer Dolores O'Riordan. It really hit me as I wrote that post. Part of me was trying to identify what are the things I really want people to know and love about me. Again, not facades and masks but what are the things I think are most important from a creation and art standpoint. What are those things I want to leave behind? Not just how people think of me from a personal branding standpoint, like the Starbucks guy. I also want to leave behind things that are useful. For example, what are the things that are important to me? What are the lessons I want to teach? What are the things I want people to come away with? When you think of creating in those terms, then you can craft things a certain way and provide for people who I think there's a huge need for.

Key Takeaways

- The best way to create a workplace that works is to surround yourself with things that make you feel comfortable.

- "What is it I want to do and what's keeping me from doing it?" is one of the most important questions we can ask ourselves.

- An important question you can ask the people you work with and for is, "Are you doing the things that make you happy and are you doing the things you love?"

- Being "Authentik" is about being intentional about things, open, and honest.

- Many people in life and in business have a tendency to do things because other people are doing them—not because they want to be doing them. That leads them down a path of nonsustainability, boredom, and resistance to success.

- The ability to go against the norm or even what is expected of you really is at the core of being authentic.

- Life is best done with other people and better together.

- Where your passion meets their need, that is your calling.

- You solve the "Authentik Equation" removing limitations so you are able to create freely.

- The more you focus on how many people your work will reach, the less impact it has.

- Channel your inner uniqueness and be comfortable with and living off of that.

- The more we focus on being great, the less we succeed at being good.

- What are the things I think are most important from a creation and art standpoint that I want to be known for?

Tom Thomison

Partner, encode.org

How Do We Start and Make It Real?

Tom Thomison is a founding member and partner at encode.org llc and cofounder at HolacracyOne. Tom is an entrepreneur and a recognized leader in self-organization practices and methods. In 2007, he cofounded HolacracyOne, LLC to further develop and mature Holacracy, now a gold standard replacement for conventional management hierarchies.

I connected with Tom Thomison when he was one of the featured speakers in a webinar I hosted on Holacracy and Beyond.[1] What I find interesting about Tom's story is that it's like my own journey at Exploring Forward-Thinking Workplaces. It's a story about going deeper to uncover what's underneath. Rather than limiting our focus to the latest "bolt-on" system, we are exploring to change what really matters that makes a real difference.

Bill Fox: How can we create a workplace where every voice matters, everyone thrives and finds meaning, and change and innovation happen naturally?

Tom Thomison: Those are very aspirational goals. I think we all want to work in that type of environment. I know I do.

---

[1] https://youtu.be/vg-e-hJawwo

© Bill Fox 2020
B. Fox, *The Future of the Workplace*,
https://doi.org/10.1007/978-1-4842-5098-3_22

> How do we start? By making it real for ourselves first. Figuring out how to do that—not relying on others to do it for us and that can go many different ways.

If you're an entrepreneur, you might start something. If you're an innovator, you might find a company that wants to innovate with you. It's taking accountability and responsibility and figuring it out for yourself.

Then from my perspective and my work over at least the last 20 years, it's figuring out the answer to that question of how to make that real. For me, I tried, like most consultants and most business owners and entrepreneurs, with all the usual things—incremental improvements like business process reengineering, total quality management, higher-performance teaming, self-directed teaming, lean systems, agile systems, and agile development.

I was at the top of my consulting game about 10 to 15 years ago working with a lot of large enterprises and competing with all the big consulting firms like PWC, McKinsey, and others. Yet I was feeling like we're beating our heads against the wall trying all these cool, clever techniques and not getting the results we wanted long term. It's not that the techniques are bad. In fact, they have embedded in them kernels of brilliance, wisdom, and good practices. But what I found is they go back in the very same system that's been around for a couple of hundred years—the authority system, the power hierarchy, the management hierarchy.

> Inevitably over about 18 months, all that goodness that was in business process reengineering, or total quality management, or lean manufacturing atrophied, withered away and died.

So about 10 years ago, I got tired of beating my head against the wall. I was continuing to look for better ways to answer that question that you posed and that led me to all sorts of innovations. I crossed paths with Brian Robertson who was experimenting with the same question and with different approaches in his software company. What emerged from that was a company called HolacracyOne that we launched together in 2007 to change that management hierarchy, to change the power distribution system, to change the core fundamental operating system of an organization to make that kind of workspace that we want, and to bring into reality a place where you can show up—a place where you can lend your time, energy, and talent toward a purpose that you care about.

I think one of the fundamental ways of getting there is addressing and changing the core operating system, which gives a healthy environment for people to show up to innovate, participate, and have a sense of what might be possible for the organization—to do something about it. This environment would provide a pathway to do their work without the fear of being ignored or overruled and without the burden of trying to seek or reach consensus in ideas. Instead they would have a self-organizing system, and this is at its roots what Holacracy is. It's a self-management and self-organizing system to rethink the fundamental operating system or an organization completely.

For me, this is how I make that manifest. Starting a company 10 years ago to bring Holacracy into the world helps to address those issues. Another definition for it is a continuous improvement process. Holacracy is a self-organizing system that allows everyone to sense and respond to what's needed—that is innovation. It's continuous innovation because you're continually sensing into what might be possible, and you have a clear pathway to do something about it on an ongoing basis.

My story is like your story in the work you are doing here at Exploring Forward-Thinking Workplaces. It's addressing what's underneath. Sometimes the language we've been focused on is on the bolt-on ancillary systems, tools, and practices. But we haven't addressed the core, which has been around a couple of hundred years or more—management hierarchy—top down and predict and control. It's hard to address the core, but I think it's one of the most fundamental shifts that you can make to change the fundamental concept or understanding of what an organization is and change that core operating system.

Bill: What does it take to get an employee's full attention and best performance?

Tom: First, don't make them employees! [laughs] At my new endeavor, encode.org, we're working to move beyond employees. With these new operating and self-management systems in place, we're grounding those systems legally, so it allows for individuals to show up as full legal members wherever they are in their career. This does not have the connotation that it's big and heavy weight with lots of responsibility and capital investment. It just means a member that cares about the purpose of the organization can show up to sense and respond to whatever's needed to participate in the running instruction of that organization and not be an employee.

I think your question is a perfectly valid question because 99.59% of the world is employer/employee relationships, but we need to change that.

I think embedded in the question is the problem. It's the assumption that that's how the world should be—an employer/employee relationship.

We need to change that. I'm working hard to make that a reality. It's not just aspirational, but a concrete legal reality where we can take these very same self-organizing principles that we find in Holacracy and now embed those in our legal structures, so that individuals who want to contribute to a purpose can do so as a legal partner, not as an employee.

Then we change the game completely because that person can now be an investor. Even if it's just a little bit, the person can benefit from sharing in the profits of the organization and contribute toward the purpose they care about. They're not following a leader; they're not under a power hierarchy. They're showing up consciously because they care about the work. And they contribute to that work through a self-managing or self-organizing process like Holacracy. This changes the game completely.

I have the opportunity to share this vision and the concrete reality we're making with a lot of folks. People will often say to me, "What about the ordinary worker that just wants a paycheck?" I tell them that's perfectly fine! In fact, even better! I've worked with a lot of organizations that would be classified as classic blue collar kind of work. In those kinds of workers, there's passion for their craft, for their art, for their industry. They love what they do, and that is just fine. It doesn't need to be any more than that.

An example I often use is an aviation company I work with. They are some cool folks that just love aviation. They love aircraft; they love the mechanics, the avionics, and the repair. They de-ice the planes, they refuel the planes, they maintain the planes—they love aviation. That was their craft. They can work as independent agents pursuing their purpose in an organization and just show up doing their work—participating and lending their time, energy, and talent to a purpose they care about in that format. Not as an employee, but as a legal partner. That's how you get engagement.

Bill: What do people really lack and long for at work?

Tom: I'd say they lack meaning, connection, purpose, growth, and development. Work is where we spend the clear majority of our time. It's our extended or second families in some cases. In a sad number of cases, we're working in a dysfunctional environment with an unwanted dysfunctional family.

Fundamentally, we want a sense that my contribution matters and that I can see it. We want a sense that my contribution matters, and I have the feedback to let me know that that's true. I want to see that I can make a difference.

We all want to make a difference and do that in big or small ways—in whatever ways make sense. That could be that I do meaningful work, and I get compensated fairly for that meaningful work to take care of my family. Then that means that work has meaning for that individual. I think those of us in the consulting field or in the organization design or development field sometimes project grandiose ideas onto ordinary situations. We make it more complicated than it needs to be. We all just want to find meaning in our work, and that meaning takes many forms. It spans a broad spectrum if you will. Allowing for that meaning to show up for each individual is what's important.

Bill: What is the most important question leaders should ask employees?

Tom: I've not lived or worked in a management hierarchy for a decade. But of course, I've helped other organizations who are still in a manager/employee model. I would like to shift this question to my context if you will because I think underneath the question in a conventional frame is the question, "How can we align better around the work, manager to employee?

The right question I think is, "How can we redirect everyone's focus to the purpose of the organization? How can we get everybody aligned with purpose—not with management?"

Purpose is the new cohering force—not good management. In fact, management just needs to end! I had an interview a couple of days ago in Bucharest, Romania, with one of the leading employer organizations. They asked a very similar question about management and employees, "What's the future of management?" I said, "It's dead, but it doesn't know it yet!" His jaw dropped, and he said, "I can't publish that!"

The whole notion of the manager/employee relationship I think just needs to die. I'll just be that blunt. The new question is, "How do we get everyone, without that artificial distinction of manager or employee, working for purpose?" How do we get everyone in a system that allows their gifts and talents to be applied to or expressed for the organization's purpose? That's the new question. How can we all get engaged in getting this purpose into the world?

But I think there are two fundamental components of this new world of work—being clear on purpose and having a clear power distribution system to energize toward that purpose. In Holacracy, there's a language cue of having the right relationship with power. Power and purpose very closely correlate. I think in the coming years that purpose work is going to be reemergent.

In Tim Kelly's book *True Purpose*,[2] there are some very concrete ways of understanding purpose and breaking down purpose. Also, there is this notion of an evolutionary purpose that is key. Frederic Laloux writes about this in *Reinventing Organizations*,[3] and it's a fundamental aspect of Holacracy that the organization pursues "its" evolutionary purpose. I think we as individuals have an evolutionary purpose. In other words, we have an always evolving understanding of our purpose in the world. It's never a fixed purpose. In

---

[2] Berkeley: Transcendent Solutions Press, 2009.
[3] Brussels: Nelson Parker, 2014.

effect, I kind of hold the Forrest Gump definition—purpose is as purpose does. In one regard, you can't ever not be on purpose; you're always doing what you're doing. But having a better, deeper, more nuanced understanding of your work in the world, your purpose in the world, your gift or blessing or mission in the world—as Tim Kelly might put it—is super important.

Bill: What is the most important question employees should ask leaders?

Tom: In a world with no employees or no managers, this question drops to, "What can we all do to manifest purpose in the world?" And just to restate what I said above, everyone should be working on lending their time, energy, and talent toward a purpose that has meaning for them. This shifts the focus of organizations to purpose. Organizations for a purpose. Work for a purpose.

That purpose is presumably something that the world needs and something that would be missing from the world if not being delivered by this organization, so it has deep meaning. And employees getting an opportunity to usher that in, not as employees but as individuals who happen to care about that purpose in the world. I think that is the reframe for both managers in the prior question and for employees in this question. Remove the artificial distinction and get everyone energizing the work of the organization for purpose.

Bill: What is the most important question we should ask ourselves?

Tom: I think true to the theme of my prior responses; it's to make conscious choices. I believe the following questions are important: "What questions can we ask ourselves? Is this a conscious choice I'm making to lend time, energy, and talent toward something other than self?"

Be conscious about your work. Be intentional about your work. Be introspective about how your work has meaning for you and the organization. Wake up more. Be more engaged in that process. Both as a self-development process and just a clear choice making process about what you do with your life, your time, your energy, and your talent.

I think that's the question, "How do we grow up and wake up?" which is just a general theme overall.

I think that's an evolutionary thing that's happening no matter what. There's a trend line there. We're all becoming more awake or more conscious over time hopefully. And that's where our organizations need to be—inviting all of us to be more conscious, to have more choice making, to bring more intention to our work without fear. And just trying to face your own reality in that as well. Be honest about what you need. Ask for what you need in that process too. More conscious choice making.

Also, I want to caveat what I just said above. For me, that's all true, and the danger is it often gets conflated or inflated in a way. Being more conscious about what you need and not apologizing for it and not trying to be developed to be any different from where you are. Let me go back to my aviation worker example above, and knowing why you work…

For example, I work because I love my craft. I love my industry. I get gratification from working in this field, and it takes care of my family. And just being honest. It's back to that being conscious. Being honest about why I am working and not trying to meet other people's expectations of why you should work. I think it's just honest and real too. It's being almost unapologetic about why you're doing what you're doing. I do that to only contrast against our current system that feels like—to put it simply—it puts people in the position of having to "sing for their supper," or compromise, or show up differently than they are naturally, or put up with it to get the paycheck to take care of their other needs. What I'm pointing to is to consciously choose to work without being compromised.

Bill: What is the current state of Holacracy in the world today?

Tom: Right now, today, we have a decade of experience with Holacracy. Hundreds of organizations all over the world are running under the Holacracy Constitution. In the Holacracy Constitution, which is legally adopted, by policy, by the power holder of the company. It makes everybody a partner. A partner in the Constitution. And that partner has an equal voice. That partner can sense and respond to opportunities or issues that need to be addressed without fear of any management hierarchy getting in the way because there is no management hierarchy.

We can do this exactly today to address the issue of employee engagement, but we're failing. We all know we're failing with employee engagement. We have been for decades. My short answer is to stop doing that and do something else!

That something else is getting everybody involved on an equal basis with equal voice but not in a flat structure, but in a deep hierarchy of how the work self-organizes according to the purpose and what it takes to fulfill that purpose.

Then let everybody participate in the running, structuring, and expression of that work in that hierarchy.

We can do that today. Any organization anywhere in the world that is tired of the management hierarchy and sees the limits of that can adopt the Holacracy Constitution to transform employees to partners to get the work done.

Now legally, if they haven't made the other legal shifts, those individuals are legal employees. There's some downside to that, but we can only fix a little bit at a time.

Key Takeaways

- Make a forward-thinking workplace real for ourselves—we can't rely on others to do it for us.

- Many of today's most popular solutions don't last long term because they rely on the systems of the past.

- The right question can lead to all sorts of innovations that bring into reality a place where you can show up.

- Change the core operating system to create a healthy environment for people to show up to innovate, participate, and have a sense of what might be possible.

- Focus on what's underneath rather than bolt-on systems. It's one of the most fundamental shifts you can make.

- Create an environment where people can sense and respond to whatever's needed and move beyond being an employee.

- Allowing meaning to show up for each individual is what's important.

- How can we get everybody aligned with purpose—not with management?

- How do we get everyone, without that artificial distinction of manager or employee, working for purpose?

- Healthy companies focus on how we can be more of service to the customer, not problems.

- What can we all do to manifest purpose in the world? Everyone should be lending their time, energy, and talent toward a purpose that has meaning for them.

- We're all becoming more awake or more conscious over time. How do we grow up and wake up?

- We've been failing with employee engagement for decades. Transform employees into partners.

Bob Schatz

Agile and Transformation Leader

Exploring Forward Thinking Workplaces with Bob Schatz

Bob is a leader in agile product development, process improvement, organizational fitness, scrum training, and lean management at Agile Infusion LLC. Bob specializes in training, consulting, and coaching in the practice of successfully using agile project management techniques to transform organizations and improve the performance of their software development project teams. He is a longtime Certified Scrum Trainer (CST) with Scrum Alliance. He began his practice as a result of leading the first large agile transition at Primavera Systems in 2002.

I first met Bob in 2011 when I attended his Scrum Master training. I really appreciated the practical, authentic, and experienced presence Bob brings to his training. I initially interviewed Bob in 2012 for *5 Minutes to Process Improvement Success*[1] and knew he would have great insights to contribute to the Forward-Thinking Workplaces conversation. Bob's Twitter profile states in part, "Improving the quality of life for companies and the great people that work in them." That's a mission that resonates highly with the intention behind my interviews.

---

[1] Fox, Bill, 2012.

© Bill Fox 2020
B. Fox, *The Future of the Workplace*,
https://doi.org/10.1007/978-1-4842-5098-3_23

Bill Fox: How can we create a workplace where every voice matters, everyone thrives and finds meaning, and change and innovation happen naturally?

Bob Schatz: This is a great question. I've always been someone that really wants to create a workplace described in those words. I know in my career as a leader, I've tried to create that type of environment for people. Now, as a consultant, I go from company to company and see what they're doing, and I try to help them get to a better place where continuous improvement is the daily goal. In my heart, I want to believe something like you're describing here can happen, but then I think about it and see what the reality is.

I don't think this type of workplace will emerge in most organizations. It takes a lot of work, excellent leadership, and a special culture all being in alignment at the same time.

What we can do as leaders is put people that want that type of workplace into an environment that fosters that kind of culture.

But I also think there are some people that might not want that—or it may not fit every situation. Some people just want to show up. They want to do good work. They want to know that the work has some meaning to it, but they may not feel the need to own the process. There are some types of work that fit well with these people. I don't think everybody needs to be a hard-charging change agent and an innovator, and if there are too many, is that a good thing?

I also think that some people at different levels of the organization—all the way from the top to the bottom—might not have that gear. They just don't have that gear to get to where they can do this. It doesn't really match every type of situation. I'm thinking in highly structured operational environments where the work is more standardized and procedures must be followed. It's just about getting things done.

In John Kotter's latest book, *Accelerate*,[2] he writes about organizations developing a type of dual operating system. One operating system is for "keep the lights on" type of work and executing the steady-state business, while the other operating system is for innovating new products and services, which requires a whole different culture. A lot of companies are trying to build in these dual operating systems that have a connection—one feeds the other, but it's a very hard thing to do with companies having the pressures they have today. It's becoming more and more a need, but trying to figure out how to make it happen is something fully different.

---

[2] Boston: Harvard Business Review Press, 2014.

Bill: What does it take to get an employee's full attention and best performance?

Bob: I think if you give people purpose and meaning in their work, so they're not just doing it to do it. It's especially important in work that's more operationally focused where meaning sometimes gets lost. However, people do want to know that their work has purpose, and it does have meaning—certainly to the people who benefit from their efforts.

Getting people immersed in a problem to solve is also important. This is especially true for people who do knowledge work. Give people the tools to do their work and basically get out of their way. If you're a manager or a leader, you can't be on top of these people. They need autonomy to be able to do their work.

I think some of the great ideas and products we come up with often come out of environments where there's scarcity and desperation. Look at where many good products have come from, for example, startups, crises, and postwar-type conditions where countries, individuals, and companies must reinvent themselves to build backup. You can't just give everybody everything they need. There's going to be some basic tools you want to provide and then let people sweat it out a little bit. There's some of that natural energy and open thinking that comes from scarcity. When everything has been destroyed, we are forced to rethink of what to do next instead of having to fit a change into some predefined pattern or model that's in our head that might be holding us back.

Getting people into an interesting problem-solving situation where they are challenged with some type of scarcity and they have to work as a team is what brings out the full capacity of people.

I know for myself, when I've been in those situations where you don't have anything and you want to solve a problem that you have passion for, that's where I did my best work. We all have much more to give and it really comes out in a crisis. That's where people really shine, using their brain power to get themselves out of that situation.

Bill: What do people really lack and long for at work?

Bob: I feel that people are missing a sense of family. It used to be if you went to work for a company, there was an informal agreement that you were going to take care of each other. You take care of the company, and the company will take care of you. Today, there's more career mobility, so people are moving around a lot more—a lot of job changes. Because of this mobility, companies are not as loyal as they used to be to employees. And in return, the employees are not really loyal to the companies.

I was thinking back to when I worked for GE Aerospace and GE was known as a highly collegial company where they would take care of you. We had t-shirts that said, "GE Is Me." You felt like when you wore that t-shirt, you were part of the GE family. They took care of me. They trained me. They gave me opportunities to work on complex problems. And in return, I gave them my best. Every time I did something, I said to myself, "I owe this back to the company." I felt like there was an informal contract between us, and I was part of something very special. Of course, that all changed when we got kicked out of the family by Neutron Jack Welch! But this was part of the deal. It was his informal contract that every GE business had had to be number one or number two in their industry sector, or that business unit would be shut down, moved, or sold—and that's what happened.

First, we became Martin Marietta then eventually merging with Lockheed to create Lockheed Martin. But it was interesting just to go through that transition from GE Aerospace to Martin Marietta. As soon as it happened, it felt like I just got kicked out of the family. There was a different feel to it; the sense of family was GE. I think that's missing in many companies today. Companies really rely on people to get into their work, solve problems, and make customers happy. They want that full commitment, but with all that mobility, how much of yourself do you want to give to a company that's not necessarily taking care of you and treating you just like a number? You know that it's going to end, so you have to build and manage your own career.

And, if somebody does want to change something in a company, can they find a way to really get that out and be heard? If they do, is it welcomed? Is the company open to hearing these people? Is the narrative, "Well, it's a great idea, but you're going to be leaving in three months, so why should we do that?" Maybe someone has a great improvement idea but doesn't want to say anything because of the fear of how others will react. Any good change idea will be challenged. How am I going to be treated since everyone is a short-timer? Is it going to be accepted or am I going to be ousted? I think that sense of belonging, that sense of family. I think that's what people are missing.

Bill: What is the most important question leaders should ask employees?

Bob: What I've always done is just walk around and talk to people and ask, "How are you doing?" Not how's that project coming or how's your task coming but really to ask how are you doing as a person? Is there anything you need to do your best work? Is there something you're missing to do the job the way you need to do it? Do you have any ideas about something we could improve?

As a manager and a leader, that's what I need to know. I want to find out from people which areas need to improve so that we can serve our customers better. Get their ideas and involve them in moving to action. "How can we do it? What do you see that we need to do?" I've seen too many companies where it's survey after survey after survey, but then fails to move to action.

I like to use this little acronym GSD—Get Shit Done! You already know 90% of what these people need to do their job. Just get it done. Stop asking. Sometimes you get tied up in the analytics of organizations. For example, we want to know what does employee engagement translate to in terms of revenue. Well, that's great, but if somebody is sitting there in a job and they don't have a tool they need, or they don't have access to a customer to get information or knowledge, that's not a question we should find out about from a survey. Managers should continuously work on getting people the things they need to do their job and remove any obstacles in their path.

Overall, managers must find out what their employees' state of being is and ask if they have the right people, processes, procedures, techniques, and tools to do it well. Then make sure you provide that environment where people can do their best work and get out of their way.

Bill: What is the most important question employees should ask leaders?

Bob: I think people are missing insight into how their organization is measured. Not so much in terms of operational metrics but more of the throughput. What is our organization's throughput measure? What do we do to track ourselves and our ability to satisfy the customer?

And at a lower level, if you dive into that and look at a specific group or a team, employees should be asking, "How does what we do contribute to that?" Employees need to know how their piece fits into the value that is delivered to the customer. It would also be a good idea for employees to ask their management, "What do you see as our biggest obstacle to our growth?"

Employees should be talking to their management and asking, "What do you see?"

Sometimes as an employee I know what I'm thinking about how things are going, but what does the manager think about the obstacles? Then ask them, "What's your plan to address it?" Many of the obstacles that people face are under the control of management, so ask them, "What are we going to do about this issue?" This is all to get management thinking about how we grow, and how do we measure that growth of what we're doing to produce value for the end user or customers?

It's tough at the middle-management level. There are requests and obstacles coming up from employees, and there's pressure to execute coming from the top. Most middle managers are just trying to survive and not rock the boat too much. But they know there are problems, and they do have the power to improve. They must have the courage to be better. If they're not willing to give their total effort there, the organization loses its capacity to serve the customer.

Bill: What is the most important question we should ask ourselves?

Bob: This is a question that I constantly ask myself, "Am I doing everything I can as a professional to improve my skills and contribute to the goals of the organization?" I'm putting it on myself to say, "Am I doing everything?" Am I complaining about things or proposing solutions?

Complaining is a regular practice for most people. It's a natural human response to a problem. But at some point, the complaining must stop. It doesn't solve the problem. It sometimes makes it worse. Maybe this is a better way to handle a problem at work, "OK, let's complain about the problem for a little bit and get it off our chest, but then let's figure out what we can do." I think it would be good for employees to ask themselves that question.

I also think on a regular basis it's good to check in on yourself by asking, "What have I learned and applied in the last month?" Give yourself an iterative way of growing to check yourself by first asking, "Am I learning things?" And secondly, "Am I learning just theory or am I learning by applying it?" That can help the organization get better, which should help me get better.

I think just constantly asking ourselves these questions transcends a particular job or a role you might have. It's just my value system that no matter who I'm working for or what I'm doing, I'm going to be the best that I can be when I'm there by continuing to learn and grow and give them what I've got.

Bill: Before we started the interview, you shared with me that you are enrolled in a doctorate program that I thought was very interesting. Can you share more information on your area of focus?

Bob: I'm always curious about the role that fear plays in organizations. What led me into my doctoral program is this constant question that keeps surfacing for me about why leaders fear changing things. Part of it is just basic human psychology. We're just so pattern based. We follow a pattern, we get paid (rewarded). It takes the stress off us. Changing how we do something, and usually if it's not going well that means major changes, can be a big risk. It takes courage to drive this. You can't be in a constant state of change either because it's too stressful, so there's something in between those two poles. In today's work environments, we need to be changing in numerous ways, constantly, to meet the needs of the market.

I do think where we get into these times where we need to change radically—whether it's personal or professional—how do we activate the part of us that is the change agent? We all have this change agent capability because in different situations, people will exhibit that and suppress the fear of what's going to happen. That's my area of interest I'm looking at. Not just the dynamics of it, but if a company really did want to have change agents and needed that to fuel an innovative practice or product development initiative, how do you free people up so they're not living in a sense of fear and start making decisions based on what's right vs. what's not going to get them fired? That's always an interesting discussion to have with people.

The program I'm taking is in the domain of Strategic Leadership. There's a lot of writing on change models and the different types of personalities that are required to lead change. But if you think about it, who is the person that's really going to put their neck on the line to drive a radical change? It's not just about their personality, it's about whether that person is willing to give up everything. Because ultimately in a radical change, you're most likely going to be out of that organization. It's going to happen because you choose that or the organization does.

In other words, people who are not comfortable with change might put up with it for a while, but then as soon as it reaches a new plateau (pattern), even though you want to push more, they don't want you to push more. When that happens, you're done. If you really think you want to do more, you might get frustrated and say, "I can't take it here anymore, and I have to go." I think this topic is interesting, and there's not a lot of writing that "Go" moment when you decide I'm going to sacrifice myself for everybody else.

Key Takeaways

- As leaders we can put people who want this type of workplace into an environment that fosters that kind of culture.

- Some people just want to show up and do good work. Not everyone needs to be a hard-charging change agent.

- Getting people immersed in a problem to solve is key to getting full attention and best performance.

- Many people do their best work when they are challenged with an interesting problem-solving situation and have to work together as a team.

- Do we have a sense of family and are we taking care of each other?

- How are people treated when they express an idea? Are they accepted?

- Walk around and talk to people and ask, "How are you doing?"

- Provide an environment where people can do their best work and get out of the way.

- What do we do to track ourselves and our ability to satisfy the customer?

- Employees should be talking to their management and asking, "What do you see? Am I doing everything?"

- Am I doing everything I can as a professional to improve my skills and contribute to the goals of the organization?

- Check in on yourself by asking, "What have I learned and applied in the last month?"

Steph Holloway

Body Language and Communication Expert

Compassionate Communication Is the Key to Everything

Steph Holloway is the founder of Elemental Potential and a body language and communication expert. She is also the creator of Compassionate Assertiveness in Action. Steph is on a journey to make compassionate assertiveness and body language a native language for the masses. She uses a unique communication approach as a catalyst for transformation in personal or corporate life. She holds a total commitment to uncovering the secrets to exceptional communication and believes it is her calling in life.

I connected with Steph Holloway after learning of her groundbreaking work on compassionate communications. We started a conversation and discovered each other's passion for making a difference and bringing change to the workplace and world. Steph is, in her words, "on a journey to make compassionate assertiveness and body language a native language for the masses."

Bill Fox: How can we create workplaces where every voice matters, people thrive and find meaning, and change and innovation happen naturally?

Steph Holloway: Of course, I love everything communication, so my answer is going to be through communication. It's always communication. Communication is the key to everything.

© Bill Fox 2020
B. Fox, *The Future of the Workplace*,
https://doi.org/10.1007/978-1-4842-5098-3_24

Where I'm coming from, I've worked with over 1000 businesses and 10,000 people since founding Elemental Potential. Everything I've learned from that has taught me that not only are human beings complex, but we all have our own little quirks, learned behaviors, and idiosyncrasies. But one thing I often say in my workshops is that intelligence, IQ score or how articulate people speak, doesn't actually mean that they're a good communicator.

Most companies I go into have some issue with communication, that's why I'm there. I often talk about the pure mechanics of communication. I see my aim as getting people back to basics. That's why I call my business "Elemental Potential."

What I see is that people often forget they've got a real human being on the other end. Or in the heat of the moment, they appear to throw fairness, reason, and all those other things out of the window.

The model for compassionate assertiveness I designed came about to answer some of these issues. I found whether I was presenting to parents, couples, organizations, or corporates, it was invariably about people feeling stifled and unheard—at home, in a relationship, or at work. I knew there had to be a simple way to form a bridge back to people when communication had broken down. A way to reintroduce communication that was more meaningful and effective and reprogram "toxic" behavior—both incoming and outgoing.

Bill: So how do we create workplaces where more voices matter?

Steph: For me, I encourage people to ask the right questions. Question one is always about self-analysis—flipping it back to people. "Is there a reason you're doing this...?" "Why do you think that?" "What would you do Bob/Julie?" How do we create workplaces where more voices matter? I think in some businesses people aren't used to being asked, they are used to being told. So, create an environment where people can ask the right questions.

Bill: How do we ensure people thrive and find meaning?

Steph: If you ask people how they want to work, not just tell them the outcome you need, that helps people thrive. I've only had a few jobs where I worked for somebody else, but one I remember went from a manager that was very good who let me run with things to a manager who micromanaged, which resulted in me leaving within 2 months. The minute I started to get micromanaged, I switched off completely.

So how do people thrive? Ask people how they want to work. Don't just tell them how you want them to work because some people like to work in very different ways.

Once I was interviewed by a man who asked me, "What would I need to do to ensure you are successful while working for me?" I thought it was a great question (still do) and answered, "You will need to leave me alone, trust me, and let me fly! Just know that I will never rip you off for time, money, or energy." He took me at my word and during his management, the company thrived.

Bill: Change and innovation?

Steph: I think it will just happen naturally where you leave an open channel for it to happen—from the top to the bottom of your business. Often it's not the people at the top who have the answer, it's someone somewhere else in the business. What I would say about change and innovation is just see everyone as important (because they are of course)—not just your high flyers. Quite often it's the people who are dealing with the aftereffects of what's not working who've got the answers.

Bill: What does it take to get an employee's full attention and best performance?

Steph: This is an easy one because I work with so many people. It's to feel recognized and valued as a person. Many people (including ones on this platform) have mentioned feeling valued as an employee. This is something different I am talking about—it's feeling valued as a person!

The reason I say that is because a lot of my work is going into toxic workplaces and trying to detoxify them. In an age where narcissism and toxic behavior are rife, the reality is that many of the people I come into contact with in my work have lived with, are living with, have someone in their life, or have a boss, manager, or someone else at work that communicates to them unreasonably or inappropriately.

To me, there is a really obvious answer to this question. Graciousness. Treat others as you would like to be treated. If you wouldn't treat someone like that in front of your kids or mother because you'd be embarrassed about it, then don't do it. What will people say about your communication style after you've gone?

Graciousness is at the heart of everything I do. It is the ultimate tool and benchmark for getting the absolute best out of people and their full attention.

We notice those people. We feel inspired by them, and it is a learned behavior—not everyone is born with it.

If there's a formula for graciousness, it might be to create time and space and stay present. People who "run" on busyness and think it's clever struggle to be gracious to people or stay present. Take the time to be fully present. Ask opinions. Include people and watch in wonder as the results unfold before you.

Bill: What do people really lack and long for at work?

Steph: The biggest thing that I feel that they lack is transparency. Many employees in the businesses I work with talk about lack of transparency being the number one problem they have with the management. Rumors take over instead of facts. The toxic people have a field day spreading malicious gossip, and management does nothing to stop it.

Of course, some things cannot be divulged to the workforce, but where many businesses fail in their communication is either no follow-through in communication or the knowledge is hoarded by one person and not filtered down. People then get frustrated and stop contributing all together knowing that whatever they say will never get actioned or heard or to the right person.

If ever I need proof that this is happening in a company, the first question I ask (an employee not a manager) is how are your meetings run? Does everything get done before the next meeting, or are they just carried forward in future minutes or forgotten?

Bill: What is the most important question leaders should ask employees?

Steph: What do you bring to the table that I don't know about?

 It is my profound belief that somewhere in your workforce is the answer to everything that you need to succeed beyond measure in your business.

But due to managers who knowledge hog, they keep the knowledge to themselves. Sometimes it's ineffective management that is top heavy, or sometimes it's management that never gets to know your team. Quite often for me, it's differing communication styles—there is a massive effect from this.

So often people feel undervalued, underutilized, and undermined. How frustrating to be sitting there with the solution and know that your boss—due to ego, dismissiveness, or lack of appreciation of your qualities and attributes—will never hear what you have to say.

Sometimes it's about busyness. Bosses will say to me, "Who has time to get to know everyone when I have 140 emails a day to deal with and pressure etc., etc.?" My reply is, "Who has the time not to?" Because you could be missing out on a lot of things if you don't ask them what they could bring to the table that you don't know about.

And by the way, busy isn't clever anymore. It probably means you are ineffective or defective in some way. Look into a leader or manager's inbox further and within a few minutes, you can note signs of control, micromanagement, and people below them who have gotten used to passing the questions uphill instead of sideways or down.

I hear this often from teams when I run a simple exercise called The Good, The Bad, and The Ugly. That's where everybody that's present in the room gets a chance to say what's the Good, what's the Bad, and what's the Ugly about working with that business. I find out by the end that many employees have "given up" trying to have a voice. They just do what they are told—even if they at heart know that it won't work. They just see it as "same old, same old."

Invariably by the next time I inquire into that business, if they haven't changed their ways or individuals haven't addressed their behavior, a few more of their best people have moved on. They've moved on to somewhere that gave them a voice and enquired about how they can help the business succeed.

Bill: What is the most important question employees should ask leaders?

Steph: Is there a reason we do it in that way? Sometimes even managers have inherited practices, processes, and procedures from other managers. That doesn't make them right or mean they are the best fit for the business.

I think sometimes people just go along with things. Then the day becomes really boring or mundane or stressful or frustrating just because they don't ask the question, "Is there a reason we do it that way?" I think some people just go along with the flow and turn up for work, take the paycheck, and never bother to ask.

Bill: What is the most important question we should ask ourselves?

Steph: If you're not true to yourself and live a life that you want across all aspects of your life, then what people get is a lesser version of you. As a result, **the most important question to ask yourself to me is, "Am I true to myself?"**

What I mean by that is, do I speak my truth? Do I ask for the truth? Do I encourage others to be a better person by how I communicate with them and the questions that I ask? If not, then what everyone else gets is a lesser version of you. They will never have your full potential... and who knows what that would mean?

If you see it (or hear it), you deal with it there and then—don't wait.

Part of Compassionate Assertiveness, my communication model, is based on a little mantra called, "See it, say it." I've got businesses that have been working with me for 3 or 4 years now, and it's transformed their business just by working with that saying. That means if you see it (or hear it), you deal with it there and then—don't wait. If you do wait and address it later, it often sounds like "blame and shame" by that time.

Bill: I've been enjoying reading your book, *Ping Pong: Compassionate Assertiveness in Action.*[1] **What is the book's core message?**

Steph: The core message about Compassionate Assertiveness in Action is that it's all about getting to the truth as quickly as possible—so regrets, recriminations, and resentment don't set in.

There are a few qualities you would need to have to call yourself compassionately assertive:

You would look for the win-win in situations rather than having to be the winner. Compassionately assertive people look for collaboration, inclusion, and cooperation; they check their ego at the door.

You would seek first to understand others, rather than be understood yourself first. So not just waiting for your turn to talk and subjecting others to your opinions and judgments—but staying present and really listening and observing.

You would talk in a low and slow tone, which aids conflict resolution and helps your body language to respond appropriately. When your tone of voice changes to aggressive/loud, your body language steps in to "help you out," and this means that your body language can become choppy, high, bigger, and can look oppressive.

If you "see it," you will "say it." Address issues and unacceptable behavior early; don't enable it so you have to carry on dealing with it.

Have courageous conversations which "corrective coach" unacceptable behavior. My model works on a simple premise of four stages—self-analysis, feelings, consequences, and choice/surrender.

Key Takeaways

- Create an environment where people can ask the right questions.
- Ask people how they want to work—don't just tell them.

---

[1] Steph Holloway, self-published, 2018.

- Leave an open channel for change and innovation to happen naturally.

- People want to feel recognized and valued as a person.

- Graciousness is the ultimate tool and benchmark for getting the absolute best out of people.

- The biggest thing people lack is transparency.

- People get frustrated and stop contributing when knowing whatever they say won't get actioned or heard.

- What do you bring to the table I don't know about?

- Many people are frustrated because they have the solution but aren't asked.

- Is there a reason we do it that way?

- Am I true to myself?

- It's all about getting to the truth as quickly as possible.

- Be compassionately assertive by looking for the win-win in situations rather than having to be the winner.

Nick Hughes

Founder, Founders Live

How to Incorporate Purpose and Values to Build a Thriving Community

Nick is the creator of Founders Live with business achievements in social media, digital payments, and e-commerce. Besides creating the global entrepreneur network Founders Live, Nick stays busy as an advisor to many startups. Previously he founded the mobile payment startup Seconds and helped start Coinme, a company built around expanding bitcoin and digital transactions into the physical realm via Bitcoin ATMs. As a sought-after advisor, entrepreneurial speaker, and writer with guest appearances on popular technology and media outlets, Nick enjoys helping others discover their unique entrepreneurial path.

As I looked for ways to build a community for people attracted to the ideas and work of Forward-Thinking Workplaces, I looked for others who were building successful communities. My search led me to Founders Live where I found a vibrant, growing, and engaged community. Nick has built a global community with over 10,000 members in 2 years. Founders Live provides a great example of the results we can achieve when purpose and values are incorporated in ways that influence how people communicate and treat each other.

© Bill Fox 2020

B. Fox, *The Future of the Workplace,*

https://doi.org/10.1007/978-1-4842-5098-3_25

Bill Fox: How can we create workplaces where every voice matters, everyone thrives and finds meaning, and change and innovation happen naturally?

Nick Hughes: It starts from valuing transparency and communication within the organization. If you think about the basis of your question, it's frankly around, do people feel their voice matters? That definitely comes from the leadership that institutes values that are baked into what it means to be an employee of that organization.

It shouldn't matter what level people are in the organization. People should feel that their voice matters.

It also revolves around the DNA of the organization. From leadership down, what it means to be a member of that organization? How does their voice matter and are they heard? I think communication and the methods of communication implemented throughout the organization are very important.

For example, weekly touchpoint and all-hands meetings. Even large tech companies still do town hall or all-hands meetings that may be viewed or listened to virtually. But people are gathering where the CEO and/or leaders are open to addressing and answering questions in a very honest, open, and authentic way. Those are just some examples of how you can bake those types of experiences into the organization providing a mechanism to recognize voices.

What's interesting is when having an open idea forum fosters innovation within the organization. Let's say a junior employee brings ideas to the table that end up being implemented and become a revenue-generating new feature or product. If we recognize them as the original idea generator for this new feature that now publicly known, then recognizing people for something like that goes a long way in having voices heard.

Bill: What does it take to get an employee's full attention and best performance?

Nick: It's funny you ask that question because if you think about the scenario I described, which is when people have new ideas and bring an idea to the table, the worst thing is to have the leadership or others take that idea and get credit for it.

Giving credit to individuals openly and publicly makes them feel like they're having an impact and their voice matters.

Public recognition goes a long way. When people see others recognized based on their production or their great quality of work, it inspires others to do the same thing. Public recognition for the betterment of the company is what I've experienced as a very strong indicator of getting the most out of your employees.

Leadership is a lot about human psychology. When you get into human psychology and thinking about what is inspirational and gets the best out of people, a lot of that is intrinsic. You need to understand psychologically what do they desire? Often people desire public recognition and status. If someone does something great, you publicly acknowledge it and attribute it to them. That reinforces the positive activity vs. not recognizing it. Letting a great quality action go unrecognized is a lost opportunity to reinforce activities and habits of your employees. Baking into the company the habits of leadership that recognizes quality work and celebrates these individuals inspires them to continue to do more of that activity.

Bill: What do people really lack and long for at work?

Nick: There are many things but probably it comes down to purpose and impact. If people are longing for something or have a sense of a lacking in their company, it's what's my purpose here? Why is my work impactful and meaningful in the world? If you feel you're doing meaningful work improving people's lives, whether that's through technology or through social impact, or quality of life living whatever the case may be, then that's what I've noticed with many people. They want to know what they're doing and how it's a part of this larger entity. Where does it actually make an impact? The more granular you can make it, the better.

We see larger technology companies that do stories profiling customers using their products or services. An engineer sitting in Seattle, Washington, or New York or whatever sees that their work is impacting a human being possibly on the other side of the world. That seems to tie things together to help make sense of the impact they're making and the meaningfulness.

You get up every day and go to work, but your job and your efforts are actually meaningful and impacting people. I think that's what they desire.

If I'm doing this every day, it needs to make sense, have an impact, and matter. Human beings want to do things that matter and impact other human beings. You're doing good work if you can tie those together.

Bill: What is the most important question leaders should ask employees?

Nick: The most important question is, how can I empower you? How can I help you? If leaders can ask, how can I help you be more successful? That's a great question. Leadership is there literally to impact someone's life positively and help them be more successful because if we can do that, then we are more successful. That's how the pieces fit together in the right way. As a leader, you are helping others achieve their goals and be more successful. That's what you need to do. Help those individuals achieve their goals rather than, "You're here to serve me and make me better." No, that's not the right way for leadership.

If a leader can ask the employee, how can I best serve you and help you be successful, then the equation is better. It works better because if that employee is more successful then that leader will be successful.

Bill: What is the most important question employees should ask leaders?

Nick: How can I help you? Not only how can I help you, but what are your expectations of me? As an employee looking toward your leadership, you need to know what's expected. Second, how am I being evaluated? And third, what is success?

If you can ask those questions and get clear answers, you're going to at least know the path ahead and how you will be judged or evaluated to determine if you're being successful in your position. It's unfortunate—and it happens more often than I think we know—that an individual doesn't know what's expected of them and/or how they're being evaluated. How are you supposed to go about your job and do a good job when you don't even know what the criteria are? It would make most sense to ask the questions of what's expected of me? What does success look like? How am I being evaluated? How do we get there? Those are good questions to ask your leadership.

Bill: What is the most important question we should ask ourselves?

Nick: The most important question we should ask ourselves is, is this the right path? What path am I on? What impact am I trying to make? I think all these questions fall into the category of, am I driving toward my purpose? What is my purpose and how can I continually manifest that and make a positive impact?

Just to make this more personal, I am the CEO and founder of Founders Live. We are a global platform for entrepreneurship. We inspire, educate, and entertain entrepreneurs globally. I recently started on a year-long world tour to be on the road to visit local Founders Live groups around the world. We have events in 30 cities globally and we're growing. I had to ask myself, where am I at on this path? What do I need to improve? What steps do I need to take to get further into this vision?

I needed to go on the road and to go to these communities and cities. We are in eight countries right now and that's growing. That's what I did. So I think constantly asking ourselves, what's the vision? What's the purpose? Where am I at in the journey and how can I improve that? That changes on a monthly and yearly basis. So that's a question that we should always ask of ourselves, what feels right at this moment? What do I need to move forward with and what risks do I need to take to make that happen?

For me personally, I'm now on the road for the entire year of 2019, maybe longer to go to these communities globally to meet our team. Work with our team to be a part of the event and to grow the mission of entrepreneurship and Founders Live around the world. So that's me asking that question, and I'm now on the road.

Bill: In the past 2 years, you've created a global community for entrepreneurs that has attracted over 10,000 members and a network of over 40 local groups worldwide. What is it about Founders Live that has allowed it to flourish when so many other entrepreneurial groups exist already?

Nick: Founders Live is a community that is both an online Internet community and a local event. It's also a global system and platform for entrepreneurship. What seem to be attractive are our core values and the things we baked into it that make it meaningful. So you're right, there are many startup entrepreneurial communities, but I don't see many that so openly speak about their core values. I don't even see they have them.

The first core value is about respectful authenticity, embracing the uniqueness of everyone, and including people of all genders, races, and background.

The first core value is respectful authenticity. In actuality, it's really about inclusion and respecting each person as an individual. Not only are you there as your authentic self but you also respect everyone else. This is also about inclusion and accepting all people because entrepreneurship is about everyone. It doesn't look like a certain skin color or gender. Unfortunately, many communities don't act that way. Our first core value is about respectful authenticity, embracing the uniqueness of everyone, and including people of all genders, races, and background. That's why people are very much interested in Founders Live. It's our core number one value.

The second core value is storytelling. As an entrepreneur, you need to craft a compelling story about what you're building or creating. What problem are you solving? What's your solution? What product are you bringing to the market? Why is it important? Crafting a story that inspires people to follow you and use your product—that's hugely important. Successful companies have figured out a way to market and tell a story that brings people together. Storytelling is our second core value. It's about how to embrace storytelling in a unique way.

The third value is open the door. That's about doing great things for people without expecting a return. It's about helping others without expecting to get paid because it will come back to you. When you help someone else, it will come back to you in an unexpected way. It's that energetic yin and yang. You're in a great community when people do that for each other.

The last core value is what we call no name tags. It's an analogy for how we strive to create a fun, enjoyable atmosphere without the awkwardness. If you've been to any business networking events, they can be awkward. We've placed a value on keeping things fun and fresh, recognizing there are certain things you include in an event that keep them loose and enjoyable.

People find Founders Live attractive because there's a purpose behind it. What I've learned is that building a community is putting meaningfulness and purpose behind it. With the right core values, you attract the right people and you probably repel some people. It makes sense.

Bill: In an interview here,[1] Jon Mertz introduced the idea of workplaces as communities. As the founder of a successful worldwide community, how does that idea translate into the workplace from your point of view?

Nick: As Founders Live internal organization and operating team grow, we'll bring a lot of that thinking into our organization. I believe what he's saying is that the basis of community is the commonality of values that people either outwardly or inwardly accept. Communities can be identified by their values.

When you look at your workplace, incorporate your purpose and values in the way that a community communicates and in the way people treat each other.

If you go the opposite direction and proclaim these are our rules, it's a very stern environment. A community is more about shared values, communication, and openness. How does the leadership relate toward everyone else? What's the communication style? How are we respecting everyone? How is our voice valued? That's all community based.

---

[1] Chapter 27.

Key Takeaways

- People should feel that their voice matters no matter what level people are in the organization.

- The way and methods of communication are very important in how voices matter and are heard.

- Giving credit to individuals openly and publicly makes them feel like they're having an impact and their voice matters.

- Letting a great quality action go unrecognized is a lost opportunity to reinforce activities and habits of your employees.

- What people really desire is that their job and efforts are actually meaningful and impacting people.

- It happens more often than we know—that an individual doesn't know what's expected of them and/or how they're being evaluated.

- What path am I on and is this the right path?

- Having and openly speaking about core values is very important.

- When you look at your workplace, incorporate your purpose and values in the way that a community communicates and in the way people treat each other.

Aviv Shahar

Founder, Aviv Consulting

How to Elevate Yourself, Your Conversations, and Your Future

Aviv Shahar is the founder of Aviv Consulting and helps leaders create new futures by unleashing strategic innovation. He is also the author of *Create New Futures: How Leaders Produce Breakthroughs and Transform the World Through Conversation.*[1]

I read Aviv's book to prepare for this interview, and the depth and coverage on conversations were impressive. When I started this interview series, I had this idea to ask a series of questions that could help us create a better workplace, but I didn't fully appreciate the powerful role of conversations. One big learning I've had from my work is the power of conversations. Several executives and CEOs who I interviewed have gotten back to me after they were observing what I was doing and said we need to have this conversation in the workplace. There's a wonderful convergence between Aviv's work and the Forward-Thinking Workplaces 2.0 conversation.

[1] Kora Press, 2016.

© Bill Fox 2020
B. Fox, *The Future of the Workplace*,
https://doi.org/10.1007/978-1-4842-5098-3_26

Bill Fox: How can we create workplaces where every voice matters, everyone thrives and finds meaning, and change and innovation happen naturally?

Aviv Shahar: Let me for a second or two just turn the tables around and ask you first back because I know this is the core of the first question you ask to people you've interviewed.

It is important to ask you, what was the genesis of this question in you? What was the trigger that catalyzed it? And then I can try to thread my way through this compound question.

Bill: That's a great question and I love starting with your question. I'll try not to go back too far because there are a number of places to start, but really it started 10 years ago when I was leading a transformation project. For the third time in my career after getting a transformation project to a great point of success, new executives take over and all the work that was done just falls away. So that's when I set an intention to have an impact on how organizations transform.

I left that job without a job in hand, and my intention seemed to set synchronicity in motion. One of the first things I came up with was an interview series called *5 Minutes to Process Improvement Success.* The leading question was, "What is your best Improvement strategy that has worked really well for you?"

From the beginning, I rarely got an answer about process improvement. It was always something deeper. It was all about trust, understanding the status quo, and things of that nature. It was surprising to me (and others), and that ignited an inner leader journey for me as I started to look at the deeper side of things.

After I did 50 interviews, I felt this was never about process improvement, and it was silly to go on in this direction. I set it aside to see if something new would show up. A year and a half later, these new questions came together.

Aviv: I'm glad I asked you. Would you mind restating the question one more time? Then let's see how I can best approach this delicious inquiry.

Bill: How can we create workplaces where every voice matters, everyone thrives and finds meaning, and change and innovation happen naturally?

Aviv: My experience and sense with powerful questions like this, in the context of the background you offered, is that they often emerge from a place of want and lack.

Therefore, such questions often are not optimally conducive or attractive to bringing forward the intelligence and the energy we hope will help us redress and sufficiently address the want. I prefer to reframe your question just slightly to help me find a different entry, one that can provide for both of us an elevated access. Here is how I will reframe the question.

I would say:

> Imagine a workplace where every voice matters, everyone thrives and finds meaning, and change and innovation happen naturally. Imagine such a workplace. Now tell us please what had to become true to enable such an emergence.

It's the same question just restated, and this is a formulation that provides a faster entry and a life-affirming path because it is anchored in the desired state rather than in its absence which is a place of want and scarcity.

Two Short Answers and One Longer Answer

To now attempt to respond to that question, I'll say there are two short answers I can offer and one longer answer. The first short answer is interior focused, so when I imagine a workplace where every voice matters and where people thrive and find meaning and change and innovation happen naturally, I imagine a place where we have made a leap forward. A place where we've evolved as people.

Actually, we've evolved as a species where sapient sapiens is not merely a name but an actuality.

That's the short inner or interior answer. Now we can then talk about what had to become true to enable that outcome and that would naturally lead us to the longer answer.

The second brief answer is more exterior, outward focusing. Here again, the short version is that when I imagine a workplace where people thrive, and where they find meaning, and where change and innovation happen naturally, and where the reciprocity of work and its benefits bring the replenishment and the enhancement to all people involved.

I can envision a place where the entire socioeconomic framework and the capital system were transformed.

This is a future enabled by a transformational shift from the short-term extractive bias that governs many companies and organizations today to a more sustainable and even life-giving seven generations forward orientation. That's the second and the more exterior leaning framing of the answer.

The third longer answer, which will build on those two, is that when I imagine a naturally arising and evolving workplace where people thrive by bringing forward the best ideas and best contribution and where the economic framework is aligned to help facilitate and bring forward the organizational and social equities that people want to cultivate and build, and is aligned with the entire ecosystem emergent purpose and health—when I imagine that kind of ecosystem, I envision that we have overcome at least seven blockages. You can call them seven evolutionary or developmental blockages or stop situations.

The first is the **leadership blockage** or stop situation. In this future space we are together envisioning, I imagine that we now have enlightened and illumined leaders. Obviously, we can talk about what's the journey that will facilitate that, but that's the number one stop situation and blockage that we have broken through to realize a transformative future.

The second is the **human development blockage** or stop situation. When I imagine that we are breaking through that one, I envision employees who engage with work as a development opportunity and in a way that enables them to transcend and embrace higher levels and higher stages of development, of creativity, of innovation, and of expression. So that's the second breakthrough in terms of human development.

The third breakthrough is one where we can transform the **winner/losers' impediment blockage**. Instead of the equation that for every winner, there must be many losers in the now especially potentized and aggrandized winner-takes-all scenario, we can envision a socioeconomic algorithm and paradigm that enables somewhat a rewired dynamic of companies and the marketplace. One that enables many winners and where a new paradigm has been established. One that facilitates and rewards the creative and generative capacities and capabilities in people even much more so than today.

Then I imagine in the fourth place that to enable these breakthroughs, there had to have been some kind of new **energy source breakthrough** where we shifted from an extractive paradigm to a multisource sustainable and generative sources and resources. I'm talking about some technologies that are coming online and other technologies and capabilities that I imagine, and I believe will come online in the next decade or two.

In the fifth place, I imagine that to propagate these and all we talked about so far, that the entire market machinery and its **incentive structures** are being rewired to enable a system-wide realignment and repositioning of the organizations that thrive in this newly realigned system.

And sixth, that what happens then is that as those utopian transformations proliferate, that then the third blood system—**the blood system of distrust and suspicion**—is replaced. Because that's what's flowing and motivating and powering today many people in the workplace and in business. And I imagine a marketplace where distrust and suspicion were absolved and replaced with a currency of trust and cocreation.

Finally, I'd say in the seventh place that this entire utopian future I'm describing is enabling (supported by a series of breakthroughs) an **evolution in consciousness** where enlightenment and illumination are the bread and butter of everyday living. It's no longer the property of a secluded elite that has embarked on that specialized journey.

So in summation, I'd say this is obviously an audacious utopian future, but remember that utopian visions often get realized and actualized a century later. Perhaps on this occasion we will not have to wait for a hundred years.

So I'll offer these as a three-layered response to the question.

Bill: Thank you for that comprehensive, insightful response, Aviv. That's a lot to consider and think about. I'll just briefly comment on a couple things. First, I really appreciate the way you rephrased the question and where that takes the conversation.

Then you talked about the changes to our inner selves. That's really the story underneath me doing this work. When I began to uncover what was underneath from my conversations with leaders, I realized that I was creating the conditions where I was open, and they felt comfortable speaking whatever was on their mind. The experience was changing me from the inside out. It changed my state of being. It changed my consciousness, and that's a journey that continues, but I see that's so important in bringing about this transformation.

Aviv: That's awesome. Essentially, you are validating what I've offered in my response.

Bill: Yes, absolutely! There's more I could validate from your response, but we probably should take that up at another time.

Bill: What does it take to get an employee's full attention and best performance?

Aviv: My experience with this very important question is that nothing energizes and liberates people more than the opportunity to shape and create their own future. That's why this is the central element of my work.

Nothing energizes and liberates people more than the opportunity to shape and create their own future.

I believe that what leaders and companies must do is get people involved in cocreating and shaping their futures. By that I mean the future of the organization, the future of the business, the future of the department, and the future of the function. By doing so, they will gain their full attention, best performance, and greatest contribution.

I believe it so strongly that I have created a whole thriving practice around that belief and core tenet. In my work with senior teams in Fortune 100 companies, we find that to create and unleash an organizational movement, you must bring people into that kind of conversation. That's how I will offer you to think about the conundrum of creating and facilitating fuller engagement and unleashing the fullest creativity of your people.

Bill: What do people really lack and long for at work?

Aviv: I believe there are two aspects to this. There are the interior and the exterior dimensions to consider. Whether people know it or not, they long for self-insight and for getting themselves back.

When you get yourself back, that's a big part of perhaps what you're looking for. Because inside it, you get to appreciate the human condition and your own conditioning too.

And these insights lead to finding your strength and appreciating that inside your strength, there also may be a weakness.

And also that inside your weakness, there may be a latent strength. As you know, there are many dyslexic people who are brilliant and found ways to lead and transform to bring tremendous innovation into a variety of spaces. It's just one example of the transformative power of self-insight and how understanding your superpower, including appreciating how inside your weakness there may be a latent strength, can be a game changer. These are mission-critical insights if you are to manifest your gifts and talent to bring forward your greatest contribution.

I think also that people long for a variety of other properties or qualities or energies if you like. We all need and seek connectedness. We all seek and/or need respect, dignity, and opportunity. Human beings need to be seen and recognized. We hope to be given the opportunity to influence and shape our destiny.

All those are naturally arising longings in human beings.

When core human needs are met at work, they unleash incredible power, creativity, and resourcefulness.

This naturally would include the opportunity to contribute to a meaningful purpose. One that affords us the feeling we are serving and are part of something even bigger than ourselves.

Cocreating your own future and contributing to a greater cause and a novel purpose are truly the biggest creativity and innovation release factors. The sense that we are serving a purpose and a mission we can identify with and that we can believe in. And that through that mission, purpose, and contribution, we get to express our talent and capabilities. That I believe is what people long for at work.

Bill: Your response spoke to me in several ways. The whole idea of self-insight and doing the work I am doing is based on operating from a level of intention and having a more meaningful impact. It really allows you to harvest who you are and the creative part of you. I think the other fascinating thing for me has been how that connects you to everything where ideas and people come from somewhere else. The right people show up. The right ideas show up. You become a vortex or focal point for that conversation and those ideas to unfold.

Bill: What is the most important question leaders should ask employees?

Aviv: I'd encourage leaders to ask their employees, what will help you create your biggest contribution?

And perhaps in broader framing, I'd offer they ask:

> "Imagine a day at work when you feel energized and excited about what we are doing here and about your contribution. Describe what you're doing. Specifically, what enables you to perform so well at such a high level?"

That's the question I'd encourage leaders to ask their teams.

Bill: What is the most important question employees should ask leaders?

Aviv: I'd encourage employees to ask their managers, leaders, and senior management the following question:

"Describe to us please, the most inclusive and most energizing future you imagine for our organization? What are we doing differently in this future? What new outcomes will we create? How are we showing up in the world differently?"

Bill: What is the most important question we should ask ourselves?

Aviv: The central inquiry of my life since I was a teenager all the way to age 60 next week has been the question of purpose.

"Why are we here on Earth? What purpose are we here to serve individually and collectively? What do we hope future generations will say about us and about the contribution we worked hard to leave behind?"

Bill: You've written the book *Create New Futures: How Leaders Produce Breakthroughs and Transform the World Through Conversation*. What prompted you to write the book?

It's probably a combination of three impulses. The first is the natural desire and need to share and transfer to others the work that I do and what enables me to produce the outcomes I help leaders and teams create. That sense of wanting to give back and offer the experience of my development journey. That's the first impulse.

The second is the observation that a group of smart people, when they come around the table, will often produce collective stupidity instead of collective wisdom. I attempted in the book to help teams transcend the collective stupidity syndrome to instead produce collective wisdom through the techniques, processes, insights, and questions I describe. There is something disconcerting, depressing, and upsetting when brilliant people can only produce suboptimal outcomes instead of the multiplication of their natural brilliance. Addressing that need is the second impulse.

The third is the game-changing realization insight that conversation is the currency of work. It's also the currency of leadership. We lead and transform our environments and organizations through conversation.

Conversation is the core mechanism to enable and facilitate change, transformation, and the evolution of an organization on the path to enabling and creating a whole new future.

Bill: In your book, you say...

"Conversations are game-changers. Through conversations, we transform ourselves, those around us, and our environments. Ultimately conversations allow us to shape possibilities, choose the best future imaginable, and make it a reality."

Is there a story you can share that brought you to that understanding?

Aviv: First, let me say it is curious and validating that of everything in the book, you have chosen this one quote because if you said "What is the one takeaway I hope people will take from *Creating New Futures*," then it would be exactly that.

Conversations are that kind of a game changer, and through conversation, we can transform ourselves and the world around us. Thank you for sharing that.

The story or perhaps where this begins for me, the first defining moment was during the 1973 war in Israel. I was a 14-year-old in the Kibbutz where I was growing up. At the time, my father was serving as the Secretary General of the Kibbutz. Every evening he convened gatherings to facilitate conversations to help people process the shock, grief, anxiety, and fear because for a few days the survival of Israel was hanging in the balance. What I observed was that through dialogue, you could convert despair into hope, fear into encouragement and confidence, and pain could be transformed into bonded conviction in a better future.

I recognized, even if not fully consciously but over time, that this was the function and the job of a leader: to unleash possibilities. To help people discover how they can bring forward their best contributions. I realized that you did those things as a leader through conversation and through the facilitation of transformative inquiry. Little did I know back then that this would be defining and setting in motion the direction and work I will be doing many years later. Today that's what I am doing with leadership teams.

People tell me that when they're with me in the room, they're able to listen to each other differently. Through those dialogues, they ask each other new questions, and these conversations enable and help them see challenges through new lenses to unleash innovative ideas. As a result, they are able to come together in days to reach agreements and decisions that otherwise would take 3 or 6 months or more likely never be reached.

As part of that process, I help teams identify the difference between displaced and efficacious conversations, which is something I explain and go into in *Create New Futures*. The point is to create effective and efficacious conversations, conversations that mobilize movement and action. Displaced conversations do not address a need. As a result, they are often captured by complaints and blame. I offer that complaint is a misdirected energy of an unaddressed and unmet need. Blame is the externalization and projection of the complaint. These are discussions that are two steps removed from the point of efficacy, where we meet a need in a transformative and innovative way.

Efficacious conversation is one that leads to requests and proposals and ultimately to agreements on how to address the need. They enable us to unleash positive movement and action. That's the story I will offer on the defining genesis of conversation as the game changer that facilitates transformation.

Key Takeaways

- If we reframe our questions so that they are anchored in a desired state rather than in a place of want and scarcity, we can bring forward the intelligence and energy to address the want.

- Nothing energizes and liberates people more than the opportunity to shape and create their own future.

- People long for self-insight and for getting themselves back, which can bring you to a place of appreciating the human condition and your own conditioning.

- When we are given the opportunity to influence and shape our destiny, it unleashes incredible power, creativity, and resourcefulness.

- Imagine a day at work when you feel energized and excited about what we are doing here and about your contribution. Describe what you're doing.

- Describe to us please, the most inclusive and most energizing future you imagine for our organization. What are we doing differently in this future?

- Why are we here on Earth? What purpose are we here to serve individually and collectively?

- We lead and transform our environments and organizations through conversation.

Jon Mertz

CEO, Activate World

How to Lead More Holistically by Learning the Secrets of the Aspens

Jon Mertz is the CEO of Activate World, a modern think tank that explores CEO and business leader activism through a podcast and articles while bringing together the best of business with the best of society. Jon is one of the Top 100 Thought Leaders in Trustworthy Business and highlighted as a Leader to Watch by the American Management Association. He also is the author of *Activate Leadership: Aspen Truths to Empower Millennial Leaders.*[1]

I got to know Jon through the Lead Change Group where we have both engaged in contributing articles. Jon was a highly regarded contributor to this community, and he always impressed me with the quality of his writing and ideas. Recently, I reconnected with Jon after reading his article "Personal Branding is Over. Start Anew with a Societal Brand."[2] What was interesting in Jon's article was that Forward-Thinking Workplaces embodies many of the same practices and values that Jon writes about in his article.

---

[1] Self-published, 2015.
[2] www.thindifference.com/2018/06/personal-branding-start-societal-brand/

© Bill Fox 2020
B. Fox, *The Future of the Workplace*,
https://doi.org/10.1007/978-1-4842-5098-3_27

Bill Fox: How can we create workplaces where every voice matters, everyone thrives and finds meaning, and change and innovation happen naturally?

Jon Mertz: That's a great question and a question that many leaders need to think through a little more clearly and thoroughly. I believe the first place to start is to think of the workplace as a community. In our communities, we have life and work that happens. We need to get to know our neighbors, and we need to help out when needed. Communities have threats but in general they are places where people feel like they can be themselves. They can challenge others. They can challenge themselves, and they can contribute and share and learn as part of that community.

It's a subtle mind shift, but we think of workplaces as being more cubicle or office oriented, which are staler and more sterile.

If we think of our workplaces as a community, our mindset begins to shift.

Not only as people working there but as leaders. We start treating people a little differently, and we collaborate a little more closely in the work that we do. Through that we'll get better results and more innovative solutions as well.

Bill: What does it take to get an employee's full attention and best performance?

Jon: I've been thinking a lot about that in a number of ways more recently. I've been involved in a doctorate program in interdisciplinary leadership. Right now, the class is on strategic management and the whole idea of how you encourage strategic thinking. I think it's fascinating. It plays directly to an answer to this question as far as how you get employees more attentive and higher performing.

I think the way you do that is by how you encourage strategic thinking within your organization. There's an interesting book that came out a couple years ago called *WorldMaking: The Art and Science of American Diplomacy* by David Milne.[3] It was a fascinating read because it showed how different generations worked between each other and how they offered ideas to build a better world together.

Some characters in the book were not big names as far as people that we may know, but yet they did very creative and innovative work to try to make the world a better place. Part of that was through encouraging strategic thinking within the organization.

---

[3] New York: Farrar, Straus and Giroux, 2015.

We need to be centered a little more on the process of how people think.

If we want to get the best out of our teams in our organization, it goes to how are we really encouraging people to think differently. Or how to think about how they are approaching certain challenges and solutions. Questioning some of that thinking because out of that we'll get better thoughts, plans, and results.

Bill: What are people really lacking and longing for at work?

Jon: I believe it's that sense of belonging. Everyone is unique, and we can't try to make everyone the same. That would not be a good thing. So how do we give people an opportunity to have that sense of belonging within our workplace? What is the sense of purpose within that organization? Not just at the high level but even at the project level. Why are we doing this work? How does it relate to the higher goal, mission, or purpose of the organization or team?

When we get that right as far as ensuring that we are doing things that are more purpose centered rather than self-centered, and we figure out how to give people that sense of belonging with an organization, then I think it's an opportunity for them to bring their best self to work. They'll also collaborate more productively and fully with others in that team.

It goes back to the question of shifting the mindset from workplace to community. Within a community, we need to deliver that sense of belonging, or provide that opportunity to achieve that sense of belonging, and through that we will get much better mindsets and better work within our communities. I think you fall into becoming parts of actions rather than an overall sense of belonging within the overall organization and the mission of the organization or the team. If we can provide a culture that has a better sense of belonging that will eliminate more of those factions and have better collaborative work.

Bill: What is the most important question leaders should ask employees?

Jon: It goes back to the idea of strategic thinking. I think the most important question is, what are you thinking? Part of that goes to what's on your mind, which could relate to the organization or the plans or the results that the organization is experiencing at that point in time. But I think a corollary question to that too is, why do you think that way?

When we start to dig into why we're thinking about certain things in a certain way, we start to discover biases in our thinking as well as the mindset that we have or some of the logic that may or may not make sense. It just provides for a much more open conversation when we focus on the thought process rather than the end result. By focusing on how we're thinking, we'll get better plans and results through that process.

Bill: What is the most important question employees should ask leaders?

Jon: This question has been on my mind for the last year, so my response is really related to that. As the generational shift continues within the workplace, it's going to become more important. The question is this, what is the role of our business in society?

You could say that it relates directly to the business, but you could say it doesn't relate to the business. But each organization plays a role within the society. The answer can be very straightforward that we create jobs. We grow by doing that, and we provide a tax base and revenue back to our communities. That's the role of our business.

But I believe that, especially with millennials and Generation Z after them, they are looking for not only that, but I also think they're looking for a more balanced approach to how business operates within society. We're seeing a lot of that shift begin to happen from moving away from focusing solely on maximizing shareholder value to looking at a broader stake of stakeholders. With Conscious Capitalism and B corporations, we're seeing more of that influence of business as a force for good.

I think the question team members should be asking is, what is the role of our business in our society?

Bill: What is the most important question we should be asking ourselves?

Jon: For me, it goes back to thinking. I think the question is, why do I think that way? It goes to mindset and purpose. It's understanding, why do I think that way? What is the underlying causes of that or mindset, or information, or whatever the case may be?

Asking these questions opens myself up to challenging my thinking a little more. It opens me to greater self-awareness of why I am thinking that way. It goes to not getting stuck. Too often even our thought processes get stuck in a certain gear. We tackle everything in the same way or we don't change our way of thinking about how to approach a problem—or how to solve the situation. So, we get stuck. We become more dogmatic in our approach, which in my opinion is never a good thing.

I think we need to think through our experiences and through those figure out how we can better adapt and grow in how we approach things. How we think about things and challenge ourselves to rise up to not only deeper thinking but better thinking as we move forward.

Bill: You've written a book called *Activating Leadership: Aspen Truths to Empower Millennial Leadership*. Why did you write it?

Jon: It came out of an interesting intersection point between work and life. Writing was part of my life, and at work, I was starting to interview new college graduates to hire. This was the millennial generation coming in. I'd seen and read all the negative stereotypes about millennials, and at least in my experience both through the interviews and working with them, it didn't match up. Not only that, I didn't think it was a good thing to be so negative about a developing generation. That was part of it, and then second, I was doing a lot more writing around different leadership topics. This all weighed on my mind as far as why leaders would be doing this. Or why others would be putting on a new generation these negative stereotypes.

As with many things when you go out to nature, you learn more than you expect. It's an opportunity to clear your mind but also an opportunity to have different ideas begin to coalesce around a moment. Why I wrote the book is that moment came among the Aspen trees where how to continue to empower the next generation and lead in a more purposeful way sprung from being among the Aspens.

Bill: What did you learn from the Aspen trees?

Jon: I'm not a skier, and so I was out with my family on spring break. They were skiing, so I decided to go snowshoeing. I went to rent snowshoes and my plan was just to go out of my own, but when I rented them, the person there said that that probably would not be a good idea. There were some avalanches that had happened in the area recently. It would be better to go out with a guide. I didn't want to do it, but I ended up going with the guide.

As with most things, sometimes the unexpected happens. If I hadn't gone with my guide, I wouldn't have learned about the wonder of Aspens as much as I did. The wonder of Aspens is that there are just so many elements that are amazing about these trees. For one, you'll never see just one single Aspen tree. There're always multiple trees within a grove. That's because underneath it, they're all connected through a root system, and through that root system, they share nutrients to the different trees that need it at the different times.

Another amazing thing about Aspen trees is that they can remain dormant for many years. Underneath the ground, you may not know it, but there's still an alive root system. Then at some point in time, it could be decades later, all of a sudden growth will spring from that root system again. Aspens also help others. Their bark is a salve for animals with an aspirin-like quality or even a kind of sunscreen for humans. The way their leaves are designed to flutter in the wind allows them to absorb more sunlight and grow in more diverse places than other trees.

Within those Aspens, it became evident to me that a lot of the lessons within that applied to this next generation of leaders. Or any leader as really how do we build that sense of community? How do we collaborate with each other? How do we help others? How do we keep that sense of purpose? And then also, how do we convert what we absorb into more action or better thoughts or whatever the case may be? How do we convert what we do to produce better work? The Aspens in my opinion provide wonderful lessons to leaders and more particular very aligned to millennials coming into the workplace.

Bill: What question is at the heart of your book?

Jon: That's a good question because I hadn't really stopped and thought about that.

I believe the question that's at the heart of my book is this, "How can I lead more holistically earlier?"

When I was in my 20s, I was full of energy and excitement. I worked hard and thought I had a possibility of a great career ahead. But I never really took a step back and thought about the way I lead, the purpose of my life in work and in life. I think what the Aspens share as well as my own life experiences is that for people starting out in their careers, it's important to take that step back and really consider how to lead more holistically. Not only within my workplace or my work community but also within my larger community, neighborhood, and society to deliver more fully on mission within that.

Bill: You say in your book that the number one skill to excel in is the ability to convert. What do you mean by that and how do we learn to excel in this area?

Jon: To me the skill or talent of converting relates directly to outcomes and results. I can read a book, or I can read an article, or I can write a product plan. I can think it through thoroughly, but if I don't take the next step of what happens next, then the value of it decreases pretty quickly.

The ability to convert relates to the Aspens as far as how do we absorb information in or observe? Then what do we do with what we've taken in? It could be going back to the point of thinking a little differently about a problem. It may convert to action steps to take in building a specific plan. It may result in a different strategic direction.

It goes to the point of being focused on meaningful results. Rather than sitting in "overanalysis" or taking new information in and not doing anything with it, if we're going to be better leaders, we need to understand that we need to change over time. We do take information in, but really the question is what do we do with that information. If we're not converting it to a better mindset, philosophy, or plan, then we're missing out on a big opportunity to grow and expand our organization as well.

Bill: What are the key takeaways you'd like readers to get from your book?

Jon: There are a lot of different directions I could go, but I think I'll stay with the simple one and that is—spend time in nature because by doing that you will always learn.

Nature is a great cleanser of our thoughts and also for recentering ourselves in what we should be doing and in life and work.

I think what nature brings back to us is encouraging us to be more thoughtful in our approach and recentering us not to be just caught in the moment but instead determine how we can string moments together to achieve more meaningful results. Not only in our career and our work but also in our life and community.

It could be simple as simple as go for a hike. Go for a run in the park. Forest bathing is the new thing where you just sit in a forest and absorb it all in. I think nature is a great cleanser, and I think we need to spend a little more time in nature to unplug and to recenter.

Key Takeaways

- Think of the workplace as a community because in a community people can be themselves, contribute and share and learn as part of that community.

- If we think of workplaces as a community, our mindset begins to shift and start treating people differently.

- How are we encouraging people to think differently to encourage strategic thinking?

- Be more purpose centered than self-centered to give people a sense of purpose within the organization.

- By thinking of organizations as communities, we get much better mindsets and work.

- What are you thinking and why do you think that way?

- What is the role of our business in society?

- Asking "Why do I think that way?" opens us up to greater self-awareness.

- When you go out to nature, you learn more than you expect.

- Underneath we're all connected.

- Aspens provide many wonderful lessons for leaders.

- It's important to take a step back and think the purpose of our life.

- Nature is a great cleanser of our thoughts.

Andy Yen

CEO, Proton Technologies

Space to Speak Honestly Gives Us Power

Andy Yen is the founder and CEO of Proton Technologies AG. The Swiss-based Proton Technologies is building a suite of security software solutions including ProtonMail, the world's largest secure email, and ProtonVPN, a security-focused VPN service that enables Internet access without surveillance. Andy was a researcher at CERN from 2009 to 2015, where ProtonMail's founding team met. He has a PhD in Physics from Harvard and a degree in Economics from Caltech. He is a longtime advocate of privacy rights and has spoken at TED, SXSW, and the Asian Investigative Journalism Conference about online privacy issues.

Our ability to create a forward-thinking workplace and a better world hinges on our ability to have open and honest discussion to share our knowledge and ideas. Fortunately, there are companies like Proton Technologies and people like Andy Yen who are delivering the means to do so. Helping to ensure the privacy of our words survive in the digital age is the reason Andy and his team get up every day passionately motivated to go to work. Discover how creating spaces where we can speak honestly gives us power.

© Bill Fox 2020

B. Fox, *The Future of the Workplace*,

https://doi.org/10.1007/978-1-4842-5098-3_28

Bill Fox: How can we create workplaces where every voice matters, everyone thrives and finds meaning, and change and innovation happen naturally?

Andy Yen: Inside our company, one thing that's helped us a lot is having a rather flat hierarchy. Everybody can contribute ideas no matter what their level is in the organization.

The open sharing of knowledge and ideas helps us be more innovative and allows us to change and adapt more quickly.

We have a culture where anybody who wants to talk to the upper management can. This allows everyone to have a sense that their voice matters. It also allows ideas to come from any corner of the organization. Even ideas for one department can come from a different department. This open sharing of knowledge and ideas helps us be more innovative and allows us to change and adapt more quickly.

Bill: What does it take to get an employee's full attention and best performance?

Andy: You need to have an efficient workforce to be competitive. For getting the best performance and full attention, it's getting the right fit for people.

Getting the best performance and full attention means getting the right fit for people.

There's always a job description, but it's very rare when someone is 100% perfect fit down to last detail. Everybody has their individual quirks, habits, strengths, and weaknesses. It's important to tailor people's duties to leverage their strengths and weaknesses. This requires management to be more flexible and tentative at the beginning. When you get people into a role where they fit, then you see that the results become dramatically better.

Bill: What are people really lacking and longing for at work?

Andy: The key thing that people miss is having real meaning to their work. Many people do jobs without knowing what is the purpose or the big picture of how their work is changing the world. This is what we call a dead end or even a bullshit job.

It's important to reduce those types of jobs. Make sure that everybody has a lot of meaning in their work, so people can see the impact their work has on the world. It's management's responsibility to convey that to the workforce.

Bill: What is the most important question leaders should ask employees?

Andy: It's very important for management to ask questions to employees. The most important question is to ask employees, how can you do your job better?

Often there's a tendency to tell employees how to do their jobs. But in fact that's not effective because many times managers themselves don't know how to do the job. It's much better to ask the employees, who are experts in their area, how they actually could do their job better. What resources do they need? What changes would help them be more effective? Then incorporate that feedback into the way they do their jobs.

Bill: What is the most important question employees should ask leaders?

Andy: The key factor is to make sure people have the right motivation. Then people can learn faster, adapt faster, and will work harder.

As an employee, you need to be at a job that keeps you motivated. So it's important to understand the vision or the big picture of the company and where the business is going. The key question employees need to ask management is, what is the vision for this company? Where is it going? If the answer doesn't motivate the employee, then they are probably in the wrong place.

Bill: What is the most important question we should ask ourselves?

Andy: Whether you're a manager or an employee, the main question I'll ask is, are we proud of our work? Is your job making the world a better place? Is it something that is improving people's lives? Is it something that 40 years later you can say, "You know, my life was well spent. I made a difference."

The main question is, are we proud of our work?

That's a question we all can ask ourselves. If you're working at a tobacco company, that may not be a job you look back at and say, "Wow, I improved people's lives. I did well there." Maybe we shouldn't have the world's best talent working on that.

Companies who are building new technologies, innovating, and making life better, that's where we need to focus the world's talents. Therefore, it's very important for everybody to ask, is this work we can be proud of?

Bill: It's very interesting to note that Proton Technologies' mission is to protect people's privacy and how that intersects with a recurring theme in our interviews is the critical need for people to share their point of view without editing themselves. Care to comment on this?

Andy: That's a very interesting point. For safety and providing people a place to speak honestly, a key part of that is confidentiality. We can encourage this in the workplace with HR policies, but the same idea also applies to all aspects of human life.

We believe a respect for privacy is a must in the digital age. Look at the tech giants like Google, Facebook, and others that are obsessively capturing data and selling it. That's a very poor business model for society when we remove the privacy, confidentiality, and security required to have an honest discussion. If you're a citizen living in China or Russia today, you can't have an honest or transparent discussion because you don't know who's listening. If you're not careful, you might end up in jail.

The cornerstone lesson of democracy is freedom of speech, which stems from privacy rights. This is why the work we do at ProtonMail is so important. We're helping to ensure that democracy survives in the digital age. This is the reason we get up every day passionately motivated to go to work.

Key Takeaways

- Having a relatively flat hierarchy allows everybody to contribute ideas no matter what their level is in the organization.

- The open sharing of knowledge and ideas helps organizations be more innovative as well as change and adapt more quickly.

- Getting the best performance and full attention means getting the right job fit for people.

- It's important to tailor people's duties to leverage their strengths and weaknesses.

- Make sure that everybody has a lot of meaning in their work, so people can see the impact their work has on the world.

- Leaders should ask employees, "How can you do your job better?"

- It's important for people to have the right motivation, so they can learn faster, adapt faster, and work harder.

- The main question we should ask ourselves is, "Are we proud of our work?"

- It's a very poor business model for society when we remove the privacy, confidentiality, and security required to have an honest discussion.

Sue Elliott and John Ryskowski

Personal and Organizational Transformation Leaders

How to Get Beyond the Way Most of Us Are Working Today

Sue Elliott is the CEO and founder at Easier Way, Inc. Through her work with leaders, as well as her writing and media appearances, Sue has empowered and uplifted millions of people. She has been immersed in the personal transformation field for 25 plus years, and for more than a decade, she has been offering a unique blend of transformational coaching, conscious business mentoring, and energy healing. Sue is currently cofounding a very different kind of college—focused on life skills, self-awareness, and collaboration—to help people thrive in a future filled with rapid change.

John Ryskowski is chief of organizational transformation at Easier Way, Inc. As a change catalyst, John has 30 years of experience helping organizations get unstuck from their current state, facilitating transformation in measurable, meaningful ways. John is a Certified Scrum Master, a CMMI High Maturity Lead Appraiser for services and development, and a Problem-Solving Leadership graduate.

© Bill Fox 2020
B. Fox, *The Future of the Workplace*,
https://doi.org/10.1007/978-1-4842-5098-3_29

I sought out Sue Elliott and John Ryskowski for this interview because I know and have worked with both of them. Sue has a rare gift for spotting people's dysfunctional patterns and dissolving them quickly and easily, and she's an exceptional listener. John has a gift for connecting with people—and for discovering what's really going on within organizations. Together, they bring a fascinating blend of personal and organizational transformation expertise to the conversation.

Bill Fox: How can we create workplaces where every voice matters, everyone thrives and finds meaning, and change and innovation happen naturally?

Sue Elliott: This is a question that's near and dear to my heart, because the vast majority of workplaces suck the life out of people. We don't always think of it this way, but organizations are actually entities.

Organizations have their own collective consciousness, which is created, in part, by the business's culture and core values.

And unfortunately, most workplaces today are incredibly draining: People drag themselves home at the end of the day, exhausted and often demoralized.

I believe now is the time to raise the consciousness of organizations so that they uplift and energize people. Then people will want to get out of bed and go to work in the morning. They'll be able to contribute more. And instead of being completely depleted and drained at the end of the day, they'll be excited about the contribution they made, and they'll go home and have energy to interact with their families and friends.

This kind of organizational transformation is, to a great degree, a process of personal transformation. In other words, it's about how we're showing up at work. And it definitely starts at the top: Is the CEO somebody who is closed off and unavailable, or somebody who's open and receptive?

When something goes wrong, do we approach it with an attitude of interrogation, as in: We must get to the bottom of this! Or are we coming at it with curiosity, asking, What's really happening here? I wonder what caused that... When I say it like that, it's pretty easy to feel which approach is going to get people to open up and share what's going on, and which approach is going to trigger people into being defensive and protective and closed off, right?

John Ryskowski: I believe it's really important to "give people the time of day." We recognized this a long time ago with the Hawthorne effect. During this study, they did all these experiments to try and figure out what made people more productive. They gave workers more lighting, and production went up. They played music, and production went up. They put workers in a special room, and production went up. And after many gyrations, they discovered that the only reason production went up was because the workers were being treated like they were special. Management was giving them the time of day.

This doesn't have to be elaborate. Here's an example from when I was doing CMMI (Capability Maturity Model Integration) appraisals: I was leading a team of 13 people. We had a lot of work to do in a very short period of time, and it was intense. I had one person on the team; we'll call her J. And midway into the work, we had another person come onto the team; we'll call her H. And suddenly, there was this territorial tension in the room. And I thought, *In today's world, how on Earth am I going to handle this one?*

Well, all I did was meet with each of them for about 20 minutes in a side room, and I just thanked them. I recognized each of their unique situations. For instance, with one of them, I said, "I know you're dealing with some health issues that are not small, and I'm happy that you can still be a part of this, and I think I speak for everyone else, too."

And that tension in the room? It went away! I didn't need some brilliant strategy. I didn't have to say some magical things. I just gave each of them some special moments.

It's so powerful when we give people the time of day, and it's so rare that it happens!

Bill: What does it take to get an employee's full attention and best performance?

Sue: One powerful way is to listen. When we allow somebody to talk about something that matters to them, we're getting their full attention, which can lead directly to getting their best performance. So as a leader, it's important to go in, ask a powerful, open-ended question, and then listen.

Bill: How do you define listening? How do you really listen?

Sue: That's a great question. People are starting to use the phrase *deep listening*. I like *active listening*. I believe that active listening requires us to be fully present. We have to let go of preconceived notions of how things should be, and we have to stop thinking about what we want to say next, or what we want the other person to understand.

We have to get out of our heads and, instead, fully focus on what the other person is saying. And not just the words coming out of their mouth: Does their body language go with what they're saying? Are they getting more tense? Are they getting more relaxed? Asking very simple questions can help, like: *I just noticed a shift in you. What happened there?*

Simply be present and show interest.

John: To get people's full attention and best performance, you have to recognize their dilemmas and somehow be able to show you are concerned and taking action. You can invest literally 90 seconds in a meeting, and you can shift the perspective and kind of light up or ignite people.

But just remember: After that, they'll be watching, so the follow-up needs to happen, and it needs to be righteous and it needs to be heartfelt. If you don't follow up, you're just "full of it." You don't get many tries, right? So you've got to take advantage of each one. Even if it doesn't work, people will forgive you for that, but you've got to at least give it a shot.

Leaders that are good at this spend a lot of time *not* doing things: They spend a lot of time not reacting or not overreacting. They're very careful about where they inject themselves, and how. And when you see somebody very carefully doing it, it's like artwork. It's quite beautiful to see.

Bill: What do people really lack and long for at work?

Sue: People long to feel seen, heard, and appreciated. We've touched on helping people feel seen and heard, so let's talk about appreciation. Your people are giving you their 8 hours or 10 hours or however long it may be every day, and they want to feel like somebody notices and cares: not just that there's a butt on the seat, but that it's *my* butt!

They also want to feel connection. They want to feel camaraderie.

Studies show that the #1 key indicator of happiness in life is having a friend at work.

That's so simple. But it takes a certain kind of workplace for that to even be possible, right?

Also, people want to feel like they're contributing to something greater. We may show up and do our one little piece of the puzzle every day, but we want to know how it connects to the bigger picture.

There was a study of college students making calls to raise money for scholarships. If the students just did the fundraising calls with minimal training or support, most of them had minimal success. But if the students read a letter from one of the scholarship recipients and *then* made the calls, their performance went up dramatically. And if one of those students on scholarship came in and spent just 5 minutes with the fundraisers, talking about how the scholarship made a difference in their life, then the fundraisers' performance went off the charts! They could see the effects of what they were doing, and it was meaningful.

In other words, connecting what people are doing with something meaningful doesn't take a lot of time. It doesn't take a lot of energy. Yet there's a huge payoff: People are way more willing to do the work, and they're going to do that work at a much higher level.

John: I agree. I believe what people lack and long for at work is a purpose … and a vision. Being a leader and having a vision and mission that you actually believe in—that you stand behind, that you really mean—is a very big deal. It's imperative.

I was just a speaker at the IEEE Aerospace Conference in Big Sky, Montana, and I ended up being the MC for our track. This is actually a very interesting conference. It's "real aerospace," meaning the people there are at the top of the game, in the top 5% of the world of getting things into space, managing space, orbital stuff. People from MIT, Caltech, JPL…

In probably half of the talks I went to, I heard SpaceX mentioned, and every one of the speakers said things like: *SpaceX told us what they were delivering was going to be within THIS window of performance, and they delivered within an even smaller window.* Everything SpaceX told them that the ship was going to do, or the rocket was going to do, it did flawlessly. Amazing stuff.

How do they do it? Well, I talk to a lot of the young people who work at SpaceX, and they *like* working there. Yes, they're there all the time. They don't have much of a life if they work at SpaceX. But they don't care. They love it. Why? Because they know what they're doing and why they're doing it. Their leader basically tells Wall Street to go screw itself. He's on a mission. They know it, and they're behind him on it. His vision is clear.

So what's important is having the vision—and the courage and ability to articulate it. Then people will come with you on that journey because they're passionate about it, too.

Bill: What is the most important question leaders should ask employees?

Sue: *What don't we know?* Obviously, frontline employees know more about what's going on in the day-to-day aspects of a business than anybody else. At every level, there's a certain amount of information that gets lost as it moves up. So *what don't we know?* is a great place to start.

Other great questions are:

How can we help you accomplish your work and your purpose? Do you have the people and the tools you need to accomplish what we're asking of you?

Are we doing things—or asking you to do things—that don't match up with our mission, our purpose, and our core values? Where are we out of alignment?

John: The most important questions (using words that are appropriate for the culture) are: *What's your greatest pain point? What is your greatest roadblock to feeling efficient and flowing forward? What is the thing that bothers you the most?*

Going after those pain points, you could ask: *What isn't working?*

Or say: If you had superpowers, what's the ONE thing you would change?

Leaders are desperate to hear honest answers from their folks, which are hard to get because you're the Big Cheese, and that's a big deal to people. When you walk into a room, people behave differently.

So that's kind of hard to deal with, especially for those leaders who *are* receptive and who *are* interested in what people have to say. But there are mechanisms that you can use to hear the voice of the people.

One of those tools is appraisals, where someone from the outside comes in to ask lots of questions. I've been doing appraisals for many years, and a long time ago, I worked with some really cool people in Arizona. They were way ahead of their time. They were a healthy organization, and they were transparent. One of their sayings was, "All data is good data. Some data requires extra work," meaning: Let the truth be known.

In this case, I was doing CMMI appraisals, and when I was presenting my findings, the managers, who were in the front row watching, were bored. Why? Because they already knew what I was going to tell them. They knew what was going on. They knew they were a high-functioning organization.

But toward the end, I shared the answers to some questions those managers weren't expecting. One was: *If you had superpowers and could change anything—but you could only change ONE thing—what would it be?*

As soon as I got to the charts with the answers to that question, the leaders in the audience sat up in their chairs and read every single word. THAT is what they cared about: the pain points of the people. *What needs to be worked on? What needs to be changed?*

They also were interested in the second "surprise" question, which was: *If everything were to change, what's the ONE thing you would keep?* That reveals what their people value most.

That's what leaders in a really high-functioning organization cared about, and they learned from it. Things actually changed as a result of the answers to those questions.

Bill: What is the most important question employees should ask leaders?

Sue: *Why are we doing what we're doing? What are we aiming to accomplish, big picture? And what are we aiming to accomplish with these specific tasks and initiatives?*

As an employee, when I have clarity around how what I'm doing fits into the big picture, that helps me make all kinds of day-to-day decisions that affect quality, productivity, and so much more. For example, maybe I can do a project several different ways. When I know what we want to accomplish, then I can do the project in the best way to move us closer to that goal.

Understanding how what I'm doing fits into the big picture also helps me determine what matters and what doesn't. Each of us, during the course of our day-to-day work, is going to come upon some information that "doesn't fit." It could be an exception to the rule. Or it could be a behavior that we didn't expect to have happened as a result of what we're doing.

Whatever it is, if we know the big picture, then we know if this is an important data point or an unimportant data point. We know if it's something that we need to share with others right away because it's an urgent potential problem, or if it's insignificant and we can just keep going about what we're doing.

John: I would follow up on that with *Why do we exist? Why are we all here?*

If you as a leader cannot answer that clearly—if you don't have a clear mission and vision statement that you firmly believe in—then that's where you've got to start. Otherwise, that's going to be at the base of everything people are troubled by.

When people have the long-term vision in mind, it makes what's going on in front of them at the moment less concerning. If you *don't* have that big picture in mind, then all you have is what's in front of you: like my cubemate talks too loudly or farts all day. Unfortunately, this becomes your life at work. Instead of *Yeah, I can put up with that because what I'm doing is part of the mission of the company and I believe in it.*

Bill: What is the most important question we should ask ourselves?

Sue: *Am I showing up as my best and highest self?* If not, then there are lots of great follow-up questions, like: *What's stopping me, and how can I change or release that? What's triggering me in this moment?*

John: Exactly. One of the most important questions to ask ourselves is: *What do I need to clear out of the way to be effective?*

If you're a psychologist, what is your goal? Your goal is to be able to respond to your client who's sitting there, talking to you, in a rational and non-emotional way—instead of bringing your own baggage into your reaction.

It's the same in business.

> You need to clear out your baggage so you can be present in the moment without dragging your own stuff in.

That's hard to do. It can be painful, but it's necessary in order to be fully present and have clarity when you're dealing with people at work or anywhere else. You're more effective if you don't have your own baggage.

Bill: Sue, I was reminded of one of the most remarkable things that stands out for me from when I've talked or worked with you from this statement on your web site, "Sue effortlessly spots patterns, blind spots and other 'hidden' limitations." Can you share the story of how you came to do this and what you see happen to people when you do this?

Sue: This is one of my superpowers. It's as natural as breathing for me, so it took me a while to recognize that not everybody on the planet can do this…

I believe that we go on a journey through life, and the journey may not look very linear at the time. But when we look back on it, we can see: *Oh, I did THAT so I could pick up this skill. I did THAT so I could hone these talents.* So, all those years I spent being a magazine editor and an author helped me really tune in to words. I also studied poetry in college, so I'm very much aware of rhythm and pacing.

I've also been on this personal transformation journey for 25 years, which tuned me in to the energy of people—including whether what they're saying is congruent with how they're acting or feeling.

Those things probably seem unrelated, but they actually converge in a way that makes it possible for me to connect dots and spot patterns that have never been spotted before. Most of them are related to what I call our "core wounds," often from childhood, which color the way we experience life. Put together, they act like one big filter—the world we see is completely "colored" by this filter. There are some really common core wounds, like feeling abandoned (perhaps by a parent who left when we were young) or feeling disrespected.

Other dysfunctional patterns that we carry as adults come from "rules" we made for ourselves when we were very young. Perhaps it wasn't safe to be angry in your family of origin: If you expressed anger, you were punished. Or maybe your dad was so miserable in his job that when he came home and you laughed out loud, your joy was annoying and he smacked you. As a small child, you made rules for yourself about how it was safe to be in the world based on how you perceived things in your home—and your school and community.

As adults, we still have those rules. They're subconscious now. And they often feel like a matter of life or death, because when we were 3 years old, it *was* a matter of life or death. If those "big people" didn't take good care of us, then we wouldn't get fed. We wouldn't have a safe place to sleep or clothes to wear. We really depended on them to get our needs met.

But now, when we notice these rules at age 30 or 40 or 50, it's pretty easy to say: *Oh, I don't need THAT anymore. I can see how it served me before, but it doesn't serve me anymore. So I'm willing to let it go. I'm willing to allow myself to feel anger (or sadness or joy). Or: I'm willing to let myself really care about someone, even if they might leave me someday.*

Once we see those patterns, then I have this gift for being able to dissolve them effortlessly. It's a process of clearing out the "gunk," or baggage, or emotional debris, and it's quite beautiful.

People have so much more energy for life—and so much more joy and creativity—once we do this work.

For example, I was working with one business leader recently who's the head of a sales team for a luxury brand. His team was the #1 sales team in the world for this brand, but then it would drop down to being #2. Then it would go back up to being #1, then it would drop down to number #2. For years, they had this pattern.

This business leader and I were having lunch one day, and he was telling me how much he loves to root for the underdog. And I blurted out, "That's the thing!" That was the pattern affecting his business!

It seems so innocuous, right? Lots of people love to root for the underdog. But, in this case, it was such a core value for this leader that it literally caused him and his team to *become the underdog*. They had to drop out of the #1 position in order to be the underdog. Over and over, they would win, and then they would become the underdog again. Then they would win, and then they would become the underdog again.

Needless to say, as soon as he saw this pattern, he was like, "I'm so done with this underdog thing!" We dissolved the pattern right there on the spot, and his team has been #1 nonstop since then.

We *all* have these kinds of blind spots. And we all have triggers—buttons people can push—that cause us to respond in a big, dramatic way to some minor little thing.

I'm very grateful that I've been gifted with the ability to see these blind spots, triggers, and dysfunctional patterns and help people get rid of them permanently. This enables people to be fully present in the moment and to show up as their best and highest selves.

Bill: What is the #1 takeaway you'd like people to get from this interview today?

Sue: For businesses to thrive in a future that's filled with massive, ongoing change—at an incredibly accelerated rate—we each need to show up as our best and highest selves. We need to let go of our baggage and show up fully present and open in each moment.

We need to have a clear vision and purpose and make sure our people—and our actions—are in alignment with that vision and purpose.

We need to open up the channels of communication. We need to make sure people feel seen, heard, and appreciated and address their pain points.

And we need to help everyone within our organization—at every level—be fully present, ask powerful questions, tune in to inspiration, and take inspired action.

This will enable us to accomplish amazing things, to be more innovative, more creative, more collaborative. And it will enable us to navigate the massive change and disruption on the horizon, so our businesses and our people can thrive.

Key Takeaways

- Organizations have their own collective consciousness, which is created, in part, by the business's culture and core values.

- It's so powerful when we give people the time of day, and it's so rare that it happens!

- Simply be present and show interest.

- As a leader, pretty much everybody in the company is going to have some information that would be really valuable for you to know. It pays to spend a little time connecting with people, asking a question or two, and getting people to open up.

- Studies show that the number one key indicator of happiness in life is having a friend at work.

- So what's important is having the vision—and the courage and ability to articulate it. Then people will come with you on that journey because they're passionate about it, too.

- If you had superpowers, what's the ONE thing you would change?

- When I have clarity around how what I'm doing fits into the big picture, that helps me make all kinds of day-to-day decisions that affect quality, productivity, and so much more.

- Identify what your baggage is so that you can be present in the moment without dragging your own stuff in.

- We each need to show up as our best and highest selves. We need to let go of our baggage and show up fully present and open in each moment.

Marcel Schwantes

Human-Centered Leadership

Human-Centered Leadership Empowers People to Scale Mountains

Marcel Schwantes is the founder of Leadership from the Core and a leading expert in helping companies develop exceptional servant leadership cultures. He is also an entrepreneur, executive coach, keynote speaker, and syndicated columnist for *Inc.* magazine.

I first met Marcel Schwantes when I discovered an article in *Inc.* magazine based on my interview with Howard Behar in *Starbucks' Former President Reveals 6 Leadership Traits That Led to His Wild Success.*[1] The insights that Marcel highlighted from the interview were remarkable, so I reached out to connect with him. It was then I discovered his passion for servant leadership, which led to this interview.

---

[1] Marcel Schwantes, "Starbucks' Former President Reveals 6 Leadership Traits That Led to His Wild Success," Inc. Magazine, August 29, 2017, www.inc.com/marcel-schwantes/starbucks-former-president-reveals-6-leadership-tr.html.

© Bill Fox 2020
B. Fox, *The Future of the Workplace*,
https://doi.org/10.1007/978-1-4842-5098-3_30

Bill Fox: How can we create workplaces where every voice matters, everyone thrives and finds meaning, and change and innovation happen naturally?

Marcel Schwantes: You know that's a loaded question because it implies that you have the right people in the right leadership spot. I think it was John Maxwell who said "everything starts and ends with leadership." So I have to point at the people you have within your organization that are making decisions and question whether those people are human-centered leaders.

Human-centered leaders have a natural understanding of what it takes for humans to succeed.

I won't even call them servant leaders yet. I'm going to call them human-centered leaders who have a natural understanding of what it takes for humans to succeed. Human-centered leaders who tap into human emotions and understand what behaviors drive high performance. That solves the culture question and everything else you mentioned in your question.

When you tap into the human potential, people are going to go above and beyond. They are going to be more creative and innovative when they feel psychological safety and valued intrinsically. That's what happens when you have human motivation. People just give their best. When you remove fear from the workplace, you set up those kinds of work environments that lead to all the things you just said in your question.

Bill: How do we get an employee's full attention and best performance?

Marcel: I think every answer I give will be biased based on my working philosophy of leading by valuing the human. Valuing them not only as employees but also as a people. There's always a person before they're an employee. To me it always starts with building the relationship because when you do that, you show people that you value them as an individual and show that you care.

Meeting the needs of others empowers people to scale mountains.

This philosophy is also consistent with the research on servant leadership. The research says that when you meet the needs of others, it empowers them to scale mountains, which addresses the business outcome question. Sure you want reasonable relationships, but not at the expense of results. When you do that, you get both.

Bill: What do you think people really lack and long for at work?

Marcel: People lack so many things but let me boil it down to what keeps coming up for me in client surveys and the people I interview. People lack being recognized. They lack having the spotlight put on them for the work they do. I believe that executives and high-level managers now have the self-awareness to give their employees the credit. But what happens at the end of the year and who gets the big fat bonus and more stock options?

The recognition part has to extend beyond an "attaboy" for good work.

When I say put the spotlight on people, I mean recognize them not only for their work and contributions, but continue to recognize them through compensation.

That really separates the most humble and human-centered leaders from the pack because it shows that "Hey, I'm not above you." Because as an executive who achieves some measure of financial performance, they get more money, more notoriety, and the parking spot in front of the building and so on. So as leaders, we must level out the playing field so that employees are recognized through various means on an equal par.

Bill: What is the most important question leaders should ask employees?

Marcel: This is not going to be so much on a strategy or 30,000-ft level answer, but every leader has to put themselves in the position to ask themselves a very look in the mirror question and that is, whose life am I impacting today? But it's really a two-part question, and the second part of that question is, what gifts am I giving that are going to help people improve themselves and their lives as a worker? And as a human being?

These questions are the ones that I would start with from the perspective of self-reflective leadership.

Bill: What is the most important question employees should ask leaders?

Marcel: If you are an employee that has the mindset of a servant follower, then your best question to ask a leader is to help empower and support that leader. One question could be, what is it that you need for me to make this team better or to support you better as a manager? Another is, what's that one thing that you need from me as an employee to make this work environment better?

In the best workplace environments, it's never about me. It's about *we*. It's about how does the team win? This question might be a little different from most other questions where the employee focuses on himself or herself. But the reason that I tossed that out as potential questions to ask is because it already implies that the employee is experiencing a level of engagement to begin with because that's what we're after.

Bill: What is the most important question we should ask ourselves?

Marcel: Because I see the level of toxicity of so many work environments, the question is, how do we alleviate suffering in the workplace? That's my big question. I try to address this question in 90% of everything I write including the book manuscript that I'm developing now.

How do we alleviate suffering in the workplace?

I had my own encounter with workplace toxicity in the past. I felt it to the point of physically and emotionally impacting me. This suffering literally took a physical form where I was on disability for a few weeks and suffered a stress fracture on my back because of toxic management. Before I even read up on any of the studies on a correlation between toxic management structures and employee health and well-being, I was a casualty. I see now that research is saying toxic work environments lead to stress, anxiety, or even death. When people are exposed to horrific work environments, it takes a toll on their health. Psychosomatically, whatever goes on in the mind will manifest in disease. Whatever is going on emotionally will eventually lead to things like heart disease and other serious ailments.

Bill: You've written many excellent articles for *Inc.* magazine. If you had to select one most important article for people to read, which one would it be and why?

Marcel: As I was doing my research to inform my book on love and leadership on how the best leaders lead through actionable love, I stumbled into compassionate management. It's a thing that's actually highly espoused by Jeff Weiner, CEO at LinkedIn. Jeff sent out a tweet last year that said one of the benefits of getting older is a far greater appreciation for three things that are too often taken for granted. Then he listed the three things. Number one is health. Number two is love. And number three is time. So I ran with his tweet and made it into an article for *Inc.* magazine.[2] In the article, I talked about how we can't ignore our health and how that greatly impacts our well-being and ability to perform at a high level.

---

[2] www.inc.com/marcel-schwantes/with-a-single-tweet-linkedins-ceo-taught-a-major-lesson-in-managing-people-successfully.html

Obviously, the time part is the time we have to focus on the things that matter the most to us. For the love part, I highlighted Jeff Weiner's interest in compassionate management. I quote him as saying that compassionate reaction has more value than an act of empathy. Compassion is basically empathy on steroids. Weiner said that a leader is someone who in their heart of hearts wants to do everything to alleviate suffering. They have the power to make decisions in the workplace to alleviate the suffering or to remove the obstacles. That's compassionate management. What is it that you can do to be more compassionate in the workplace without falling for the soft fuzziness of the word? It's a powerful word when you put yourself in the position of removing obstacles so that other people can succeed.

That should be a huge strength of leadership that more people should tune in to, and so I truly admire that one of our most well-known CEOs is advocating for compassionate management. So I wrote about this in the article, and lo and behold Jeff Weiner read it. He then tags my name and posts a status update on LinkedIn. The next thing I know my phone is blowing up with requests. I'm literally getting one connection request per minute for 7 or 8 hours. So that made an impact on me that was on his radar screen, and he was kind enough to share it with this global audience.

Bill: What has been the biggest surprise that has come out of your work in servant leadership or writing for *Inc.* magazine?

Marcel: Writing for *Inc.* magazine does provide a fair amount of exposure globally, so you never know who's going to come knocking on your door. The government administration that we're under currently I would not call as having an interest in servant leadership. So I was quite surprised when I was asked to provide a speech at the CIA.

I wouldn't think that there would be an interest in that topic, but the CIA asked me to speak and do a workshop on servant leadership. As it turned out, I discovered that it was the second in command at the CIA who was the one that had an interest. That's the best-case scenario when you have somebody at the top wanting to champion the cause.

I'm not saying that she is championing that cause now because I don't know what happened since I left a few months ago, but just the mere fact that I was invited to speak on servant leadership indicates that something triggered deep inside the leadership structure there to risk bringing somebody like me to speak on something that's so counterintuitive under this administration.

I delivered the talks and I can tell you that there were many deer-in-headlights looks in the room. At the same time, there were people that were soaking up every word coming out of my mouth. It was a 50/50 split in the room, but it gave me hope that maybe there are enough people banging the drum about more human-centered approaches of leadership.

If we can affect government space, then we've done a great service not only on behalf of government but on behalf of our citizens as well.

Bill: What's the single best piece of advice that you'd like to pass on to people?

Marcel: I thought about a quote from Ken Blanchard who once said that "servant leadership is love in action." Many people misconstrue the word love in the worst possible ways, and what Ken meant and what I mean when I write articles about leadership and love in the same sentence is agape love. It's an actionable love—a verb, not a feeling. It's not the emotion as much as it is what you are doing for other people.

Going back to Jeff Weiner and his compassionate management philosophy, it is a practical love. When you love your people, they will run through walls for you. So that's what I want to leave leaders with as they think about how to elevate their game.

Bill: What question is at the heart of Marcel Schwantes?

Marcel: I'll go back to the self-reflective question that every aspiring leader should ask and that is, what are you doing to improve the life of an employee? What are you giving them as gifts that they can take with them? And maybe even pay it forward and make leaders of other leaders to create a leadership culture? Not only in your company or organization but in our society.

What are you doing to improve the life of an employee?

That's what I would leave behind as the question that's in my heart. I think it defines my work. When I wake up in the morning, it's the running question in my head. What I think about is, how can I help shift the mindset of one person to look at leadership in the sense of improving someone else's life?

Key Takeaways

- Human-centered leaders have a natural understanding of what it takes for humans to succeed.

- Meeting the needs of others empowers them to scale mountains.

- The recognition part has to extend beyond an "attaboy" for good work.

- Whose life am I impacting today?

- What is it that you need for me to make this team better or to support you better as a manager?

- In the best workplace environments, it's never about me—it's about we.

- How do we alleviate suffering in the workplace?

- We can't ignore our health and how that greatly impacts our well-being and ability to perform at a high level.

- A leader is someone who in their heart of hearts wants to do everything to alleviate suffering.

- Leadership is actionable love—a verb, not a feeling.

- When you love your people, they will run through walls.

- What are you doing to improve the life of an employee?

- How can we help shift the mindset of one person to look at leadership in the sense of improving someone else's life?